THE NATURAL HISTORY OF CATS

Mrs. Necker is also the editor of
Cats and Dogs: An Anthology

THE NATURAL HISTORY OF CATS

Claire Necker

A DELTA SPECIAL

A DELTA BOOK
Published by Dell Publishing Co., Inc.
1 Dag Hammarskjold Plaza
New York, New York 10017

For information contact A. S. Barnes and Co., Inc., Cranbury, New Jersey 08512.
Manufactured in the United States of America
Reprinted by arrangement with A. S. Barnes and Co., Inc.
Delta ® TM 755118, Dell Publishing Co., Inc.

ISBN: 0-440-56356-9

First Delta printing—October 1977

Designed by Joel Schick

My thanks to the following who have given permission to reprint copyrighted material. If omissions have been made inadvertently they will be corrected in future editions if notification is sent to the publisher.

American Mercury for "Concerning Cats" by Alan Devoe.

The Cornell Veterinarian and Dr. Neil B. Todd for excerpts from "Behavior and Genetics of the Domestic Cat."

Doubleday & Co., Inc., for "The Tom-Cat," © 1917 by The Sun Printing & Publishing Association, from *Poems and Portraits* by Don Marquis; an excerpt from *An Explorer Comes Home* by Roy Chapman Andrews, © 1939, 1940, 1945, 1946, 1947 by Roy Chapman Andrews; and an excerpt from *Penrod and Sam* by Booth Tarkington, © 1916 by Doubleday & Co., Inc.

The Folk-Lore Society for a selection from *Rumanian Bird and Beast Stories* by M. Gaster.

Harper & Row, Publishers, Inc. for "Seven Cats" from *Lives* by Gustav Eckstein, © 1932 & 1960 by Gustav Eckstein; and for portions of "Time: A Cat That Knows Monday" from *Everyday Miracle* by Gustav Eckstein, © 1948 by Gustav Eckstein.

Houghton Mifflin Company for excerpts from *Man Meets Dog* by Konrad Lorenz.

The Journal of Parapsychology for excerpts from "A Test of the Occurrence of a Psi Effect Between Man and the Cat" by Karlis Osis and "A Test of ESP in Cats" by Karlis Osis and Esther Bond Foster.

The Journal Press for excerpts from "Development of Behavior in the Fetal Cat," by J. D. Coronios.

J. B. Lippincott Co. for "In Honor of Taffy Topaz" from *Poems* by Christopher Morley, © 1929 & 1957 by Christopher Morley.

Methuen & Co., Ltd. for excerpts from *Man Meets Dog* by Konrad Lorenz.

New Scientist for "How Does a Cat Fall On Its Feet?" by Donald McDonald.

The New Yorker for "Catalog" by Rosalie Moore, © 1940, 1968 by The New Yorker Magazine, Inc.

The Royal Society for the Protection of Birds and The Society of Authors for an excerpt from *The Book of a Naturalist* by W. H. Hudson.

CW

For All Who Would
And All Who Should
Know More About
CATS

Contents

Introduction

Tri paces on the kitchen counter. Mot-Mot, talking as usual, sits on the porch table. Fairchild, the boisterous busybody, chases psychotic String, Long-Girl swatting at both of them as they race past her. Carbonel, aloof in all things, waits close by my feet until Fairchild reappears to rub my legs. Beta Boy, late again, comes zooming through the cat door skirting around Omega who lies far from the activity, hating and hated by all. Tabitha, on the stairs, stretches in an attempt to see all and yet remain apart from the commotion. Outside, Specs waits impatiently to be let in through the front door—why should he bother coming through the cat door in the rear? Juno, feeling the same way, waits on the porch roof to have an upstairs window opened for her.

It's 6 A.M. and their breakfast is ready to be served. The filled dishes are handed round in the rotation least likely to produce dissension, and all annoyances and animosities are forgotten for the time being in food and drink.

Living with cats is fascinating and exasperating, joyous and heartbreaking, anything but monotonous. And no matter how many you have, you always will miss those who have gone. How could you possibly forget them? Each is and always will be a rugged individualist. No cat knows what it is to conform. True, all *tend* to concede to some things like letting young cats (and, for that matter, the young of all species) off easy, but just wait, the time will come . . . Champfleury summed all this up when he said, "The cat is *natural,* and for that reason it is calumniated. Playing its little part in the world unaffectedly, when it is hungry it says so. If it wants to sleep, it lies down and stretches itself out. When it wants to go out, it asks to be let out."

But make a statement about the cat and you'll discover that invariably you'll have to qualify that statement with "ifs," "probablys," "howevers," and the like. For those who like cats and want to know as much as possible about them such limitations are irritating. Viewed from another angle, however, it is these unknown quantities that enhance our feelings for them. The unknown intrigues, and that being the case, cats will always appeal.

Over the centuries we have known them they have continued to be an enigma, and the longer we live with them, and the more we read about them, the more we wonder. What are they really? Where did they come from and when? Why and how do they act as they do? An attempt to find the answers to these questions has resulted in this book. I hope its contents will bring you, as they did me, greater understanding and enjoyment of your companion, the ever-inscrutable cat.

Cat Quiz

QUIZ YOURSELF—THEN FIND THE ANSWERS

True, false, or unknown?

Domesticated cats are easy to distinguish from wild cats.

Cats can see in the dark.

Cats are color-blind.

Catnip and valerian are the only plants that excite cats.

A cat's whiskers tell it whether or not it can safely pass through a small opening.

Cutting off its whiskers deprives a cat of its sense of smell.

Cutting off its whiskers causes a cat to lose its courage.

Only a cat's feet and nose tip are equipped with sweat glands.

Landing on its feet is a reflex act in the cat.

How a cat usually manages to land on its feet is completely understood.

A cat's personality is related to the color of its fur.

Tortoiseshell tomcats are always sterile.

Tortoiseshell tomcats are rare.

Both the voice and purr of a cat arise from its vocal cords.

Cats who have accidentally lost their tails often get short-tailed kittens.

Cats dislike getting wet.

Black cats generate more electricity than other cats.

If its nose is hot and dry a cat is sick.

Cats scratch wood in order to sharpen their claws.

A good mouser can be spotted by the number of ridges on the roof of its mouth.

Cats are unable to taste sweet substances.

Cats can't be taught anything because they are stupid.

Cats learn to do things through imitation.

Cats were living with man prior to 2000 B.C.

The Egyptians were the first people to domesticate cats.

Cats were unknown to the early Greeks and Romans.

There was once a breed of cats with hanging ears.

Cats are preferred animals in laboratory experiments because their anatomy and physiology is so similar to ours.

Only cats and humans possess Cowper's glands.

Siamese cats originated in Siam, Persian cats in Persia, and Manx cats in the Isle of Man.

PART ONE

HISTORY

I

Origin and Domestication

I know of course cat's origin—the incubation of "greybeard."
The cat was gotten on a stove—has a girl's nose, a hare's head,
A tail of snake's venom, claws of a viper,
Feet of cloudberries, the rest of its body is of the wolf's race.
(one of the magic songs of the Finns)

ONE of the last animals to be domesticated by man, the cat is, at present, cosmopolitan in distribution. But how it spread over the globe, where it originated and who its ancestors were remain obscure and no doubt always will. The major reason both recent and paleontological history of cats is shrouded in mystery is the impossibility of distinguishing small wild cats from each other or from the domestic cat by means of their skeletal remains. There *are* differences but there is such an overlapping of characteristics from one species to another that no positive identification is possible.

Today's small cats apparently look very much like their ancestors of eight million years ago. Bone fragments of cats have been discovered from the Lower Pliocene in France and the Upper Pliocene in Italy which are so similar to those of modern wild cats that they do not actually warrant a new species name, and none was given to those found in France.

A great variety of cat bones has been discovered in Europe which date from the Pleistocene, that is around one million years ago, when the cat was contemporary with prehistoric man. These have been ascribed to the European and African wild cats, and the Steppe cat as well, the confusion arising from their skeletal similarities as mentioned above. None of the bones has been ascribed to the domestic cat. Even though cat remains were found among the Lake Dwellers, these were always in association with other wild carnivores; this negates the possibility that cats lived in close association with man as a domestic animal.

From the meager evidence at hand it is now generally agreed that house cats had their origin in the African wild cat, *Felis lybica,* which later hybridized with the European wild cat, *F. silvestris,* to give our present-day cat a mixed inheritance. Over the centuries it has retained characteristics from both of its ancestors and acquired some of its own.

Roughly speaking, domestic cats having a coat color and pattern similar to wild cats can be distinguished by shorter fur and a smaller average size. Measurements of the skull and lower jaw are most significant, body dimensions tending to be unreliable in domestic cats due to their range, particularly in leg length. Domestication has greatly shortened the faces in some breeds, making the skull broad across the eyes, a characteristic that has been exaggerated through artificial selection by cat fanciers. Another general change is that the gap between the canines and premolars of the lower jaw is bigger in domestic cats than in wild cats. This is due to a decrease in the size of the teeth, particularly the first molar.

Skull measurements of Egyptian cat mummies indicate that these cats were much larger than ours. Pocock considered them a subspecies of *F. lybica.* It is now suggested that they were a hybrid between the smaller North African race, *F. lybica,* and the larger *F. Chaus nilotica* or *F. Chaus* itself which is bigger than its subspecies. But all the Egyptian cats appear to have been tabbies, and *chaus* is not. Whatever their origin, it is now questioned whether they were ancestors of the modern cat.

Supporting the theory that *F. lybica* and *F. silvestris* are, at the least, the principal ancestors of domestic cats is the fact that the only common coat pattern for domestic cats throughout the world is the striped tabby. This pattern is shared by *lybica* and *silvestris* and is not found in any other *Felis.* There are only minor color and fur quality variations between the two species and these overlap as do the bone structures already discussed. Interbreeding between the two occurs in zoos, which leads to the assumption that it also takes place in nature. The hybrids in captivity have the appearance of typical striped tabby housecats.

For many years it was argued that *lybica* alone was the housecat's ancestor. This contention was based on the color of the soles of the hind feet which are black in *lybica* and most domestic breeds and pale in *silvestris*. Pocock, however, in his study of a large series of animals, found this to be an unreliable characteristic. Another argument favoring *lybica* is that it is easily domesticated whereas *silvestris* is completely untameable.

Serological evidence is now being used to determine the taxonomic relationships of higher animals. Its worth as a criterion for comparison has been demonstrated by a number of tests: results verify both anatomical and paleontological evidence and sometimes reveal unsuspected affinities that could lead to a better understanding of the animal kingdom. For example, ostriches and parrots have been found to be more closely related than wolves and hyenas.

A housecat and interbred spaniel were compared in one test and were found to be closely related serologically, as their placement in the same order of mammals, the *Carnivora,* would indicate. If and when the technique is refined it may become possible to compare closely related species. The domestic cat's relationship to the different species of small wild cats could then be determined and thereby indicate its probable ancestors.

Relatively recent records of cats have been found in two prehistoric sites, the earliest in Pre-Pottery Jericho, c. 6700 B.C., the other in Harappa in the Indus Valley, c. 2000 B.C. The first is almost certainly that of a wild cat, but the second could easily be domestic. In Egypt the earliest indisputable evidence dates the cat's domestication at c. 1600 B.C. Those cats depicted around 1900 B.C., the earliest possible date now given for their domestication in Egypt, can as readily be considered wild cats as domestic animals. A few scientists continue to maintain that cats were already domesticated in Egypt by 3000 B.C. but the evidence for this assumption is even more ambiguous than for the 1900 B.C. date.

There is little point in conjecturing about the cat's domestication as such. No other animal is as capable of seeing how or why it will benefit from something than is the cat, so it undoubtedly made the overtures toward a communal life with man. It gained much in the pact and gave up nothing. To this day the most pampered housepet is able, if necessary, to revert to the wild state with a minimum of inconvenience on its part. And the most feral cat is capable of coming to some terms with humans when it finds it necessary. This ability is treated in the section on the cat's innate wildness. The scanty records of its domestication in the Western World from the earliest times to the 16th century are itemized in the historical outline and its expansion which follow.

Unlike science, folklore has had no difficulty in explaining the origin of the cat, but here, too, there are many possibilities to choose from. The one best known relates how a glove was transformed into a cat so that it could destroy pesky mice. The identity of the man who owns and throws the glove-become-cat at the mice varies. Usually it is Noah, but Adam and Jesus have also been credited with the miracle granted by God.

Whether the cat made its appearance during the creation of earth's animals or on the Ark, it came in answer to the need for controlling mice, a fact that indicates man's preoccupation with rodent control from the earliest times. The devil, in most cases, is blamed for the rodents, and God solves the dilemma they cause man by introducing the cat. But divine origin didn't save cats from persecution or from being considered lowly creatures any more than did their proclivity for destroying rodents. If not from a glove, they were said to have risen makeshift from the leftovers of more lordly animals or through a spiteful gesture between antagonistic deities. All things considered, folktales about the cat's origin reflect the same low opinion of it that all early recorded material does after its initial reign in Egypt.

Here are some of the tales told about how our animated mousetraps were created and domesticated.

THE SUN MYTH

"The cat is more harmful than useful, its caresses are more to be dreaded than desired, and its bite is fatal. The cause of the pleasure it gives us is strange and entertaining. At the moment of the creation of the world, says the fable, the Sun and the Moon emulated each other in peopling the earth with animals. The Sun, great, fiery and luminous, formed the lion, beautiful, sanguinary and generous. The Moon, seeing the other gods in admiration before this noble work, caused a cat to come forth from the earth, but one as disproportionate to the lion in beauty and courage as she (the Moon) is to her brother (the Sun). This contention gave rise to derision, and also indignation on the part of the Sun, who, being angry that the Moon should have attempted to match herself with him,

Créa par forme de mépris
En même temps une souris.

As, however, 'the sex' never surrenders, the Moon made herself still more ridiculous by producing the most absurd of all animals, the monkey. This creature was received by the company of stars with a burst of immoderate laughter. A flame spread itself over the face of the Moon, even as when she threatens us with a tempest of great winds, and by a last effort, in order to be eternally revenged upon the Sun, she set undying enmity between the monkey and the cat, and between the cat and the mouse. Hence comes the sole advantage which we derive from the cat."

PIERRE PALLIOT 1664.
La Vraye et Parfaicte Science des Armoires.

A similar story is told about Apollo and Diana who were personifications of the sun and moon respectively. Apollo created the lion to terrify his sister Diana (Hecate). Scornfully she ridiculed his beast by mimicking it in the form of a cat.

ARK STORY

During the first day or two on the Ark the animals didn't mingle with each other, but the monotonous life soon became too much for them. The monkey was the first to tire of it. His roving eye spotted the lioness and it wasn't long before he had persuaded her to forget her marital vows to the lion. The result of this unnatural union was the cat.

ARABIA

The following is one of several variations of the story of the cat coming forth from a lion's sneeze:

When Noah built the Ark he made no provision on it for waste disposal. It soon became so overladen with the animals' excrement that it threatened to sink.

Noah prayed to God for guidance and was told to take an elephant to the latrines. From its droppings and those of man the pig was engendered. The pig set to work immediately to distribute all the other animals' dung, levelling it off so that the Ark regained its equilibrium.

In doing this the pig's nostrils became filled with the dung which caused it to sneeze, and out sprang a mouse. The mouse began to cause Noah more trouble than the ordure had. Once again he prayed to God for guidance, whereupon God told him to strike the lion's head. The lion became so incensed at such treatment that he roared in his wrath and from his nostrils issued the cat. She immediately gave chase to the mouse and order was once again restored on the Ark.

EUROPE

When Noah had built the Ark, he kept the door wide open for the animals to enter. After they had all gone in, his own family came, and last of all his wife.

Noah said to her, "Come in." She obstinately said, "No." Noah again said, "Come in." She again said, "No." Noah, getting angry, said, "Oh, you devil, come in." That was just what the devil was waiting for. He knew that Noah would not allow him to come in otherwise, and so he waited for an invitation, of which he promptly availed himself. Getting into the Ark the devil changed himself into a mouse.

When the devil has nothing to do he weighs his tail. But here he found plenty to do, for, he thought, now is an opportunity of putting an end to the whole of God's creatures. So he started gnawing on one of the planks, trying to make a hole in it. When Noah surprised him at this devilish work he threw his fur glove at him. It turned into a cat and in the twinkling of an eye the mouse was in the mouth of the cat.

But Noah could not allow the peace of the Ark to be broken; the animals had to live in peace with one another. So he seized the cat, with the mouse in her mouth, and flung her out of the Ark into the water.

The cat swam to the Ark and, getting hold of the door step, climbed on to the sill and lay down there to bask in the sun.

There she remained until the water had subsided: and ever since then, the cat likes to lie on the doorstep of the house and bask in the sun.

M. Gaster, 1915.
Rumanian Bird and Beast Stories

Another tale has the devil in mouse form attempting to drown Adam in his boat. The glove-become-cat eats the devil who causes the cat's fur to bristle and make sparks and its eyes to glisten in the dark. Cats have continued to have these characteristics to this very day—the sparks of the devil still reside in them.

NEGRO

Long ago Jesus often strolled around among the colored folk to see how they were making out and help them if they needed it. One day he stopped at the home of a very poor woman, stepped through the doorway and greeted her. For a while she answered nothing, merely standing and facing Him. Suddenly she burst out in all her misery, "Lord, I'm just miserable!"

In all her lifetime she had never heard of Jesus, but seeing Him stand before her His identity seemed to fill her entire being, and she poured out her woes to Him. It appeared that rats and mice were eating and destroying what little she owned. Her cornmeal and meat had been consumed long ago. Her clothing had been chewed to shreds. Her mattress was gnawed full of holes, and the pests were by now so bold that they were getting ready to gnaw on her. Her misery was made worse by the fact that she didn't know how to cope with the invasion.

Jesus watched her quietly during this recital. When she had finished He looked at her long and hard and then exclaimed, "Woman, behold your God!" While saying this he pulled off his right hand glove and flung it on the floor. No sooner had the glove touched the floor, than it became a cat. The four fingers of the glove became the cat's legs, the thumb its tail. And no sooner was the glove a cat, than it set about catching all the rats and mice that plagued the old woman, doing better than any cat has done since.

That's why cats are the enemies of rats and mice and why it's a sin to kill one and unlucky to hurt one. Cats are of divine origin.

JAPAN (AINU)

After God had rested from creating the world, He decided to visit it one day to see how things were progressing. Having descended from Heaven He was strolling around admiring His latest creation when He suddenly came face to face with the Devil. The Devil had been watching

God's apparent pleasure over the world and decided to taunt Him about it. He looked hastily around for something to deprecate and his glance stopped at a thicket of brambles and thistles. "Of course I don't mean to criticize any of Your work," he began. "I know You do the best You can, but I can't see why You've done certain things. Take that thicket for instance. What, may I ask, is that good for?"

God grew angry from these words but said nothing and began pacing to and fro, His hands working feverishly behind His back. Soon they had created a rat. The Devil meanwhile was smiling at the discomfort he had caused, but not for long. No sooner was the rat completed, then it raced over to him and climbed up to his mouth. Before he could get over his surprise it had bitten off his tongue and made him dumb.

This so outraged the Devil that he swore revenge. Debating about what he should do he finally decided to make rats multiply so rapidly that Man, whom God apparently liked, would be harassed by them continually.

Soon plagues of rats were bothering men all over the world. The Ainu, however, were troubled by them more than anyone else. Nothing seemed to halt their destructive habits or decrease their numbers. It was decided that only God could do this and they began to pray for Him for help. God was happy to come to their assistance. After much thought He solved their dilemma by creating cats. For this reason cats cannot help but be enemies of rats.

ICELAND

The Devil competed with God in creating the animals. His attempt to create a man, however, was not altogether a success. The creature appeared not in man's shape but in that of a cat without fur.

Peter, looking at this miserable creature, pitied it and made it some fur. And that explains how the cat made its appearance on earth and why only its fur is of any use to man.

FINLAND

After God had created man He showed him to the Devil. The Devil wanted to make something peculiar, too, and created the mouse, saying to God, "I have made a jumper." God replied, "And I will make a

"Cat" by Toko, Meji Period, Japan. (The Metropolitan Museum of Art, Gift in memory of Charles Stewart Smith, 1914.)

wrestler," and proceeded to make the cat which He sent after the mouse. The Devil, however, seized the cat firmly by its head and tail causing it to bend in the middle. And that is why to this day cats always have arched backs.

In another cat-origin tale from Finland, an eagle mistakes a stick of wood for a fish. When it seizes the stick its talons get caught in the wood's grain. The wind blows off its feathers and makes fur, and still further transformations finally produce the cat.

RUSSIA

God and the Devil were creating the animals, and God decided that He wanted to make a cat. The Devil said, "Make a cat, if you will, but remember that the head belongs to me." And so, although the cat's body belongs to God, its head belongs to the Devil.

BOHEMIA

When in the beginning of the world man's crops had been planted and were growing well the Devil created the mouse. He did this so that the mouse would destroy the grain and other growing things and cause man to go hungry. God, however, was taking care of man and created the cat so that it would destroy the work of the Devil.

HOPI INDIAN

A long time ago a Hopi boy went out to hunt. It was winter, and snow lay on the ground in the valley where he searched for game. To his surprise he found some tracks in it that were like no tracks he had ever seen before, and he followed them. Out of the valley they went, ending at last at a large rock. The boy put his hand into the opening under the rock and pulled out a strange animal by its leg. He tied its legs together and started back with it to his village.

When he reached home and asked his father what the animal was he was told that it was a cat and that it ate mice, rats and rabbits. On hearing this the boy went again into the valley and caught a rabbit which he brought back to the cat.

Keeping it confined in a niche in the wall of his home he continued to feed it for four days. In this way the cat became tame and has lived in Hopi houses ever since.

ASSAM, KHASI HILLS

Cat was Tiger's sister and they lived together in perfect harmony and accord. One day, however, Tiger got sick and began to shiver all over. Cat grew alarmed when his chills continued, and although she didn't like to leave him she decided she'd have to get some fire to warm him.

Man was the only one who had fire so she went to his house to ask for some. No one was at home. She went inside to get the fire herself, but what did she see as soon as she entered but some rice and fish on the floor. And how good they tasted!

In the meantime Tiger began to wonder what was keeping Cat. When his teeth stopped chattering long enough he called and called to her. Cat finally heard him. With her stomach comfortably full she had curled up at the hearthside to enjoy its pleasant warmth. Guiltily she

"Cast Bronze Cat," China, Ming Dynasty (1368–1644).
(Royal Scottish Museum, Edinburgh)

took some fire and ran back to him with it. But she had found indoor life so much to her liking that she decided to live that way from then on. She told her brother of her decision and ran back to the house.

Tiger was so angry that he forgot how sick he felt. He ran after her and prowled around the house ready to grab her and eat her if she showed herself outside. But she remained indoors, and the door remained shut.

Since that day cats have lived with the Khasi people, and tigers try to kill cats whenever they can.

CHINA

Once upon a time there lived a young man who earned his living by gathering and selling firewood. His search for wood often took him into heavily forested mountains, and one day, having wandered from his usual route, he became lost. Night was coming on and he was certain he'd have to spend it in the open when, as if from nowhere, an old man came to him and invited him to his hut for shelter.

In the morning when the youth was thanking his host for the night's lodging and bidding him farewell, the old man handed him two animals. He had never seen anything like them before. They were very small and striped all over their bodies.

"Take good care of them and you will find you have two fine companions," the old man said. "They are intelligent and will be a good addition to your household." The young wood-gatherer thanked him for the gifts and departed.

Although the animals were small they were hard to manage, and before the youth had gone very far, one of them struggled from his grasp and vanished into the forest. He searched and searched for it but finally gave up and went home with the one that remained. He took very good care of it as he had promised he would, and it grew into a very handsome domestic cat, the first of its kind.

As for the animal that had escaped into the forest, it was hard put to survive, and the more it had to struggle for its existence the larger and stronger and fiercer it grew. It was soon the terror of the entire countryside. It was a tiger.

II
Geographical and Natural History

It's bad enough that knowledge of the domestic cat's past is less than meager, but now the validity of the little that is known is being questioned. Worse yet, no new facts are turning up concerning the dissemination of *Felis catus* throughout the world or its presence during different periods of civilization. So, instead of information growing on the subject, it's beginning to shrink.

The following chronology, up to the 16th century, is an abbreviated presentation of facts now known. When any of these warrants enlargement it is presented in more detail in one of the sections that follow, and is so designated here by one of the following letters for identification.

FT—Folktales and fables which could help to unravel the time element in the cat's distribution and which also illustrate the interpretation of its nature at that particular period.

P—Poetry which gives facts about cat natural history as well as dating it.

RL—Religion and laws which, while indicating human appraisal of the cat, inform us about its natural history and geographic distribution.

NH—A selection of general natural history on the cat, principally by naturalists, to illustrate how various concepts about it continue or change over the centuries: some are repeated almost verbatim while others vary according to the times if not the writer.

THE BEGINNING

3000 B.C. *India.* Cats mentioned in Sanskrit writings.

1900 B.C. *Egypt.* Cats represented in art; these are now usually considered to be wild rather than domestic cats.

1700 B.C. *Palestine.* Ivory statuette of a cat discovered from Lachish.

1600 B.C. *Egypt.* Cats definitely established as domestic and holy animals. To kill a cat was a sin punishable by death, and mourning for the death of a family cat was enforced.

Around this time cats were also beginning to spread throughout the Mediterranean Region through thefts from Egypt.

1500 B.C., *or earlier. Greece.* Cretan wall painting of a cat stalking a pheasant, Palace at Hagia Triada.

1100 B.C., *or earlier. Greece.* Terracotta head of cat found in Crete.

1000 B.C. Homer, the great epic poet, possibly alluded to the cat under the word *gale* in his "Battle of the Frogs." However, most authorities believe that at this time *gale* did not signify cat.

710 B.C. *Book of Isaiah.* "Owls shall dwell there, and satyrs shall dance there." *and* "The wild beasts of the desert shall also meet with the wild beasts of the Island, and the satyr shall cry to his fellow." Satyr is thought to mean cat but could easily be other animals.

588 B.C. *Book of Baruch.* "Upon their bodies [the idols' bodies] and heads sit bats, swallows, and birds, and cats also."

"Cats" are now thought to be wagtails which is far more logical. In Latin this bird has the same name as cat.

MOSTLY GREECE

c.560 B.C. Aesop and Pilpay created their fables. FT

500 B.C., and later. The height of Etruscan culture, from which art depicting the cat was found. One vase painting shows two women playing with a cat, teasing it with a bird.

480 B.C. Greek marble relief from the Themistoclean wall near Athens depicts men trying to make a cat and dog fight.

c.450 B.C. Herodotus, traveller, historian and anthropologist, commented on Egyptian cats. see p. 221

c.400 B.C. Tarentum (Greece) coins minted. Two depict a cat, one of which is shown leaping at a bird held in a woman's hand.

Aristophanes, the most celebrated Greek comic poet, included a cat as one of the items offered for sale by the Boetian in "The Acharnians."

c.350 B.C. Anaxandrides of Rhodes, Greek comic poet, has one of his characters in "The Cities" say to an Egyptian, "If you see a cat indisposed you weep for it. For my part I am well pleased to kill it for its skin."

Cats appear on Greek vase paintings. One shows a man throwing a ball into the air to amuse a cat; another shows a man holding one on his arm.

Aristotle, pupil of Plato, tutor of Alexander the Great, a diversified scholar but at his best as a naturalist, mentioned the cat only briefly. NH

c.320 B.C. Timocles, Greek comic poet, is credited with saying that he certainly would not fear violating cat shrines when irreverence to the great gods themselves went unpunished.

c.270 B.C. In his fifteenth Idyll, Theocritus, one of the most celebrated Greek pastoral poets, has a character called Praxinoe who is in a hurry to leave for a feast call to her slave:

"Eunoa! my cloak, you wanton, quickly raise,
And place it near me—cats would softly sleep."

Prof. Rolleston disagreed with this translation by Chapman. He argued that the word translated as cloak actually means towel. Praxinoe wishes to wash before going out and sees that cats are asleep on the towel, so she calls, "Eunoa, give me the towel, stupid. Cats always have to sleep on a soft bed."

Whether cats were actually present or whether Eunoa was merely being compared to one makes no difference. The conclusion is the same; cats must have been domestic animals in some homes at least in the third century B.C. and were already noted for their ability to choose comfortable sleeping places.

c.100 A.D. Plutarch, Greek biographer and essayist (c.50–120), wrote a little about cats. see p. 226

ROME

Romans apparently used cats principally for utilitarian purposes as did the Greeks, but cats must have been generally known because cat figurines were found in Roman settlements in France and Spain and the remains of cats themselves were found in England. They appeared on coins as well as in art and were emblazoned on shields and banners, but in literature they were ignored or maligned. Their defects and not their attributes seem to have impressed writers, except, of course, their usefulness in rodent control. Earlier agricultural treatises such as Cato's *De Re Rustica* (200 B.C.) fail to mention them in this capacity, but the later ones do.

c.200 B.C. Tiberius Gracchus, the Roman statesman (168–133 B.C.), had a temple of liberty built whose goddess held a sceptre in one hand and a cap in the other, while at her feet was a cat, the emblem of liberty.

Spain. Bronze cat unearthed in Italica.

c.100 B.C. Diodorus, who wrote a history of the world, told of a mountain in Numidia (roughly modern Algeria) which was inhabited by a commonwealth of cats so that no birds dared to nest there. Hunters supposedly carried away captive cats from here to decadent Greece. see also p. 241

Virgil, the most illustrious of Latin poets (70–19 B.C.) is said to have used as a theme for poetic allusion the cat's supposed uneasiness at the approach of rain.

Mosaics of cats found at Pompey and Orange, France.

1st Century A.D. Ovid, the popular Roman poet (43 B.C.–18 A.D.) gave slight mention to cats in his *Metamorphoses*. FT

Pliny (23–79) in his *Natural History* speaks of cat worship: "And taking the Arabian side of the Nile first, we have the catadupe tribe, and then the Syenitae, and the towns of Tacompson . . . Dumana, Radata (where a golden cat used to be worshipped as a god) . . . ." see also pp. 72 & 74

Martial, the epigrammist (c.40–c.100), wrote:

> Pannonicas nobis nunquam dedit Umbria Cattas;
> Mavult haec Domino mittere dona pudens.

Here, as in the Book of Baruch, a bird rather than a cat must be referred to considering the placement of the lines in the text.

c.220 Aelian, in his history of animals, commented briefly on the cat, borrowing in part from previous works. NH

3rd Century. On a tomb of the Gallo-Roman period is shown a young girl holding a cat in her arms.

4th Century. Palladius, a writer on agriculture, recommended that cats be kept in gardens to protect them from mice and moles.

Roman cats in Britain. Skeletons have been found in domestic situations in the following places: near Chesham and Hambledon, Buckinghamshire, c.325 and 350 respectively; Silchester, Hampshire, c.350; Lullingstone, Kent, c.350; Caerwent, Monmouthshire.

EUROPE PRINCIPALLY

c.10 A.D. *Ireland.* Cairbre the Cat-headed (or Cairbre Cat-Head), the last king of the Aitheach-Tuatha (Atticotti) was said to be so-called because his god had the shape of a cat. The meager facts available would seem to indicate it was a wildcat.

2nd–6th Century. The Talmud, the written form of the oral laws of the Jews, was gathered over these four centuries. In it we read that if we wish to see the evil spirits we must take the afterbirth of a firstborn black cat which is the daughter of a firstborn black cat, burn it and grind it to a powder, then put the ashes into our eyes. This sounds like a borrowing from early Christian superstition rather than a part of the "original" Talmud and also raises the question as to how early varied coat colors in cats began to appear.

2nd–9th Century. Gospel of the Holy Twelve. RL

2nd–10th Century. Remains of cats, presumably domestic, found in Central Europe.

6th Century. Agathias, Greek historian and poet (527–565), and his disciple Damocharis, the Grammarian, wrote poems about the former's wicked cat who killed a partridge. Only portions of these poems are reprinted here. P

Pope Gregory the Great (c.550–604) was said to have had a cat as his only companion after he retired from secular duties to live a monastic life.

Zend, the language of Zoroaster, had a word for the domestic cat—*gatu.* Zend gave place to the Persian language which dates its origin from the Arabic invasion in the 7th century. The inference can consequently be drawn that cats were domesticated in that region well before the 7th century. *Gatu,* almost identical to the Spanish *gato,* means a place. This is significant considering that cats have always been thought lovers of places rather than people.

Byzantine Greece, which reached its peak in the 6th century, also had a word to designate the domestic cats brought there from Egypt—káttos or katta.

Persian manuscripts and paintings in this period contained cats.

7th Century. Mohammed's love of cats sanctified them for Moslems. RL

Ancient Burgundians were fond of incorporating the cat in their coats-of-arms. For example, the wife of King Clovis used for hers a cat sable killing a rat.

8th Century. Ireland. The Brehon Laws or Ancient Irish Code were written down between the 8th and 13th centuries. RL

Ireland. An ancient scholar wrote the poem "Pangur Ban." P

Arabia. The poet Abn Shamaqmaq wrote a poem in 770 entitled "The Hungry Cat" in which the cat's master addresses it.

9th Century. Ireland. The Book of Kells included an excellent cat illustration.

10th Century. Arabia. The poet Ibn Alalaf Alnaharwany wrote "To a Cat, killed as she was robbing a Dovecote." This was apparently based on Pilpay's fable (see p. 26–27). P

Henry I of Saxony, called Henry the Fowler (876–936), ruled that anyone who killed an adult cat would be fined 60 bushels of corn.

Welsh laws which included the cat were issued in the reign of Hywel Dda (d. 948). RL

The Byzantine Empress Zoë (980–1054) owned a pet cat. see p. 147

The *Arabian Nights* was put into print. FT

11th Century. Teutonic mythology was written down. FT

The Crusades. The Crusaders (11th–14th century) did not bring cats back with them as has often been stated. Cats were already in England and on the continent.

12th Century. Reynard the Fox printed. FT

A bestiary mentions the cat, and the "Lincoln Bestiary" contained an excellent cat illustration. NH

Diverse forms of "Dick Whittington" printed. FT

England. 1127. A canon forebade all nuns, including abbesses, to wear any costlier skins than those of lambs and cats. Reference here is thought to be to the wild cat which was eagerly hunted.

Persia. Cats continue to appear in the art of that country.

13th Century. France. "Romance of the Rose," a poem on the art of love, was begun by Guillaume de Lorris (?–c.1240) and finished by Jean Meung (c.1280–?). Angora cats are mentioned in it, who, snug in their fur coats, are likened to beneficent canons.

Italy. Dante (1265–1321) mentions cats only once in his poetry, comparing them to demons who, with their hooks, claw the barterers when these sinners try to emerge from the hot pitch in which they are being punished. He says of one of these: among wicked cats came the mouse.

England. 1205. The Ancren Riewle (Nun's Rule) denied nuns the possession of flocks, cattle, swine, or other domestic animals except for the cat. "Ye shall not possess any beast, my dear sisters, except only a cat. An anchoress that hath cattle appears as Martha was, a better housewife than anchoress . . ."

The Moslem, Sultan El-Daher-Beybars, who reigned in Egypt and Syria c.1260, bequeathed an orchard close to Cairo for the benefit of cats. From its revenue food was bought and distributed in the outer court of the Mehkémeh to all indigent and needy cats.

Bartholomeus Anglicus touched on the cat in his "De Proprietatibus Rerum," c.1260. NH

The proverb "The cat would eat fish but would not wet its feet" first (?) mentioned.

14th Century. The Knights Templars (1309) were charged with worshipping a cat.

c.1350. A Cornish miracle play has Noah building his Ark. He is derided by his neighbors, one of whom says, "All your labor is not worth a cat." Cats then must still have had a little value.

1398–99. Scotland. In these two years cats were bought at 2 pence each. As they were bought for the service of the State, this was doubtless much higher than the market price. "In vncto empto ad vnguendos pullanos, *ijd.* In *i.j.* gatis emptis, *iiijd.*" Acc., &c. Exch. K.R., Bundle 7, No. 20, fo. 7b.

Chaucer (1328–1400) gave a good description of cats in his *Canterbury Tales.* see p. 159 and 236

Petrarch, the Italian poet, (1304–1374), owned a cat that vied with his Laura for his affections. According to some, his love for it exceeded that for Laura.

15th Century. Leonardo da Vinci (1452–1519) made numerous cat drawings.

John Skelton (1460–1529) wrote "The Boke of Phylyp Sparowe," a tirade about a cat killing a bird similar to that of Agathias 1000 years previously.

Desiderius Erasmus, the famous Dutch scholar and philosopher, (1465–1536), visited England in 1498. He found the earls there wearing cloaks trimmed with catskin (wild or domestic?). In a letter to a friend he mentioned that a visit to an English home necessitated not only kissing the host and hostess and their children, but also the family cat.

Andrea Doria (1466–1560). It is said that a favorite cat of this famous Genoese admiral accompanied him on all his voyages and took part in all the action. A painting of the admiral in his later years includes a cat, probably one of a succession over the years.

THE CAT IN THE EASTERN WORLD

The cat's history in the East parallels that in the West. In China as in Egypt cats were portrayed before 2000 B.C., but not until around 400 A.D. were they without question domestic animals. Ancient Chinese documents describe them as hunters of mice and slayers of hens, and they were valued only for their destruction of rodents as were those in ancient Greece and Rome. Confucius is said to have had a favorite cat, but as he lived in the 5th century B.C. this story is probably apocryphal.

The Japanese emperor Ichijō (986–1011) is credited with introducing the cat into his country from China. Here, too, after it became common, it was thought of only in terms of its utility and not as a house pet. We get an idea of how much it was prized before this came about from Lady Sei Shonagon's story of the imperial cat, written about 1000 A.D. and translated by Nobuko Kobayashi:

"The cat which dwells in the Presence was lately ennobled and therefore respectfully addressed by all as Myobu-no-Omoto. She is the loveliest creature, and their Majesties adored her. One day she lay on the very edge of the veranda, and her lady-attendant said in alarm: 'Pray pardon me, madam, but do move further in!'

"Not the least notice did she take and went placidly off to sleep, drowsing in the sun. At last her lady threatened her, though of course only in jest, saying: 'Where is the dog? Okinamaru, the Imperial Cat won't listen! Come and bite her.'

"Unluckily Okinamaru thought he was wanted in earnest, and he sprang at the exalted cat and she made a dash for it behind the bamboo screen where the Emperor was breakfasting. In horror he caught her to his breast and called aloud. Kuroda Tadataka rushed into the Presence.

" 'Exile this dog to Dog's Island this instant.'

"The Imperial command was given. Men assembled and made a great shouting and Okinamaru was driven away. Next came the lady's turn.

" 'This attendant can in no way be trusted. All must be changed.'

"She was imprisoned in her room. Okinamaru was exiled."

When cats in Japan became common enough to be owned by many they also came to be feared. Demons were thought to take their shape. In China they were linked with witchcraft, as were cats in the West in the Middle Ages and later. They have been associated with the occult in every part of the world, a good indication of the basic similarities of all humans and all cats. This is further borne out by Eastern literature concerning the cat, a good example of which is Kaibara's short summary appearing in volume 16 of *Yamato Honzo,* written in 1708:

"The cat differs from all other mammals in these nine points. First, it cleanses its face when it feels contentedly. Secondly, it purrs to express gladness. Thirdly, it sharpens its claws when full of valour. Fourthly, its female nurses the kittens of any other females with a perfectly good will. Fifthly, its pupils change their shapes according to the hours of the day. Sixthly, its nose is always cool at the tip. Seventhly, it rejoices when one strokes its throat. Eighthly, it perishes in a place quite out of human sight, as if it wills not to let man see its dying look, which is unusually ugly. Ninthly, it is very passionately fond of matatabi—not only does it eat it, but also it rubs its body with the roots, stem, and leaves of the plant, well knowing it is its superlative panacea."

III
Fables and Folktales

To present fables and folktales as evidence that the cat was known at a certain period of history is unsound and unscientific. Through the years translators and compilers of these ancient stories have changed them and made additions of their own, with the result that fables attributed to Aesop, for example, can actually be of more recent origin. However, the history of the cat being no less obscure than that of fables and folktales, an attempt at presenting chronologically arranged stories about them will do no harm and might help to clarify the cat's position in antiquity.

Pre-Christian Era. I choose to follow those scholars who believe that the fabulists, Pilpay and Aesop, actually existed and were not one and the same person. And I choose to begin the historical treatment of the cat in folktales with Pilpay whose source material, at least, predates that of any other cat storyteller.

Pilpay, an oriental fabulist, is said to have been a Brahman gymnosophist, a sort of hermit philosopher, living several centuries before Christ. According to some authorities his fables had their origin in the Panchatantra, a Sanskrit collection of animal fables, or in its earlier versions. Others maintain that Pilpay himself wrote the Panchatantra as we now know it.

Regardless of how they came to be, the stories attributed to Pilpay were translated from the Sanskrit into Persian during the 6th century A.D. Two centuries later this translation was rendered into Arabic which in turn was translated into Greek in the 11th century. A Hebrew translation was made somewhat later, and it was this translation of translations that became the source of a Latin version made in the 13th century and first published in 1480. Through it Pilpay was introduced into Europe, and from it stemmed the European language translation, although one English translation was made direct from the Sanskrit in 1787.

The three cat fables given here are those from a collection published in 1818 in London. Although they vary from the original Sanskrit, it is only in details which make no difference for the use they are put to here. Notice how the cat's innate drive to care for its basic needs, the theme for all three tales, is interpreted as a sign of greed or deceit. Outside of Egypt, where they were still being worshipped, cats already had a poor reputation, though why the ancients chose greed as one of their major faults is difficult to understand. Today's cat is an opportunist and an epicure but can hardly be called greedy. Were cats of an earlier date different?

In Aesop's fables cat character fares no better, usually being portrayed as villainous. One thing becomes certain from the narrations: the cat's predilection for mice hasn't changed over the years. Aesop lived from about 619 to 564 B.C., roughly in the same era as that assigned to Pilpay. Thought to be a Phrygian by birth, he became the slave of Iadmon of Samos, and, when later freed, lived at the court of Croesus where he became famous for his moralizing animal tales.

Allusions to his fables were frequent in the writings of the period but his writings weren't put into book form until around 300 B.C. As with Pilpay, many translations then followed. The first was into Latin from which it was rendered into Syriac; from the Syriac it went back into Greek. As more and more editions came out, oriental and other spurious tales crept into the collection, and it is this contamination which makes it impossible to say what is or isn't Aesop. The European countries got their so-called Aesop from the relatively late translation of Maximus Planudes, a Byzantine monk who lived in the 14th century.

Of the numerous cat fables attributed to Aesop I give the four that appear most authentic—short, simple, pithy tales with obvious morals and no human characters.

FABLES FROM PILPAY

The Cat and the Two Birds. Some years ago, said the raven, I made my nest upon a tree, at the foot of which there frequently sat a partridge, a fair and comely bird, well shaped and good-humored: our neighboring situation soon brought us acquainted with one another; and after a short knowledge of each other's talents and humor, we made a league of friendship together, and almost continually kept one another company. Some time after our first entering on this intimacy one with another, my friend, however, absented herself, for what reason I know not, and stayed away so long, that I thought her dead; but my thoughts of this kind were mistaken, for she at length returned, but had the misfortune to find her habitation in possession of another bird. The partridge pretended the house was hers, and would have made a forcible entry; but the bird refused to go out, alleging that possession was the strongest tenure of law. I endeavored, soon after this, to bring them to an accommodation, but all to no purpose; for the partridge's attorney, finding she had money, egged her on, and tickled her ears with a lease of ejectment. However, at length, the partridge, finding the law to be very tedious and expensive, said one day to herself, 'Here lives hard by, I remember, a very devout cat; he fasts every day, does nobody harm, and spends the nights in prayer: let us, in short,' said she to her adversary, 'distract our brains and empty our purses no more about law, but refer our difference to him: I know not where we shall find a more equitable judge.' The other bird having consented to this proposal, they went both to this religious cat, and I followed them out of curiosity. Entering, I saw the cat very attentive at a long prayer, without turning either to the right or left; which put me in mind of the old proverb, that 'Long prayers before people is the key of hell.' I admired his sober hypocrisy, and had the patience to stay till the venerable personage had done; after which the partridge and her antagonist accosted him with great respect, and requested him to hear their difference, and give judgment according to the usual rules of justice. The cat, in his fur gown, acting the part of a grave and formal judge, first heard what the stranger bird had to plead for itself; and then addressing himself to the partridge, 'My pretty love,' said he, 'come you now to me and let me hear your story; but as I am old and thick of hearing, pray come near and lift up your voice, that I may not lose a word of what you say.' The partridge and the other bird, on this, seeing him so devout and sanctified, both went boldly close up to him; but then the hypocrite discovered the bottom of his sanctity, for he immediately fell upon them, and in short devoured them both. (The Sanskrit tale tells of a partridge and hare rather than two birds.)

THE RAVENOUS CAT. A certain person bred up a cat very frugally in his own house. He gave her enough to suffice nature, though nothing superfluous: and she might, if she pleased, have lived very happily with him; but she was very ravenous, and, not content with her ordinary food, hunted about in every corner for more. One day, passing by a dove-house, she saw some young pigeons that were hardly fledged; and presently her teeth watered for a taste of those delicate viands. With this resolution up she boldly mounted into the dove-house, never minding whether the master were there or no, and was presently, with great joy, preparing to satisfy her voluptuous desires. But the master of the place no sooner saw the epicure of a cat enter, than he shut up the doors, and stopped up all the holes at which it was possible for her to get out again, and so bestirred himself, that he caught the felonious baggage, and hanged her up at the corner of the pigeon-house. Soon after this the owner of the cat passing that way, and seeing his cat hanged, 'Unfortunate greedy-gut,' said he, 'hadst thou been contented with thy meaner food, thou hadst not been now in this condition! Thus,' continued he, moralizing on the spectacle, 'insatiable gluttons are the procurers of their own untimely ends . . .' "

THE GREEDY AND AMBITIOUS CAT. There was formerly an old woman in a village, extremely thin, half-starved, and meager. She lived in a little cottage as dark and gloomy as a fool's heart, and withal as close shut up as a miser's hand. This miserable creature had for the companion of her wretched retirements a cat meager and lean as herself; the poor creature never saw bread nor beheld the face of a stranger, and was forced to be contented with only smelling the mice in their holes, or seeing the prints of their feet in the dust. If by some extraordinary lucky chance this miserable animal happened to catch a mouse, she was like a beggar that discovers a treasure; her visage and her eyes were inflamed with joy, and that booty served her for a whole week; and out of the excess of her admiration, and distrust of her own happiness, she would cry out to herself, 'Heavens! Is this a dream, or is it real?' One day, however, ready to die for hunger, she got upon the ridge of her enchanted castle, which had long been the mansion of famine for cats, and spied from thence another cat, that was stalking upon a neighbor's wall like a lion, walking along as if she had been counting her steps, and so fat that she could hardly go. The old woman's cat, astonished to see a creature of her own species so plump and large, with a loud voice, cries out to her pussy neighbor, 'In the name of pity, speak to me, thou happiest of the cat kind! Why, you look as if you came from one of the Khan of Kathai's feasts; I conjure ye, to tell me how, or in what region it is that you get your skin so well stuffed?' 'Where?' replied the fat one; 'why, where should one feed well but at a king's table? I go to the house,' continued she, 'every day about dinner-time, and there I lay my paws upon some delicious morsel or other, which serves me till the next, and then leave enough for an army of mice, which under me live in peace and tranquility; for why should I commit murder for a piece of tough and skinny mouse flesh, when I can live on venison at a much easier rate?' The lean cat, on this, eagerly inquired the way to this house of plenty, and entreated her plump neighbor to carry her one day along with her. 'Most willingly,' said the fat puss; 'for thou seest I am naturally charitable, and thou art so lean that I heartily pity thy condition.' On this promise they parted; and the lean cat returned to the old woman's chamber, where she told her dame the story of what had befallen her. The old woman prudently endeavored to persuade her cat from prosecuting her design, admonishing her withal to have a care of being deceived; 'For, believe me,' said she, 'the desires of the ambitious are never to be satiated, but when their mouths are stuffed with the dirt of their graves. Sobriety and temperance are the only things that truly enrich people. I must tell thee, poor silly cat, that they who travel to satisfy their ambition, have no knowledge of the good things they possess, nor are they truly thankful to heaven for what they enjoy, who are not contented with their fortune.'

The poor starved cat, however, had conceived so fair an idea of the king's table, that the old woman's good morals and judicious remonstrances entered in at one ear and went out at the other. In short, she departed the next day with the fat puss to go to the king's house; but, alas! before she got thither, her destiny had laid a snare for her. For being a house of good cheer, it was so haunted with cats that the servants had, just at this time, orders to kill all the cats that came near it, by reason of a great robbery committed the night before in the king's larder by several grimalkins. The old woman's cat, however, pushed on by hunger, entered the house, and no sooner saw a dish of meat unobserved by the cooks, but she made a seizure of it, and was doing what for many years she had not done before, that is, heartily filling her belly; but as she was enjoying herself under the dresser-board, and feeding heartily upon her stolen morsels, one of the testy officers of the kitchen, missing his breakfast, and seeing where the poor cat was solacing herself with it, threw his knife at her with such an unlucky hand, that he stuck her full in the breast. However, as it has been the providence of nature to give this creature nine lives instead of one, poor puss made a shift to crawl away, after she had for some time shammed dead: but, in her flight, observing the blood come streaming from her wound: 'Well,' said she, 'let me but escape this accident, and if ever I quit my old hold and my own mice for all the rarities in the king's kitchen, may I lose all of my nine lives at once.'

FABLES FROM AESOP

THE CAT AND THE COCK. A cat caught a cock, and because cats don't ordinarily eat cocks, let alone catch them, he tried to think of a good reason why he should eat this one.

"You're a nuisance," he told the cock. "Your crowing keeps others from sleeping, so I'm going to make an end of you."

The cock defended himself by saying, "I crow only when it is time for others to rise to a new day and set about their work. Without me many would oversleep."

"That may be," said the cat, "but I'm still not going to go hungry." And he killed and ate the cock.

THE CAT AND THE MICE. A cat settled down in a house full of mice. Day after day she caught and ate them until finally the remaining mice panicked and decided to stay in their holes.

There was only one thing for the cat to do if she wanted to eat and that was to coax the mice from their security with a trick. She hung herself by means of her hind legs from a peg on a wall and pretended to be dead.

A wise old mouse peering out of his hole saw her hanging in this way. "Oh, you're very clever, Cat," he taunted, "but you'll have to do better than that. Even if you turn yourself into a bag of meal while you hang there we won't come anywhere near you."

THE CAT AND THE FOX. A cat and a fox began a discussion about what they could do to save themselves if they were attacked by dogs. The cat admitted that she had only one good way to escape them and if that failed she was done for.

"I feel sorry for you," said the fox in his superior way. "Why, I have at least a hundred different tricks I can use to save myself from those brutes. It's too bad you're not as clever as I am."

Hardly had he said this when a pack of hounds came over the hill toward where the cat and fox sat.

The cat immediately used her only means of escape. She ran to the nearest tree and climbed it as fast as she could.

The hounds raced by underneath her after the fox, who, having been taken unawares, was unable to employ even one of his many tricks. He was soon overtaken and killed.

THE MICE IN COUNCIL. The mice had a big meeting to decide what could be done about the cat who was killing so many of them.

They were getting nowhere until one mouse spoke up and said, "To provide for our safety is a simple matter. All we have to do is bell the cat. The tinkling of the bell when she walks will always warn us of her presence."

Everyone applauded this sage advice and shouted with pleasure over having at last a solution to their problem. When the noise and excitement had finally died down an old mouse quietly said, "The idea is a fine one, I agree, but tell me, who is going to tie the bell on the cat?"

1st Century A.D. Ovid, the popular Roman poet who lived from 43 B.C. to 18 A.D. gives slight mention to the cat in his *Metamorphoses,* and even this mention is questioned. The first reference is in book V where he speaks of the flight of the gods and goddesses into Egypt to escape from Typhon, a monster giant.

> . . . "Jupiter,"
> She said, "became a ram, leader of sheep—
> Ammon of Libya wears his crooked horns—
> Apollo was a crow, Bacchus a goat,
> And Phoebus' sister then became a cat,
> And Juno a great cow, white as snowdrift,
> Venus a fish and Mercury an ibis."

The question as to whether "cat" here means our domestic *Felis* or a weasel is the usual one for this period of history, when "cat" was still an unspecific word. In this case it has generally been decided that "cat" means *Felis*. One of the principal arguments favoring such a decision is that the oldest (?) of all cat myths, which originated in India, tells of the cat moon devouring the grey mice of twilight. Diana was a lunar deity so what is more logical than for her to assume the form of a feline? In this form she is said by some to have hidden in the moon itself to spy on Typhon.

The question of cat or not-cat also arises in the legend of Galanthis where Ovid again mentions a "cat." Jealous goddesses are preventing Galanthis's mistress, Alcmena, from giving birth to Hercules. Through trickery, Galanthis foils their plot and enables the birth to take place. For this deceit Juno changes her into a cat.

There seems to be no reason in this case to assume that "cat" is anything but cat. Galanthis was deceitful, and cats have always been credited with this trait. What is more logical, then, than to turn a woman who acts like a cat into the animal itself?

Tenth Century A.D. From Pilpay, Aesop and Ovid to the *Arabian Nights* and "Dick Whittington" means a jump of many centuries, those centuries that furnish us with almost no knowledge of the cat in any discipline.

The *Arabian Nights,* or *The Book of the Thousand Nights and a Night,* reached Arabia in the 10th century through a translation from the Persian which had been made a century earlier from its supposed Indian origin. (Portions found their way into the Jewish *Book of Esther* as well.) Again, there is the problem of evaluating which tales are authentic and which are not, and which may have been tampered with.

On the 150th night we are told the story of a crow that rescues a cat from certain death, but it's hard to believe that the creature is actually a cat. It is insipid and spineless, with absolutely no initiative, and you feel that it wrings its paws in anguish as it begs the crow to save it from the leopard. No cat is that degenerate, and no matter what you think about cats you can never say that they rely on and put their trust in others. Rather, it's through self sufficiency, independence and distrust that they gain enemies. No, a cat just doesn't suit the part in this story, and that leaves the question: if the original actor was a cat, why was it chosen, or why was the plot changed to make it so uncatlike?

The story of "The Mouse and the Cat" that begins in the 900th night is in keeping with the opinions voiced in the fables, that the cat is a wicked animal without morals. The unpleasant side of the cat—the deceitful mouse-murderer side—is exposed, but at least you know you're reading about a cat and not a nonentity as in the other tale. Both tales given here are Burton's translations.

Dick Whittington's cat is a nonentity, too, but only because it plays an undeveloped part in the story, the lowly part of mouse-catcher. Here, naturally, its activities are lauded because they bring about monetary gain.

The origin of Whittington and his cat may also be traceable to the East. Sir William Gore Ousely in his *Travels* is said to have mentioned a Persian manuscript that relates a similar tale. In the 10th century, Keis, the son of a poor widow in Siraf, left for India taking with him a cat, his sole possession. The story then parallels that of Whittington, and Keis returns to Siraf a rich man. Afterwards, with his mother and brothers, he settled on an island in the Persian Gulf and named the island Keis, the Persian *Keish*.

This is the earliest mention of the Whittington story that I have found, and it conflicts with other claims made for the story's origin. Venice is usually credited with the first version (around the middle of the 12th century) in the Chronicle of Albert, Abbot of the Convent of St. Mary at Stade, while a Persian variant with an old woman being the cat's owner didn't appear until 1300.

In the latter half of the 15th century the Italians circulated still another variant, and Denmark and Tuscany also had theirs. Although Whittington lived from 1358 to 1423, the cat wasn't mentioned, so far as can be ascertained, until the beginning of the 17th century, and the first picture of him with it is dated 1536.

The question as to whether the story is fact or fiction remains unsettled. Those who believe the former claim that all the stories from all the countries are true cases because in the far past cats were as yet unknown in many rat-infested countries. Fortunes were consequently made by introducing them to these places, and authenticated cases of later dates bear this out. True or not, the recorded histories serve their purpose by offering further evidence of the cat's presence in different parts of the world in the early centuries A.D.

A TALE OF THE CAT AND THE CROW

Once upon a time, a crow and a cat lived in brotherhood; and one day as they were together under a tree, behold, they spied a leopard making towards them, and they were not aware of his approach till he was close upon them. The crow at once flew up to the treetop; but the cat abode confounded and said to the crow, "O my friend, hast thou no device to save me, even as all my hope is in thee?" Replied the crow, "Of very truth it behoveth brethren, in case of need, to cast about for a device when peril overtaketh them, and how well saith the poet,

A friend in need is he who, ever true,
For thy well-doing would himself undo:
One who when fortune gars us parting rue
Victimeth self reunion to renew."

Now hard by that tree were shepherds with their dogs; so the crow flew towards them and smote the face of the earth with his wings, cawing and crying out. Furthermore he went up to one of the dogs and flapped his wings in his face and flew up a little way, whilst the dogs ran after him thinking to catch him. Presently, one of the shepherds raised his head and saw the bird flying near the ground and lighting alternately; so he followed him, and the crow ceased not flying just high enough to save himself and to throw out the dogs; and yet tempting them to follow for the purpose of tearing him to pieces. But as soon as they came near him, he would fly up a little; and so at last he brought them to the tree, under which was the leopard. And when the dogs saw him they rushed upon him and he turned and fled. Now the leopard thought to eat the cat who was saved by the craft of his friend the crow.

THE MOUSE AND THE CAT

A grimalkin, that is to say, a Cat, went out one night to a certain garden, in search of what she might devour, but found nothing and became weak for the excess of cold and rain that prevailed that night. So she sought for some device whereby to save herself. As she prowled about in search of prey, she espied a nest at the foot of a tree, and drawing near unto it, sniffed thereat and purred till she scented a Mouse within and went round about it, seeking to enter and seize the inmate. When the Mouse smelt the Cat, he turned his back to her and scraped up the earth with his forehand, to stop the nest-door against her; whereupon she assumed a weakly voice and said, "Why dost thou thus, O my brother? I come to seek refuge with thee, hoping that thou wilt take pity on me and harbour me in thy nest this night; for I am weak because of the greatness of my age and the loss of my strength, and can hardly move. I have ventured into thy garden tonight, and how many a time have I called upon death, that I might be at rest from this pain! Behold, here am I at thy door, prostrate from cold and rain and I beseech thee, by Allah, take of thy charity my hand and bring me in with thee and give me shelter in the vestibule of thy nest; for I am a stranger and wretched and 'tis said, 'Whoso sheltereth a stranger and a wretched one in his home his shelter shall be Paradise on the Day of Doom.' And thou, my brother, it behoveth thee to earn eternal reward by succouring me and suffering me abide with thee this night till the morning, when I will wend my way." Hearing these words the Mouse replied, "How shall I suffer thee enter my nest seeing that thou art my natural foe and thy food is of my flesh? Indeed I fear lest thou false me, for that is of thy nature and there is no faith in thee, and the byword saith, 'It befitteth not to entrust a lecher with a fair woman nor a moneyless man with money nor fire with fuel.' Neither doth it behove me to entrust myself to thee; and 'tis said, 'Enmity of kind, as the enemy himself groweth weaker, groweth stronger.' " The Cat made answer in the faintest voice, as she were in most piteous case, saying, "What thou advancest of admonitory instances is the truth and I deny not my offences against thee; but I beseech thee to pardon that which is past of the enmity of kind between me and thee; for 'tis said, 'Whoso forgiveth a creature like himself, his Creator will forgive him his sins.' 'Tis true that whilom I was thy foe, but here am I a suitor for thy friendship, and they say, 'And thou wilt have thy foe become thy friend, do with him good.' O my brother, I swear to thee by Allah and make a binding covenant with thee that I will hurt thee nevermore and for the best of reasons, to wit, that I have no power thereto; wherefore place thy trust in Allah and do good and accept my oath and covenant." Quoth the Mouse, "How can I accept the covenant of one between whom and me there is a rooted enmity, and whose wont it is to deal treacherously by me? Were the feud between us aught but one of blood, this were light to me; but it is an enmity of kind between souls, and it is said, 'Whoso trusteth himself to his foe is as one who thrusteth hand into a serpent's mouth.' " Quoth the Cat, full of wrath, "My breast is strait and my soul is faint: indeed I am *in articulo mortis* and ere long I shall die at thy door and my blood will be on thy head, for that thou hadst it in thy power to save me in mine extremity: and this is my last word to thee." Herewith the fear of Allah Almighty overcame the Mouse and ruth gat hold upon his heart and he said in himself, "Whoso would have the succour of Allah the Most High against his foe, let him entreat him with compassion and kindness show. I rely upon the Almighty in this matter and will deliver this Cat from this her strait and earn the divine reward for her." So he went forth and dragged into his nest the Cat, where she abode till she was rested and somewhat strengthened and restored, when she began to bewail her weakness and wasted strength and want of gossips. The Mouse entreated her in friendly guise and comforted her and busied himself with her service; but she crept along till she got command of the issue of the nest, lest the Mouse should escape. So when the nest-owner would have gone out after his wont, he drew near the Cat; whereupon she seized him and taking him in her claws, began to bite him and shake him and take him in her mouth and lift him up and cast him down and run after him and cranch him and torture him. The Mouse cried out for help, beseeching deliverance of Allah and began to upbraid the Cat, saying, "Where is the covenant thou madest with me and where are the oaths thou swarest to me? Is this my reward from thee? I brought thee into my nest and trusted myself to thee: but sooth he speaketh that saith, 'Whoso relieth on his enemy's promise desireth not salvation for himself.' And again, 'Whoso confideth himself to his foe deserveth his own destruction.' Yet do I put my trust in my Creator, for He will deliver me from thee." Now as he was in this condition, with the Cat about to pounce on him and devour him, behold, up came a huntsman, with hunting dogs trained to the chase. One of the hounds passed by the mouth of the nest and hearing a great scuffling, thought that within was a fox tearing somewhat; so he crept into the hole, to get at him, and coming upon the Cat, seized on her. When she found herself in the dog's clutches, she was forced to take thought anent saving herself and loosed the Mouse alive and whole without wound. Then the hound brake her neck and dragging her forth of the hole, threw her down dead: and thus was exemplified the truth of the saying, 'Who hath compassion shall at the last be compassionated. Whoso oppresseth shall presently be oppressed.'

Eleventh Century A.D. Teutonic mythology is thought to have been recorded for the first time during the 11th century, and Freya, whose chariot was drawn by cats (some say white ones, others black or grey) is one of its better-known goddesses. Although the god Thor is also well known, the story about him and a grey (?) cat is not. Whether these cats were in the original Germanic oral tales or were added when they were written down, can, of course, never be ascertained. They are cited here as proof that at least by the 11th century (and probably earlier) the cat was a familiar household pet of the northern Europeans.

Thor's encounter with the cat came about in this fashion. During his extensive wanderings he comes to the castle of Utgard-Loke, and is ridiculed by that king who makes light of his great prowess. He is told that he must prove his powers, and, as with Ulysses, various tasks are set before him.

"The children here in the castle play a little game," Utgard-Loke says. "I don't want to minimize your abilities, but maybe you'd like to try what they do. Their game is to lift my cat from the floor."

No sooner does Utgard-Loke speak, than a huge grey cat appears and sits down before him. Thor walks over to it at once, puts his hands under its belly and attempts to lift it. The cat's back arches mightily from his efforts, but although he uses all his strength he manages to raise only one of its paws from the floor. Realizing that is the limit of his capacity, he angrily gives up further attempts.

What Thor did not know was that he was in an enchanted castle and couldn't possibly succeed in any of the tasks given him. Later he learns that the cat was actually the famous Midgard serpent which encircles the earth. When he had managed to raise its paw his audience, unknown to him, almost panicked because by doing this the serpent had been raised so high that its head had reached heaven.

Can we accept the fact that Utgard-Loke's cat was grey and that

Freya's cats also were of one color? If so, it would indicate that the basic tabby pattern of the ancestral cat was already well diversified.

Twelfth Century. The beast epic *Reynard the Fox* and how he bested all the animals including Tybert the cat is too well known to require much introduction. Its origin began in the Aesopic fable of the sick lion who was told by the fox that he would get well if he wrapped himself in the wolf's skin. The two earliest versions known, the work of monks, were written in Latin. The first, "The Escape of a Captive in an Allegory," appeared in the 10th century, the second, "Ysengrimus," (the name of the wolf) around 1152.

Roman de Renard, composed by the mediaeval court poets, was begun around 1170 and added to until about 1250. Tybert the cat appears in its earlier portions, and the fox is made the main character instead of the wolf who had top billing in the Latin. The poets, however, drew heavily for their material from the Latin epic, merely adding embellishments and further episodes.

Reinhart Fuchs appeared in 1180. Although this German version diverges from the loose plot of the French *Renard,* the story is essentially the same. The cat merely suffers a change of name, from Tybert to Dieprecht. Not until 1250 when the Flemish version was written did *Reynard the Fox* really become popular. From then on many variations came into print although these were limited geographically for some time to western Germany, northern France and Flanders. Beast *stories* abounded throughout the world but not the beast *epic.*

Before Caxton's translation of Reynard in 1481, beast stories were practically non-existent in English literature. Caxton's translation was from the Flemish although English translations were subsequently made from the German. It is the modernized Caxton translation made by William Swan Stallybrass that is given here.

REYNARD THE FOX

Chapter 10. How the King sent another time Tybert the Cat for the Fox, and how Tybert sped with Reynard the Fox

Then the King said: "Sir Tybert, ye shall now go to Reynard, and say to him this second time that he come to Court unto the plea for to answer; for, though he be fell to other beasts, he trusteth you well and will do by your counsel. And tell (him), if he come not, he shall have the third warning and be summoned, and, if he then come not, we shall proceed by law against him and all his lineage without mercy."

Tybert spake: "My Lord the King, they that this counselled you were not my friends. What shall I do there? He will not for me neither come ne abide. I am little and feeble. Bruin the Bear, which was so great and strong, could not bring him: how should I then take it on hand?"

"Nay," said the King, "Sir Tybert, ye are wise and well learned. Though ye be not great, there lieth not much in that. Many do more with skill and knowledge than with might and strength."

Then said the Cat: "Sith it must needs be done, I must then take it upon me. God give grace that I may well achieve it, for my heart is heavy, and evil-willed thereto."

Tybert made him soon ready toward Maleperduys. And he saw from far come flying one of Saint Martin's birds; then cried he (a) loud and said: "All hail, gentle bird, turn thy wings hitherward, and fly on my right side." The bird flew forth upon a tree which stood on the left side of the Cat. Then was Tybert woe; for he thought it was a sinister token and a sign of harm. For, if the bird had flown on his right side, he had been merry and glad; but now he was anxious lest his journey should turn to misfortune. Nevertheless, he did as many do, and gave to himself better hope than his heart said. He went and ran toward Maleperduys, and there he found the Fox alone standing before his house.

Tybert said: "The rich God give you good even, Reynard! The King hath menaced you for to take your life from you if ye come not now with me to the Court."

The Fox then spake and said: "Tybert, my dear cousin, ye be right welcome! I would well truly that ye had much good luck." What hurted (it) the Fox to speak fair? Though he said well, his heart thought it not; and that shall be seen ere they depart.

Reynard said: "Shall we this night be together? I will make you good cheer, and to-morrow early in the dawning we will together go to the Court. Good nephew, let us so do; I have none of my kin that I trust so much to as to you. Here was Bruin the Bear—the traitor! He looked so knavishly on me, and methought he was so strong, that I would not for a thousand mark have gone with him; but, cousin, I will to-morrow early go with you."

Tybert said: "It is best that we now go, for the moon shineth all so light as it were day: I never saw fairer weather."

"Nay, dear cousin, such might meet us by day-time that would make us good cheer and by night peradventure might do us harm. It is suspicious to walk by night. Therefore abide this night here by me."

Tybert said: "What should we eat if we abode here?"

Reynard said: "Here is but little to eat. Ye may well have an honey-comb, good and sweet. What say ye, Tybert, will ye any thereof?"

Tybert answered: "I set naught thereby. Have ye nothing else? If ye gave me a good fat mouse, I should be better pleased."

"A fat mouse!" said Reynard. "Dear cousin, what say ye? Hereby dwelleth a Priest and hath a barn by his house; therein are so many mice that a man could not lead them away upon a wain. I have heard the Priest many times complain that they did him much harm."

"Oh, dear Reynard, lead me thither for all that I may do for you!"

"Yea, Tybert, say ye me truth? Love ye well mice?"

"If I love them well?" said the Cat. "I love mice better than anything that men give me! Know ye not that mice savour better than game—yea, than pancakes or pasties? Will ye well do, so lead me thither where the mice are, and then shall ye win my love, yea, although ye had slain my father, mother, and all my kin."

Reynard said, "Ye mock and jest therewith!"

The Cat said: "So help me God, I do not!"

"Tybert," said the Fox, "wist I that verily, I would yet this night make that ye should be full of mice."

"Reynard!" quoth he, "Full? That were many."

"Tybert, ye jest!"

"Reynard," quoth he, "in truth I do not. If I had a fat mouse, I would not give it for a golden noble."

"Let us go then, Tybert," quoth the Fox; "I will bring you to the place ere I go from you."

"Reynard," quoth the Cat, "upon your safe-conduct I would well go with you to Montpelier."

"Let us then go," said the Fox; "we tarry all too long."

Then went they forth, without hindrance to the place where they would be, to the Priest's barn, which was fast walled about with a mud wall. And the night before the Fox had broken in, and had stolen from the priest a good fat hen; and the Priest, all angry, had set a snare before the hole to avenge him; for he would fain have taken the Fox. This knew well the fell thief, the Fox, and said: "Sir Tybert, cousin, creep into this hole, and ye shall not long tarry but that ye shall catch mice by great heaps. Hark how they pipe! When ye be full, come again; I will tarry here after you before this hole. We will to-morrow go together to the Court. Tybert, why tarry ye thus long? Come off, and so may we return soon to my wife which waiteth for us, and shall make us good cheer."

Tybert said: "Reynard, cousin, is it then your counsel that I go into this hole? These Priests are so wily and shrewish I dread to take harm."

"'Oh, ho, Tybert!" said the Fox, "I saw you never so sore afraid! What aileth you?"

The Cat was ashamed, and sprang into the hole. And anon he was caught in the snare by the neck, ere he wist. Thus deceived Reynard his guest and cousin.

As Tybert was wary of the snare, he was afraid and sprang forth—the snare went to. Then he began to shout, for he was almost strangled. He called, he cried, and made a villainous noise.

Reynard stood before the hole and heard all, and was well satisfied, and said: "Tybert, love ye well mice? Be they fat and good? Knew the Priest hereof, or Mertynet, they be so gentle that they would bring you sauce. Tybert, ye sing and eat—is that the custom of the Court? Lord God, if Isegrim were there by you, in such rest as ye now be, then should I be glad; for oft he hath done me damage and harm."

Tybert could not go away; but he mewed and cried out so loud, that Mertynet sprang up, and cried (a)loud: "God be thanked, my snare hath taken the thief that hath stolen our hens. Arise up; we will reward him!"

With these words arose the Priest in an evil time, and waked all them that were in the house, and cried with a loud voice: "The Fox is taken!"

There leapt and ran all that there was. The Priest himself ran, all mother-naked. Mertynet was the first that came to Tybert. The Priest took to Locken (Julocke) his wife an offering candle, and bade her light it at the fire; and he smote Tybert with a great staff. There received Tybert many a great stroke over all his body. Mertynet was so angry that he smote the Cat an eye out. The naked Priest lifted up and should have given a great stroke to Tybert, but Tybert, that saw that he must die, sprang between the Priest's legs with his claws and with his teeth that he tore out his right colyon or balockstone. That leap became ill to the Priest, and to his great shame . . .

The Priest fell down a-swoon. They took him up, and brought him again to bed. Then went the Fox again in toward his burrow and left Tybert the Cat in great dread and jeopardy, for the Fox wist none other but that the Cat was nigh dead. But, when Tybert the Cat saw them all busy about the Priest, then began he to bite and gnaw the snare in the middle asunder, and sprang out of the hole, and went rolling and rolling towards the King's Court. Ere he came thither it was fair day, and the sun began to rise. And he came to the Court as a poor wight. He had caught harm at the Priest's house by the help and counsel of the Fox. His body was all beaten-to-pieces, and blind on the one eye. When the King wist this, that Tybert was thus arrayed, he was sore angry, and menaced Reynard the thief sore; and anon gathered his Council to know what they would advise him how he might bring the Fox to the law, and how he should be fetched . . .

Sixteenth Century. Straparola, Basile, Perrault and Tieck—these are the four writers who gave us "Puss in Boots," which originally came from India like most of our folktales. Perrault is the one usually credited with this fairytale, but Straparola had already narrated it early in the 16th century and Basile early in the 17th. Perrault's version came during the last decade of the 1600s and Tieck's almost 50 years later.

Unsurprisingly, the cat in this tale once again plays the role of deceiver. As in Dick Whittington the deceit is condoned because it brings about human gain, and Puss is portrayed as a beloved rogue rewarded for his cleverness. So we are told by Perrault, and it is his "Puss in Boots" that has been related year after year after year.

Compare it with Basile's version given here, a moral tale if there ever was one; it is more in keeping with stories of this type and the reason for their having come into existence in the first place. Here the cat carries its deceit one step further than in Perrault's story, to give us a surprise ending.

It is immaterial which variant you prefer. What is important is that the cat has been given a higher status than in previous tales. It has a personality and its intelligence, rather than its basic so-called craftiness, is stressed.

GAGLIUSO; A FAIRY TALE FROM THE PENTAMERON

GIAMBATTISTA BASILE

There once lived in Naples a poor old man named Gagliuso, so squalid and destitute that he was as naked as a worm. Feeling himself at the point of death, he said to his two children, Oratiello and Pippo, "My sons, I am summoned to pay the debt of nature. Believe me, Christians as you are, that my only regret in quitting this sad abode of toil and pain is that I leave you without a farthing. Alas! you will have less than a fly could carry off on his foot. I have led a dog's life; I have dined off an empty stomach, and gone to bed in the dark. But in spite of all, I wish on my deathbed to leave you some token of my love. Oratiello, my firstborn, take that wallet hanging on the wall, and may you find in it every night what I have often sought in vain all day, a crust of bread. As to you, my youngest, take the cat. My children, remember your dear father." With these words, he burst into tears, and a little while after said, "Farewell, it is night."

Oratiello buried his father at the public expense; after which he plucked up his courage, and went down to the bay to help the fishermen draw the seine.

But Pippo, looking at the cat, cried, "See what a fine legacy my father has left me! I cannot keep myself, and here I have two mouths to feed!"

The cat heard these lamentations, and remarked, "You complain without cause, and have more luck than sense. You do not know your good-fortune, for I can make you rich if I set about it."

Pippo felt that she was right. He stroked the cat three or four times, and warmly besought the favor of Dame Puss, who took compassion on the poor lad. She went out every morning, to the bay, or the fish-market, where she managed to lay hold of some large mullet or superb swordfish, which she carried to the king, saying, "Your majesty's slave, Signor Gagliuso, sends this fish, with his compliments, as a small gift to a great prince."

Upon which the king, with the pleased air of one receiving a present, would answer, "Tell this stranger gentleman that I am infinitely obliged to him."

Another time the cat would scour the fields and marshes, and when the hunters shot down a blackbird, lark, or woodcock, would snatch up the game, and hurry with it on the same errand to the king. She used this artifice so long that at last, one morning, the king said, "I am under so many obligations to Signor Gagliuso, that I should like to make his acquaintance and thank him for all his courtesy." The cat replied, "Signor Gagliuso's blood and life are at your majesty's disposal. My master will wait upon you tomorrow morning without fail."

Morning having come, the cat hastened to the king, crying, "Signor Gagliuso begs you to excuse him for not presenting himself before you. Some of his rascally valets ran off with his clothes last night; the thieves have not left him a shirt to his back."

On hearing this, the king ordered a quantity of linen and wearing apparel to be taken from his own wardrobe and sent to Gagliuso. Before two hours had passed our hero entered the palace, escorted by the cat. The king received him most graciously, and seating him by his side, ordered a magnificent feast to be served him.

While they were at dinner, Gagliuso turned from time to time to the cat, and said, "Look here, Puss, keep an eye on our things!" to which she answered, "Hush! hush! don't speak of such trifles." The king asked what troubled Gagliuso, whereupon the cat said that he would like a small lemon, when the king sent to the garden for a whole basketful. But Gagliuso continued to repeat the same thing, while the cat tried to hush him, and when the king insisted upon knowing what was the matter, invented one excuse after another to conceal her master's meanness, in thinking that anyone there would be likely to steal his hat and cloak.

At last, after sitting long at the table, talking of one thing and another, Gagliuso asked permission to withdraw. Left alone with the king, the cat extolled her master's merit, wit, and good sense, and, above all, the immense wealth that he possessed in the Roman Campagna and Lombardy. He was just such a son-in-law as a crowned head might desire. The king, asking what his fortune might be, the cat declared that it was impossible to reckon the value of the goods and chattels of this Croesus, who did not know himself what he was worth. But if the king wished to be sure, it was a very easy matter; he had only to send some trusty messengers across the frontier, and they would learn for themselves that there was no wealth in the world like Gagliuso's.

The king summoned his faithful counsellors, and ordered them carefully to inquire into the affair. They followed the cat, who, as soon as they had crossed the frontier, ran on before, on the pretense of preparing refreshments. Wherever she found a flock of sheep, cows, horses, or swine, she said to the shepherds, or keepers, "Look here! there is a company of robbers coming to plunder everything they find. If you wish to escape and save your property, you must say, 'All this belongs to Signor Gagliuso!' and they will not touch a hair."

She repeated the same thing at all the farms along the way, so that, wherever the king's messengers went, they heard the same song. All that they saw belonged to Signor Gagliuso. Tired of asking the same question, they returned to the king and told him wonders concerning Signor Gagliuso's possessions. On hearing this the monarch promised the cat a heavy fee if she would make the match, and her friendly tongue bobbed back and forth like a shuttle till it had woven the whole intrigue. Gagliuso offered himself, and the king gave him a fat dowry with his daughter.

After a month's merry-making Gagliuso told his royal father-in-law that he wished to carry his bride to his estates. The king accompanied them as far as the frontier, after which they went to Lombardy, where, by the cat's advice, Gagliuso bought a vast domain with the title of baron.

Master Gagliuso, on seeing himself as rich as a prince, thanked the cat in the warmest way imaginable, telling her over and over again that it was to her that he owed his wealth and grandeur. The wit of a cat had done more for him than all his father's sense. She might dispose of the property and life of her dear master as she saw fit. And when she died—would to heaven that she might live a hundred years!—he pledged her his word that he would have her embalmed and put in a golden casket, which he would keep in his chamber, that he might always have her cherished remembrance before his eyes.

The cat was greatly puffed up with all these fine speeches. Before three days had passed, she stretched herself at full length along the garden terrace, pretending to be dead.

"Husband! husband!" cried Gagliuso's wife, "what a great misfortune! The cat is dead!"

"The deuce take her," answered Gagliuso; "better that she should die than we."

"What shall we do with her?" asked the princess.

"Take her by the paw and fling her out of the window."

On hearing this funeral oration, which was not exactly what she was looking for, the cat jumped up, and cried: "So these are your thanks to me for cleansing you of your filth! This is your gratitude for stripping you of rags fit for nothing but a wad for a distaff! This is the way you reward me for feeding you, you scoundrel! for clothing you, you wretch! But it is wasting soap to wash an ass's head. Accursed be all that I have done for you. You are not even worth the trouble of spitting in your face. A fine gold casket you have made ready for me! A splendid funeral you have ordered for me! Well, puss, you have sweated, labored, and worn yourself out, to be paid in such coin! Fool that you were, not to know that service is no inheritance. The philosopher was right who said, 'He who goes to bed an ass will get up an ass.' The more one does, the more one may do. But fine words and foul deeds deceive wise men and fools alike."

With these words she started for the door. Gagliuso followed, and attempted in the humblest accents to soften her. His labor was in vain; she would not return, but went straight onward, without turning her head, saying, "Beware of enriching a pauper; he is sure to turn out a villain."

(From *Last Fairy Tales* by EDOUARD LABOULAYE)

Seventeenth Century. From LaFontaine's many fables dealing with cats you get the feeling that he appreciated their qualities, good or bad, and had more than a casual acquaintance with them. He deals with the same aspects of cat character found in the previously narrated tales (in fact most of the fables are borrowed from Pilpay and Aesop) but his cats come to life as definite animals instead of being purely allegorical. There is a contemporary flavor to the tales as well as to the cats, a good indication that it is here we should take leave of the history of the cat through folktale.

What do all the tales tell us about the cat? They indicate that it must have been a well-known animal from around 500 B.C. on, or it would never have been in the oral tales of the common people. And it must have lived closely with them or they wouldn't have been able to describe its characteristics so well, albeit unsympathetically. The dating of the stories is less than approximate but it reinforces other data and in this way helps to establish facts.

Until we get to LaFontaine, it would be impossible to picture from the tales just what sort of animal a cat actually is, except that it is disagreeable. Greedy, deceitful, tricky, unscrupulous, a murderer of defenseless birds, a devourer of filthy mice—how could a beast like that be likeable? Things haven't changed much for the cat over 2000 years.

THE COCKEREL, THE CAT AND THE YOUNG MOUSE

A youthful mouse, not up to trap,
Had almost met a sad mishap.
The story hear him thus relate,
With great importance, to his mother:—
I passed the mountain bounds of this estate,
And off was trotting on another,
Like some young rat with nought to do
But see things wonderful and new,
When two strange creatures came in view.
The one was mild, benign, and gracious;
The other, turbulent, rapacious,
With voice terrific, shrill and rough,
And on his head a bit of stuff
That looked like raw and bloody meat,
Raised up a sort of arms, and beat
The air, as if he meant to fly,
And bore his plumy tail on high.

A cock, that just began to crow,
As if some nondescript,
From far New Holland shipped,
Was what our mousling pictured so.
He beat his arms, said he, and raised his voice,
And made so terrible a noise,
That I, who, thanks to Heaven, may justly boast
Myself as bold as any mouse,
Scud off, (his voice would even scare a ghost!)
And cursed himself and all his house;
For, but for him, I should have stayed,
And doubtless an acquaintance made
With her who seemed so mild and good.
Like us, in velvet cloak and hood,
She wears a tail that's full of grace,
A very sweet and humble face,—
No mouse more kindness could desire,—
And yet her eye is full of fire.
I do believe the lovely creature

A friend of rats and mice by nature.
Her ears, though, like herself, they're bigger,
Are just like ours in form and figure.
To her I was approaching, when,
Aloft on what appeared his den,
The other screamed,—and off I fled.
My son, his cautious mother said,
That sweet one was the cat,
The mortal foe of mouse and rat,
Who seeks by smooth deceit,
Her appetite to treat.
So far the other is from that,
We yet may eat
His dainty meat;
Whereas the cruel cat,
Whene'er she can, devours
No other meat than ours.

Remember while you live
It is by looks that men deceive.

THE CAT AND THE TWO SPARROWS

Contemporary with a sparrow tame
There lived a cat; from tenderest age,
Of both, the basket and the cage
Had household gods the same.
The bird's sharp beak full oft provoked the cat,
Who played in turn, but with a gentle pat,
His wee friend sparing with a merry laugh,
Not punishing his faults by half.
In short, he scrupled much the harm,
Should he with points his ferule arm.
The sparrow, less discreet than he,
With dagger beak made very free.
Sir Cat, a person wise and staid,
Excused the warmth with which he played,
For 'tis full half of friendship's art
To take no joke in serious part.

Familiar since they saw the light,
  Mere habit kept their friendship good;
Fair play had never turned to fight,
  Till, of their neighborhood,
Another sparrow came to greet
Old Ratto grave and saucy Pete.
Between the birds a quarrel arose,
  And Ratto took his side.
A pretty stranger, with such blows
  To beat our friend! he cried.
A neighbor's sparrow eating ours!
Not so, by all the feline powers.
And quick the stranger he devours.
  Now, truly, saith Sir Cat,
I know how sparrows taste by that.
Exquisite, tender, delicate!
This thought soon sealed the other's fate
But hence what moral can I bring?
For, lacking that important thing,
A fable lacks its finishing.
I seem to see of one some trace,
But still its shadow mocks my chase.
Yours, prince, it will not thus abuse:
For you such sports, and not my muse.
In wit, she and her sisters eight
Would fail to match you with a mate.

IV
Poetry

AGATHIAS (c.527–c.580), Greek Historian and Poet

To a Cat which had Killed a Bird

O cat in semblance, but in heart akin
To canine raveners, whose ways are sin,
Still at my hearth a guest thou dar'st to be?
Unwhipt of Justice, hast no dread of me?
Or deem'st the sly allurements shall avail
Of purring throat and undulating tail?
No! as to pacify Patroclus dead,
Twelve Trojans by Pelides' sentence bled,
So shall thy blood appease the feathery shade,
And for one guiltless life shall nine be paid.

[RICHARD GARNETT, *Translator*]

DAMOCHARIS THE GRAMMARIAN, Disciple of Agathias

The Cat and the Partridge

Your master grieved as though you'd savaged *him,*
When you devoured his partridge, wicked cat.
The hounds which tore Actaeon limb from limb,
Fierce man-eaters, did hardly worse than that.
And now so set on partridge is your soul,
The mice can dance and rob your dainty bowl.

[W. B. STANFORD, *Translator*]

IRISH SCHOLAR (8th or 9th Century)

Pangur Ban

I and Pangur Ban, my cat,
'Tis a like task we are at;
Hunting mice is his delight,
Hunting words I sit all night.

Better far than praise of men
'Tis to sit with book and pen;
Pangur bears me no ill-will,
He too plies his simple skill.

'Tis a merry thing to see
At our tasks how glad are we,
When at home we sit and find
Entertainment to our mind.

Oftentimes a mouse will stray
In the hero Pangur's way;
Oftentimes my keen thought set
Takes a meaning in its net.

'Gainst the wall he sets his eye
Full and fierce, and sharp and sly;
'Gainst the wall of knowledge I
All my little wisdom try.

When a mouse darts from its den,
O how glad is Pangur then!
O what gladness do I prove
When I solve the doubts I love!

So in peace our tasks we ply,
Pangur Ban, my cat, and I:
In our arts we find our bliss,
I have mine and he has his.

Practice every day has made
Pangur perfect in his trade;
I get wisdom day and night,
Turning darkness into light.

[Robin Flower, *Translator*]

Ibn Alalaf Alnaharwny (died c.930), Poet of Bagdad

To a Cat, Killed as she was robbing a Dove-cote

Poor Puss is gone! 'Tis fate's decree—
Yet I must still her loss deplore,
For dearer than a child was she,
And ne'er shall I behold her more.

With many a sad presaging tear
This morn I saw her steal away,
While she went on without a fear
Except that she should miss her prey.

I saw her to the dove-house climb,
With cautious feet and slow she stept,
Resolved to balance loss of time
By eating faster than she crept.

Her subtle foes were on the watch
And mark'd her course, with fury fraught,
And while she hoped the birds to catch,
An arrow's point the huntress caught.

In fancy she had got them all,
And drunk their blood, and suck'd their breath;
Alas! She only got a fall,
And only drank the draught of death.

Why, why was pigeons' flesh so nice,
That thoughtless cats should love it thus?
Hadst thou but lived on rats and mice,
Thou hadst been living still, poor Puss.

Curst be the taste, howe'er refined,
That prompts us for such joys to wish,
And curst the dainty where we find
Destruction lurking in the dish.

[J. D. CARLYLE, *Translator*]

JOACHIM DU BELLAY (c.1524–1560), "the French Ovid"

Epitaph on a Cat

Life I can no longer live,
Magny! If you bid me give
Cause of my despairing pain,
Of no losses I complain,
Rings or money, or of purse.
What then? Oh, 'tis something worse!
Three days since did Death destroy
My chief treasure, love, and joy.
What? The thought fresh grief doth wake,
'Tis as though my heart would break:
So to write or speak I dread—
Belaud, my grey cat is dead.
Belaud, who may well be said
Fairest work by nature made
'Mong the total race of cats;
Belaud, lethal foe of rats;
Belaud, with such charms as nigh
To earn immortality.
First of all, then, let me say,

Belaud was not wholly grey

As cats which in France are born
But like those which Rome adorn—
Silver grey, and softer far
Than either silk or satin are.
Small his head and teeth; his eyes
Shot no glance that terrifies,
But whose pupils, greenish-blue,
Somewhat imitate the hue
Which, through rain, the varied bow
'Thwart the heavenly arch doth throw.

Head to match his size appears,
Slim his neck, and his ears,
And beneath his ebon nose
Mouth like a small lion shows;
And around his mouth there grew
A small beard of silvery hue,
Nature there had seemed to place
To defend his pretty face.
Small his paws, his legs were slim,
Like soft mittens smooth and trim;
Soft his throat was, and his tail
Long as those which monkeys trail,
Barred its length with many a band,
The fair work of Nature's hand.

Such Belaud! dear animal!
Who from head to foot was all
Of such beauty that I ween
Like of him was never seen.
Greater woe was ne'er conceived,
Loss that ne'er can be retrieved.
My sad heart is wrung, I wis
That e'en Death, although she is
Like a bear for cruelty,
Yet, had she ta'en pains to see

Such a cat, how fierce soe'er
She had felt obliged to spare,
And my sad life would not now
Hatred still to live I avow.

But stern Death did ne'er survey
All the pretty tricks and play
Of my Belaud, nor the grace
Of his every moment trace:
How he deftly scratched or leapt,
How he turned about or crept,
Or a rat caught, and awhile
Let it go, but then with guile
Quickly caught again, and so
Oft would take, oft let it go.

Often, with his dainty paw,
Would he gently stroke his jaw,
Or the rogue would slyly sit
On my bed, or seize a bit
I was eating, yet he ne'er
Would offend or roughly tear,
But amused attention claims
By a thousand tricks and games.

Ah, me—what pleasant fun
'Twas to watch my Belaud run
Swiftly for a ball of thread,
Or when chase his merry head
After his own tail race
Round and round in wheeling chase,
Like a garter fasten it
Round his legs as he did sit,
And so solemn looked as he
Might a Sorbonne doctor be!
Or at times (a pretty sight),
He would make pretense to fight,
But soon as again caressed,

All feigned anger he repressed.

Belaud's sport no malice hid,
Belaud never mischief did,
Nor worse crime than but to seize
And bear off a scrap of cheese,
Or a linnet eat whose song
Vexed him. This no doubt was wrong.
But we men, Magny, are not
Perfect in all points, I wot.
Belaud went not night and day,
As some cats do after prey,
And for naught but eating care.
His expenditure was spare,
Small his appetite, and he
Took his diet frugally.

Belaud was my favorite,
Belaud my companion quite,
In my room, at bed and board,
Closer friendship did afford
Than by any dog is lent.
He by night ne'er howling went,
Like those dreadful cats who wake
Sleepers, and night hideous make.
Oh, my little Belaud! Would
To heaven I had wit so good,
And a style of such high worth,
As to blaze my merits forth;
Then Belaud I swear and vow,
That in verse as fine as thou,
You should live on earth, while cats
Wage unceasing war on rats.

PHILIP SIDNEY (1554–1586)

I have, (and long shall have) a white great nimble Cat
A king upon a mouse, a strong foe to the rat,
Fine eares, long taile he hath, with Lions curved clawe,
Which oft he lifteth up, and stayes his lifted pawe,

Deepe musing to himselfe, which after-mewing showes,
Till with lickt beard, his eye of fire espie his foes.

[from "Nico and Dorus"]

CHRISTOPHER SMART (1722–1771)

Cat Jeoffry

For I will consider my Cat Jeoffry.
For he is the servant of the Living God, duly and daily serving him.
For at the first glance of the glory of God in the East he worships in his way.
For is this done by wreathing his body seven times round with elegant quickness.
For then he leaps up to catch the musk, which is the blessing of God upon his prayer.
For he rolls upon prank to work it in.
For having done duty and received blessing he begins to consider himself.
For this he performs in ten degrees.
For first he looks upon his fore-paws to see if they are clean.
For secondly he kicks up behind to clear away there.
For thirdly he works it upon stretch with the fore-paws extended.
For fourthly he sharpens his paws with wood.
For fifthly he washes himself.
For sixthly he rolls upon wash.
For seventhly he fleas himself, that he may not be interrupted upon the beat.
For eightly he rubs himself against a post.
For ninthly he looks up for his instructions.
For tenthly he goes in quest of food.
For having consider'd God and himself he will consider his neighbour.
For if he meets another cat he will kiss her in kindness.
For when he takes his prey he plays with it to give it a chance.
For one mouse in seven escapes by his dallying.
For when his day's work is done his business more properly begins.
For he keeps the Lord's watch in the night against the adversary.
For he counteracts the powers of darkness by his electrical skin and glaring eyes.

For he counteracts the Devil, who is death, by brisking about the life.
For in the morning orisons he loves the sun and the sun loves him.
For he is of the tribe of Tiger.
For the Cherub Cat is a term of the Angel Tiger.
For he has the subtlety and hissing of a serpent, which in goodness he suppresses.
For he will not do destruction, if he is well-fed, neither will he spit without provocation.
For he purrs in thankfulness, when God tells him he's a good Cat.
For he is an instrument for the children to learn benevolence upon.
For every house is incompleat without him and a blessing is lacking in the spirit.
For the Lord commanded Moses concerning the cats at the departure of the Children of Israel from Egypt.
For every family had one cat at least in the bag.
For the English Cats are the best in Europe.
For he is the cleanest in the use of his forepaws of any quadrupede.
For the dexterity of his defense is an instance of the love of God to him exceedingly.
For he is the quickest to his mark of any creature.
For he is tenacious of his point.
For he is a mixture of gravity and waggery.
For he knows that God is his Saviour.
For there is nothing sweeter than his peace when at rest.
For there is nothing brisker than his life when in motion.
For he is of the Lord's poor, and so indeed is he called by benevolence perpetually—Poor Jeoffry! poor Jeoffry! the rat has bit thy throat.
For I bless the name of the Lord Jesus that Jeoffry is better.
For the divine spirit comes about his body to sustain it in compleat cat.
For his tongue is exceeding pure so that it has in purity what it wants in musick.
For he is docile and can learn certain things.
For he can set up with gravity which is patience upon approbation.
For he can fetch and carry, which is patience in employment.
For he can jump over a stick which is patience upon proof positive.
For he can spraggle upon waggle at the word of command.
For he can jump from an eminence into his master's bosom.
For he can catch the cork and toss it again.
For he is hated by the hypocrite and miser.

For the former is afraid of detection.
For the latter refuses the charge.
For he camels his back to bear the first motion of business.
For he is good to think on, if a man would express himself neatly.
For he made a great figure in Egypt for his signal services.
For he killed the Icneumon-rat very pernicious by land.
For his ears are so acute that they sting again.
For from this proceeds the passing quickness of his attention.
For by stroking of him I have found out electricity.
For I perceived God's light about him both wax and fire.
For the electrical fire is the spiritual substance, which God sends from heaven to sustain the bodies both of man and beast.
For God has blessed him in the variety of his movements.
For, tho' he cannot fly, he is an excellent clamberer.
For his motions upon the face of the earth are more than any other quadrupede.
For he can tread to all the measures upon the musick.
For he can swim for life.
For he can creep.

DR. ERASMUS DARWIN (1731–1802)

The Freebooter

Cats I scorn, who, sleek and fat,
Shiver at a Norway rat.
Rough and hardy, bold and free,
Be the cat that's made for me;
He whose nervous paw can take
My lady's lapdog by the neck;
With furious hiss attack the hen,
And snatch a chicken from the pen.

JOANNA BAILLIE (1762–1851)

The Kitten

Wanton droll, whose harmless play
Beguiles the rustic's closing day,
When, drawn the evening fire about,
Sit aged crone and thoughtless lout,

And child upon his three-foot stool,
Waiting until his supper cool,
And maid, whose cheek outblooms the rose,
As bright the blazing faggot glows,
Who bending to the friendly light,
Plies her task with busy sleight;
Come, show thy tricks and sportive graces,
Thus circled round with merry faces!
Backward coil'd and crouching low,
With glaring eyeballs watch thy foe,
The housewife's spindle whirling round,
Or thread, or straw, that on the ground
Its shadow throws, by urchin sly
Held out to lure thy roving eye;
Then stealing onward, fiercely spring
Upon the tempting, faithless thing.
Now whirling round with bootless skill,
Thy bo-peep tail provokes thee still,
As still beyond thy curving side
Its jetty tip is seen to glide;
Till from thy centre starting far,
Thou sidelong veer'st with rump in air
Erected stiff, and gait awry,
Like madam in her tantrums high;
Though ne'er a madam of them all,
Whose silken kirtle sweeps the hall,
More varied trick and whim displays
To catch the admiring stranger's gaze.
Doth power in measured verses dwell,
All thy vagaries wild to tell?
Ah, no! the start, the jet, the bound,
The giddy scamper round and round,
With leap and toss and high curvet,
And many a whirling somerset
(Permitted by the modern Muse
Expression technical to use),
These mock the deftest rhymester's skill,
But poor in art, though rich in will.
The featest tumbler, stage bedight,

To thee is but a clumsy wight,
Who every limb and sinew strains
To do what costs thee little pains;
For which, I trow, the gaping crowd
Requites him oft with plaudits loud.
But, stopp'd the while thy wanton play,
Applauses too thy pains repay:
For then beneath some urchin's hand
With modest pride thou tak'st thy stand,
While many a stroke of kindness glides
Along thy back and tabby sides.
Dilated swells thy glossy fur,
And loudly croons thy busy purr,
As, timing well the equal sound,
Thy clutching feet bepat the ground,
And all their harmless claws disclose
Like prickles of an early rose,
While softly from thy whisker'd cheek
Thy half-closed eyes peer, mild and meek.
But not alone by cottage fire
Do rustics rude thy feats admire.
The learned sage, whose thoughts explore
The widest range of human lore,
Or with unfetter'd fancy fly
Through airy heights of poesy,
Pausing, smiles with alter'd air
To see thee climb his elbow-chair,
Or, struggling on the mat below,
Hold warfare with his slipper'd toe.
The widow'd dame, or lonely maid,
Who, in the still, but cheerless shade
Of home unsocial, spends her age,
And rarely turns a letter'd page,
Upon her hearth for thee lets fall
The rounded cork, or paper ball,
Nor chides thee on thy wicked watch,
The ends of ravell'd skein to catch,
But lets thee have thy wayward will,
Perplexing oft her better skill.

. . . . .

John Keats (1795–1821)

To a Cat

Cat! who hast pass'd thy grand climacteric,
How many mice and rats hast in thy days
Destroy'd?—How many tidbits stolen? Gaze
With those bright languid segments green, and prick
Those velvet ears—but prithee do not stick
Thy latent talons in me—and upraise
Thy gentle mew—and tell me all thy frays
Of fish and mice, and rats and tender chick.
Nay, look not down, nor lick thy dainty wrists—
For all the wheezy asthma,—and for all
Thy tail's tip is nick'd off—and though the fists
Of many a maid have given thee many a maul,
Still is that fur as soft as when the lists
In youth thou enter'dst on glass bottled wall.

Professor Karl of Trinity College wrote the following for "Grandfather" who died at the age of 22, still in excellent health and able to climb trees, catch birds and kill mice with as much zest and activity as a kitten.

Grandfather
(Obiit July 1862, aetatis 22)

'Life to the last enjoyed,' here Pussy lies
Renown'd for mousing, and for catching flies;
Loving o'er grass and pliant branch to roam,
Yet ever constant to the smiles of home;
Philosopher of Garden and of Porch,
Whom sun and hearth have warm'd, but could not scorch;
Monarchs might envy him his regal fur,
And list the music of his household purr.
His sweet content possess'd; his feline soul
With milk of human kindness brimmed the bowl;
Nor anger nor ingratitude e'er shed
The blood of hand that stroked him, or that fed.

Blameless in morals, feared by mice and rats,
The *Preux Chevalier* of the race of cats:
He has outlived their customary span—
As Jenkins and Old Parr had that of man—
And might on tiles have murmured, in moonshine,
Nestorian tales of youth, and Troy divine;
Of rivals fought; of Kitten-martyrdoms;
While meekly listening round sat Tabs and Toms;
But, with the modesty of genuine worth,
He vaunted not his deeds of ancient birth;
His whiskers twitched not at the world's applause,
He only yawned, and licked his reverend paws;
Curled round his head his tail, and fell asleep,
Lapped in sweet dreams, and left us here to weep:
Yet pleased to know that, ere he sank to rest,
As far as mortal cats are, he was blest.

RICHARD GARNETT (1835–1906)

Marigold

She moved through the garden in glory because
She had very long claws at the end of her paws.
Her back was arched, her tail was high,
A green fire glared in her vivid eye;
And all the Toms, though never so bold,
Quailed at the martial Marigold.

CHRISTOPHER MORLEY (1890–1957)

In Honor of Taffy Topaz

Taffy, the topaz-coloured cat,
Thinks now of this and now of that,
But chiefly of his meals.
Asparagus, and cream, and fish,
Are objects of his Freudian wish;
What you don't give, he steals.

His gallant heart is strongly stirred
By clink of plate or flight of bird,

He has a plumy tail;
At night he treads on stealthy pad
As merry as Sir Galahad
A-seeking of the grail.

His amiable amber eyes
Are very friendly, very wise;
Like Buddha, grave and fat,
He sits, regardless of applause,
And thinking, as he kneads his paws,
What fun to be a cat!

ROSALIE MOORE

Catalog

Cats sleep fat,
And walk thin.
Cats, when they sleep, slump,
When they wake, pull in—
And where the plump's been
There's skin.
Cats walk thin.

Cats sleep in a lump,
Jump in a streak.
Cats when they jump are sleek
As a grape slipping its skin—
They have a technique.
Oh, cats don't creak,
They sneak.

Cats sleep fat.
They spread out comfort underneath them
Like a good mat,
As if they had just picked the place—
Then sat.
You walk around one
As if he were the city hall
After that.

If male,
A cat is apt to sing on a major scale.
This concert is for everybody,
This is wholesale.
For a baton he wields a tail.

He is also found
When happy, to resound
With an enclosed and private sound.

A cat condenses.
He pulls in his tail to go under bridges
And himself to go under fences.
Cats fit
In any size box or kit,
And if a large pumpkin grew under one,
He could arch over it.

When everybody else is just ready to go out
The cat is just ready to come in.
He's not where he's been.
Cats sleep fat and walk thin.

V
Religion and Laws

CATS have always been associated with the sun and moon, weather, fertility and chastity, love and the female sex in general, so it is not surprising that the deities linked with them should have the same associations. Bast, the cat-headed Egyptian goddess, is the first and most famous of these. Presumably evolved from a cat totem, she continued to be a major goddess when Egypt was on the wane and Greece was ascendant, and she then became embodied in Diana, to the Teutonic race in Freya, and to the Christians in the Virgin Mary.

Under all these names she retained her close association with the cat. One cannot, however, do more than speculate from this that the cat was a continuously familiar animal from its reign in Egypt on through the beginnings of Christianity. Neither can one use its close association with certain saints as conclusive evidence of its presence during their lives, it being impossible to ascertain when the cat was first associated with each. Regardless, each association is worth considering. Gregory the Great's cat, already noted in the outline, must, of course, be accepted as authentic.

1. Martha (1st century) is said to have had a cat as her companion.

2. Agatha (d. 251) is still known as Santo Gato along the Pyrenees mountain range. She angrily appears in cat form to punish women who work on her day, February 5. Like the cat deities she is connected with the weather, ruling hail and thunderstorms, and forecasts are made on her day.

3. Gregory the Great (c.550–604) See chronological table.

4. Gertrude of Nivelles (629–659) is known as the patroness of cats, gardeners, travellers and widows. She is depicted with mice running up her pastoral staff and is sometimes shown holding a large mouse. A cat is said to have been her companion and is often pictured with her.

5. Ivo or Ives (1035–1115), the patron of lawyers, is depicted with a cat, the symbol of justice.

In the Western Hemisphere the Quechua Indians of South America have a cat spirit who is partly responsible for weather and looks something like a tabby cat. He is grey with darker stripes and is two feet long with a foot-long tail. His head is large and his eyes phosphorescent and streams of hail pour forth from his eyes and his ears. He is responsible for lightning as well as hail, and being an evil spirit he uses these to kill people and ruin crops. Ccoa, as he is called, must be continually propitiated with offerings, and is greatly feared. One can only wonder how much our culture has influenced both the form and attributes of this fierce creature, if at all.

The Moslems never worshipped the cat as such or in any form; but it was held in high esteem principally, it is thought, because Mohammed, himself, cherished cats. They were allowed in the mosques and temples, and the Arabs were said to keep them in their tents for utilitarian purposes—to keep the tents free from snakes.

Practically every cat book mentions Mohammed's extreme love for all cats and how he cut off his sleeve rather than disturb his favorite sleeping on it. The following story as to why Mohammedans should cherish cats is not so well known, and the date of origin is questionable.

One day a snake crawled into Mohammed's sleeve seeking warmth. When the prophet asked it to get out it refused. "Very well," he said, "let us refer the matter to the cat." To this the snake consented. The cat then said to the snake, "Put out your head so that we may better discuss this matter," and the snake did. No sooner did it do so, then the cat pounced on it and carried it away. And for this reason no cat should ever be struck with anything except a cotton-ball.

THE BREHON LAWS OR ANCIENT IRISH CODE

In Ireland long ago, a cat was a domestic animal belonging especially to women; that is, it was deemed lawful for a woman to possess one. Women in those early days (pre 700 A.D.) were allowed to prosecute at law on their own account, and if successful could distrain the goods of the defendant. But these goods had to be confined to those things considered specifically pertinent to a woman's daily life, a list of which was given in the *Senchus Mór* which is said to predate the fifth century. The list included, besides cats, lap-dogs and sheep.

Both felines and canines were familiar pets of early Ireland. Until they were deemed "capable of action," dogs and "little cats" were regarded as children's toys. Also, there is an old story about a black and white cat, a great champion taken from the ship of Breasel Breac, in which were white-breasted cats.

The Brehon Laws as we know them today were pieced together from the remains of documents dating from the 8th to 13th century. These documents indicated that the laws had been in force long before they were recorded—handed down orally from one generation to another. When and how, then, did black and white cats make their appearance? Assuming that the facts as given are accurate, it would mean that in Ireland the domestic cat is of very ancient lineage. The ancestors of the European house cat were tabbies and although melanistic wild animals are fairly common, prominent white markings are found only in animals that have been domestic for some time. Pet animals were often dyed by the Irish from the colors left over in the dye pots from cloth dying, but no mention is made of bleaching. White-breasted black cats are common nowadays but were they then and if so, where did they come from?

GOSPEL OF THE HOLY TWELVE (2ND–9TH CENTURY)

And there were in the same cave an ox and a horse and an ass and a sheep, and beneath the manger was a cat with her little ones; and there were doves also overhead; and each had its mate after its kind, the male with the female.

Thus it came to pass that He was born in the midst of the animals which, through redemption of man from ignorance and selfishness, He came to redeem from their sufferings by the manifestation of the Son of God.

As Jesus passed through a certain village He saw a crowd of idlers of the baser sort, and they were tormenting a cat which they had found, and shamefully treating it. And Jesus commanded them to desist, and began to reason with them.

And as Jesus entered into a certain village He saw a young cat which had none to care for her, and she was hungry and cried unto Him; and He took her up and put her inside His garment, and she lay in His bosom.

And when He came into the village He set food and drink before the cat, and she ate and drank, and showed thanks unto Him. And He gave her unto one of His disciples who was a widow, whose name was Lorenza, and she took care of her.

And one of those who were with Him said, "Behold, this man loveth all creatures. How is it that He loveth all living things as if they were His brothers and sisters?"

And Jesus said, "Verily I say unto ye, these creatures are children of God even as ye are, and are indeed your brethren and sisters. And whoso giveth them food and drink giveth it to Me. And whoso doeth them harm or doth not protect them, harmeth Me and doth not protect Me."

WALES: (10TH CENTURY)

THE VENDOTIAN CODE

XI. The worth of a cat and her tiethi is this—

1st. The worth of a kitten, from the night it is kittened until it shall open its eyes, is a legal penny.

2nd. And from the time that it shall kill mice, twopence.

3rd. And after it shall kill mice, four legal pence; and so it always remains.

4th. Her tiethi are to see, to hear, to kill mice, to have her claws entire, to rear and not devour her kittens, and if she be bought and be deficient in any one of those tiethi, let one-third of her worth be returned.

THE DIMETIAN CODE

XXXII. Of Cats

1st. The worth of a cat that is killed or stolen: its head to be put downward upon a clean even floor, with its tail lifted upwards, and thus suspended, whilst wheat is poured about it until the tip of its tail be covered; and that is to be its worth. If the corn cannot be had [i.e. due to its scarcity which in turn enhances the cat's value], then a milch sheep, with her lamb and her wool, is its value, if it be a cat which guards the king's barn.

2nd. The worth of a common cat is four legal pence.

3rd. The tiethi of a cat, and of every animal upon the milk of which people do not feed, is the third part of its worth, or the worth of its litter.

4th. Whosoever shall sell a cat is to answer for her not going a caterwauling every moon; and that she devour not her kittens, and that she have ears, eyes, teeth, and nails, and be a good mouser.

THE GWENTIAN CODE

XX. [Inflation and demands for higher quality caused the value of cats to increase from the former edicts, and necessitated that the animal be more perfect.]

3rd. That it be perfect of ear, perfect of eye, perfect of teeth, perfect of claw, and without markes of fire. [Found faulty in any one of these points, a third of her price was to be refunded to her purchaser. Marks of fire were considered an indication that the cat liked to lie overly much by the fireside and was consequently a poor mouser. It was also reasoned that a singed cat could be readily smelled by rodents and therefore was easily avoided by them.]

4th. That the tiethi and legal worth of cat are co-equal.

5th. A pound is the worth of a pet animal of the king.

6th. The pet animal of a breyer is six score pence in value.

7th. The pet animal of a taeog is a curt penny in value.

XXXIX. There are three animals whose tails, eyes, and lives, are of the same worth—a calf, a filly for common work, and a cat, excepting the cat which shall watch the king's barn. [Here, again, the king's cat had more value than others.]

OTHER OLD WELSH LAWS

"Three animals reach their worth at a year: a sheep, a cat, and a cur."

"This is the complement of a lawful hamlet: nine buildings, and one plough, and one kiln, and one churn, and one cat, and one cock, and one bull, and one herdman." Appended to this was a later advisement that the worth of a cat was then a whole barn full of wheat, and so that no one would mistake what was meant by a *cath,* and through ignorance, or what have you, accidentally kill one, a picture of a cat was appended in the manuscripts of the laws.

"Let no man, apprised of this law, present even water to a priest who acts like a cat." This refers to actions like those of the proverbial penitent cat.

In the event of a separation of husband and wife, goods and chattels were to be divided, but the husband took the cat. If there was more than one cat, they went to the wife.

Katherine Simms relates that the inhabitants of Pitcairn Island have, to this day, a penalty for anyone killing a cat. These people are descendants of the sailors from Captain Bligh's ship the *Bounty,* and have every reason to appreciate the cat's use in rodent control. The law states that "if a cat is killed without being positively detected in killing fowls, however strong the suspicion may be, the person killing such a cat is obliged, as a penalty, to destroy three hundred rats, whose tails must be submitted for the inspection of the magistrate, by way of proof that the penalty has been paid."

Two other legal pronouncements almost a hundred years apart show an understanding of the cat's habits and behavior. In 1865 in Fontainebleau, France, after plaintiffs had asked for legal protection for their cats, a judge ruled:

That the domestic cat is not a thing of naught, but the property of its master, and, as such, entitled to the shelter of the law.

That the utility of the cat as a destroyer of mischievous rodents being indisputable, equity demands the extension of indulgence to an animal which the law tolerates and protects.

That even the domestic cat is of a mixed nature; that is to say, a creature which is partly wild, and which must ever remain so, by reason of its destiny and purpose.

In 1949 Adlai Stevenson, then governor of Illinois, vetoed a so-called cat bill that would have restricted cats in an attempt to protect birds. Among the reasons he gave for doing so were the following:

"Furthermore, I cannot agree that it should be the declared public policy of Illinois that a cat visiting a neighbor's yard or crossing the highway is a public nuisance. It is in the nature of cats to do a certain amount of unescorted roaming . . ."

"Also consider the owner's dilemma: To escort a cat abroad on a leash is against the nature of the cat, and to permit it to venture forth for exercise unattended into a night of new dangers is against the nature of the owner."

"Moreover, cats perform useful service, particularly in rural areas, in combating rodents—work they necessarily perform alone and without regard for property lines."

"The problem of cat *versus* bird is as old as time. If we attempt to resolve it by legislation who knows but what we may be called upon to take sides as well in the age-old problem of dog *versus* cat, bird *versus* bird, or even bird versus worm . . ."

VI
General Natural Histories

(Chronologically arranged)

Aristotle (384–322 b.c.)

The cat and the ichneumon bear as many young as the dog, and live on the same food; they live about six years . . .

The polecat or marten . . . preys on birds like the cat . . .

Cats do not copulate with a rearward presentment on the part of the female, but the male stands erect and the female puts herself underneath him, and, by the way, the female cat is peculiarly lecherous, and wheedles the male on to sexual commerce, and caterwauls during the operation . . .

Historia Animalium

A small face marks a small soul, as in the cat and the ape.

Physiognomonica

Pliny (23–79 a.d.)

Then how silently and with what a light tread do cats creep up to birds! How stealthily they watch their chance to leap out on tiny mice! They scrape up the earth to bury their droppings, realizing that the smell of these gives them away.

Natural History X:94

AELIAN (c. 220)

4:44 In Egypt the Cats, the Ichneumons, the Crocodiles, and moreover the Hawks afford evidence that animal nature is not altogether intractable, but that when well-treated they are good at remembering kindness. They are caught by pandering to their appetites, and when this has rendered them tame they remain thereafter perfectly gentle: they would never set upon their benefactors once they have been freed from their congenital and natural temper . . .

5:7 In Egypt, says Eudemus a Monkey was being pursued and Cats were the pursuers. So the Monkey fled as fast as he could and made straight for a tree. But the Cats also ran up very swiftly, for they cling to the bark and can also climb trees. But as he was going to be caught, being one against many, he leapt from the trunk and with his paws seized the end of an overhanging branch high up and clung to it for a long while. And since the Cats could no longer get at him, they descended to go after other prey . . . [What species of cat is being discussed here is questionable considering the method of hunting, especially in groups.]

5:50 (i) With its crowing a cock scares a lion and is fatal to a basilisk, and yet it cannot endure cats or kites.

6:27 The Tom-cat is extremely lustful, but the Female cat is devoted to her kittens and tries to avoid sexual intercourse with the male, because the semen which he ejaculates is exceedingly hot and like fire, and burns the female organ. Now the Tom-cat knowing this, makes away with their kittens, and the Female in her yearning for other offspring yields to his lust. They say that cats hate and abhor all foul-smelling objects, and that is why they dig a hole before they discharge their excrement, so that they may get it out of sight by throwing earth upon it. [No doubt copied from Herodotus, see p. —]

On the Characteristics of Animals A. F. Scholfield, trans.

12TH CENTURY BESTIARY

She is called MOUSER because she is fatal to mice. The vulgar call her CATUS the Cat because she catches things (*acaptura*) while others say that it is because she lies in wait (*captat*) i.e. because she 'watches'. So acutely does she glare that her eye penetrates the shades of darkness with a gleam of light. Hence from the Greek comes 'catus', i.e. 'acute'.

THE BESTIARY; a book of beasts, being a translation from a Latin Bestiary . . . T. H. White

BARTHOLOMEUS ANGLICUS (c. 1260)

He is a full lecherous beast in youth, swift, pliant and merry, and leapeth and reseth on everything that is to fore him: and is led by a straw and playeth therewith: and is a right heavy beast in age and full sleepy, and lieth slyly in wait for mice: and is aware where they be more by smell than by sight, and hunteth and reseth on them in privy places: and when he taketh a mouse he playeth therewith, and eateth him after the play. In time of love is hard fighting for wives, and one scratcheth and rendeth the other grievously with biting and with claws. And he maketh a ruthful noise and ghastful, when one proffereth to fight with another: and unneth is hurt when he is thrown down off an high place. And when he hath a fair skin, he is as it were proud thereof, and goeth fast about: and when his skin is burnt, then he bideth at home, and is oft for his fair skin taken of the skinner and slain and flayed.

De Proprietatibus Rerum translated by John of Trevisia 1397

The 1498 translation by Thomas Berthlet has the following variations. Translations in those days could mean almost anything.

The Cat is surely most like to the Leoparde, and hathe a great mouthe, and sharpe teeth, and a long tongue, plyante, thin and subtle. He lappeth therewith when he drinketh, as other beastes do that have the nether lip shorter than the over; for, by cause of unevenness of lips, such beastes suck not in drinking, but lap and lick, as Aristotle saith, and Plinius also . . . He is a cruell beaste when he is wilde, and dwelleth in woods, and hunteth there small beastes as conies and hares.

JOHN MAPLET (1567)

The Cat in Latin is called *Catus,* as if you woulde say *Cautus,* warie or wise. In Greeke she is named *Galiootes,* with the Germaines *Kaiz.* She is to the Mouse a continuall enimie; verie like to the Lyon in tooth and clawe: and useth to pastime or play with the Mouse ere she deuoureth hir. She is in hir trade and maner of liuing very shamefast: alwayes louing clenlinesse. There is also a kind hereof called the Wild Cat, which of all things is annoyed with the smell of Rue, and the Almond leafe, and is driuen away with that sooner then with any other thing.

A Greene Forest

JOHN BOSSEWELL (1572–1576)

The beaste is called a Musion, for that he is enimie to Myse, and

Rattes. And he is called a Catte of the Greekes because he is slye and wittie: for that he seeth so sharpely, thet he overcommeth darkness of the nighte, by the shyninge lyghte of his eyne. In shape of body he is like unto a Leoparde, and hathe a greate mouthe. He dothe delighte that he enjoyeth his libertie: and in his youthe he is swifte, plyante, and merye. He maketh a rufull noyse, and a gastefull, when one profereth to fighte with another. He is a cruell beaste, when he is wilde, and falleth on his owne feete from moste highe places: and oneth is hurte therewith. When he hathe a fayre skinne, he is, as it were, prowde thereof, and then he goeth faste aboute to be seene.

The Accendens of Armory . . .

EDWARD TOPSELL (early 17th century)

Extracts from *The Historie of Foure-Footed Beasts*

Once cattes were all wilde, but afterward they retyred to houses, wherefore there are plenty of them in all countries.

Eyes. Her eies glister aboue measure especialy when a man commeth to see a cat on the sudden, and in the night, they can hardly be endured, for their flaming aspect . . . they cast forth beames in the shaddow and darknes, but in the sunshine they haue no such clearnes, and thereof *Alexander Aphrodise* giueth this reason both for the sight of Cattes and of Battes, that they haue by nature a most sharpe spirit of seeing. Albertus compareth their eye-sight to carbuncles in darke places, because in the night they can see perfectly to kill Rattes and Myce.

Mouth. The tongue of a cat is very attractiue, and forcible like a file, attenuating by licking the flesh of a man . . . Her teeth are like a saw . . .

Voice. . . . she whurleth wth her voyce, hauing as many tunes as turnes, for she hath one voice to beg and to complain, another to testifie her delight & pleasure, another among hir own kind by flattring, by hissing, by puffng, by spitting, insomuch as some haue thought that they haue a peculiar intelligible language among themselues.

Claws. Her nailes sheathed like the nailes of a Lyon, striking with her forefeete, both Dogs and other things, as a man doth with his hand.

Color. Cats are of diuvers colours, but for the most part gryseld, like to congealed yse, which commeth from the condition of her meate.

The Spanish blacke cats are of most price among the Germaines, because they are nimblest, and haue the softest hair fit for garment.

Reproduction. In the time of their lust (commonly called catwralling) they are wilde and fierce, especially the males, whoe at that time (except they be gelded) will not keepe the house: at which time they have a peculiar direfull voice. The maner of their copulation is this, the Female layeth downe and the Male standeth, and their females are aboue measure desirous of procreation, for which cause they prouoke the male, and if he yeeld not to their lust they beate and claw him, but it is onely for loue of young and not for lust: the male is most libidinous, and therefore seeing the female will neuer more engender with him, during the time hir young ones sucke, hee killeth and eateth them if he meet with them, (to prouoke the female to copulation with him againe, for when she is depriued of her young, she seeketh out the male of her own accord,) for which the female most warily keepeth them from his sight. During the time of copulation, the female continually cryeth, whereof the Writers giue a double cause; one, because she is pinched with the talants or clawes of the male in the time of his lustfull rage, and thother, because his seed is so fiery hot, that it almost burneth the females place of conception. When they haue litered or as we commonly say kittened, they rage against Dogges, and will suffer none to come neere their young ones. The best to keep are such as are littered in March, they go with young fifty daies, and the females liue not aboue sixe or seuen yeares, and males liue longer especially if they be gelt or libbed: the reason of their short life is their rauening of meate which corrupteth within them.

Cleanliness. It is a neate and cleanely creature, oftentimes licking hir own body to keep it smooth and faire, hauing naturally a flexible backe for this purpose, and washing hir face with her fore feet: . . . And her nature is to hide her own dung or excrements, for she knoweth that the sauour and presence thereof, will driue away her sport, the little Mouse being able by that stoole to smelle the presence of hir mortall foe.

Homing. The nature of this Beast is, to loue the place of her breeding, neither will she tarry in any strange place, although carried very farre, being neuer willing to forsake the house, for the loue of any man . . . and although their maisters forsake their houses, yet will not these Beastes beare them company, and being carried forth in close baskets or sackes, they will yet returne againe or loose themselues.

Predation. For a cat is a watchful and warye beast, seldome ouertaken, and most attendaunt to her sport and prey . . .

This beast is wonderfull nimble, setting vpon her prey like a Lyon, by leaping: and therefore she hunteth both rats, all kind of Myce, & Birds, eating not onely them, but also fish, wherewithal she is best pleased. Hauing taken a Mouse, she first playeth with it, and then deuoreth it, but her watchfull eye is most strange, to see with what pace and soft steps, she taketh birds and flies.

Some haue said that cats will fight with Serpentes, and Toads, and kill them, and perceiuing that she is hurt by them, she presently drinketh water and is cured.

Play. Therefore how she beggeth, playeth, looketh, catcheth, tosseth with her foote, riseth vp to strings held ouer her head, sometime creeping, sometimes lying on the back, playing with one foot, somtime on the bely, snatching, now with mouth, & anon with foot, aprehending greedily any thing saue the hand of a man with diuers with gestical actions, it is needelesse to stand vpon . . .

Miscellaneous. They loue fire and warme places, whereby it falleth out that they often burne their coates. They desire to lie soft . . .

It is needelesse to spend any time about their louing nature to man, how she flattereth by rubbing her skinne against ones legges.

William S. Salmon (1693)

Catus, The Cat

II. It is bred and is an Inhabitant of almost all Countries in the World, all *Cats* were at first wild, but were a length tamed by the industry of Mankind; it is a Beast of prey, even the tame one, more especially the wild, it being in the opinion of many nothing but a diminutive Lyon.

III. It is now said to be of three kinds. 1. *The tame Cat.* 2. *The wild wood cat.* 3. *The Cat of Mountain,* all which are of one nature, and agree much in one Shape, save as to their magnitude, the *wild Cat* being larger much than the *Tame,* and the *Cat of Mountain* much larger than the *wild Cat.*

IV. It has a broad Face almost like a Lyon, short Ears, large Whiskers, shining Eyes, short smooth Hair, long Tail, rough tongue, and armed on its feet with Claws, being a crafty, subtle, watchful Creature, very loving and familiar with Man-kind, the mortal enemy to the Rat, Mouse, and all sorts of Birds, which it seizes on as its prey. As to its Eyes, Arthurs say that they shine in the Night, and see better at the full, and more dimly at the change of the Moon; as also that the Cat doth vary his

Eyes with the Sun, the Apple of its Eye being long at Sun rise, round towards Noon, and not to be seen at all at night, but the whole Eye shining in the night. These appearances of the Cats Eyes I am sure are true, but whether they answer to the times of the day, I never observed.

V. It is a neat and cleanly creature, often licking it self, to keep it fair and clean, and washing its face with its forefeet; the best are such as are of a fair and large kind, and of an exquisite Tabby color, called *Cyprus* Cats. They usually generate in the winter Season, making a great noise, go 56 Days or 8 weeks with young, and bring forth 2, 3, 4, 5, 6, or more at a time, they cover their excrements, and love to keep their old habitations.

The Compleat English Physician

THE JESUIT, FATHER BOUGEANT (1690–1743)

. . . Such is one of those big-whiskered and well-furred tom cats, that you see quiet in a corner, digesting at his leisure, sleeping if it seems good to him, sometimes giving himself the pleasure of hunting, for the rest enjoying life peaceably, without being troubled by the events which agitate us, without tiring his mind by a thousand useless reflections, and little caring to communicate his thoughts to others. Truly it needs only that a female cat come on the scene to derange all his philosophy; but are our philosophers wiser on such occasions?

(quoted in Simpson, Frances. 1903. *The Book of the Cat*)

Caroli Linnaei Systema Naturae 1758

12. FELIS. *Dentes Primores* aequales.
Molares terni.
Lingua retrorsum aculeata.
Ungues retractiles.

Catus. 6. F. cauda elongata, corpore fasciis nigricantibus; dorsalibus longitudinalibus tribus; lateralibus spiralibus.

Felis cauda elongata, auribus aequalibus. *Faun. suec.* 3. *Syst. nat.* 4. n. 6.

Felis vulgo Catus. *Gesn. quadr.* 98. *Aldr. quadr.* 565. *Raj. quadr.* 98. Felis. *Aldr. dig.* 564. *Jonst. quadr.* 180. t. 72.

Habitat in Europae *australis sylvis*

Moribus congenerum, tranquilla, ore molat, caudam erigit; excitata agilissima, scandit, irata fremit odore ambrosiaco, Murum Leo, in praedam intena caudam movet, oculi noctu lucent, inhiando praedam haurit, clamando rixandoque misere amat. Pupilla interdiu, perpendiculari oblonga, noctu tereti ampliata; unguibus complicatis incedit, parce bibit, urina corrosiva, stercus sepelit, carnes edit vegetabliaque respuit, os instante tempestate manu lavat, dorsum in tenebris electrisat; in altum acta decidit in pedes. Pulices non habet. Delectatur Maro, Nepeta, Valeriana.

GEORGES LOUIS LECLERC BUFFON (1791)

The Cat

The cat is an unfaithful domestic, and kept only from the necessity we find of opposing him to other domestics still more incommodious, and which cannot be hunted; for we value not those people, who, being fond of all brutes, foolishly keep cats for their amusement. Though these animals, when young, are frolicksome and beautiful, they possess, at the same time, an innate malice, and perverse disposition, which increase as they grow up, and which education learns them to conceal, but not to subdue. From determined robbers, the best education can only convert them into flattering thieves; for they have the same address, subtlety, and desire of plunder. Like thieves, they know how to conceal their steps and their designs, to watch opportunities, to catch the proper moment for laying hold of their prey, to fly from punishment, and to remain at a distance till solicited to return. They easily assume the habits of society, but never acquire its manners; for they have only the appearance of attachment or friendship. This disingenu ity of character is betrayed by the obliquity of their movements, and the duplicity of their eyes. They never look their best benefactor in the face; but, either from distrust or falseness, they approach him by windings, in order to procure caresses, in which they have no other pleasure than what arises from flattering those who bestow them. Very different from that faithful animal the dog, whose sentiments totally centre in the person and happiness of his master, the cat appears to have no feelings which are not interested, to have no affection that is not conditional, and to carry on no intercourse with men, but with the view of turning it to his own advantage. By these dispositions, the cat has a greater relation to man than to the dog, in whom there is not the smallest mark of insincerity or injustice.

The form and temperament of the cat's body perfectly accord with his temper and dispositions. He is jolly, nimble, dexterous, cleanly, and voluptuous. He loves ease, and chooses the softest and warmest situations for repose. He is likewise extremely amorous, and what is singular in this animal, the female seems to be more ardent than the male. She not only invites and goes in quest of him, but announces, by loud cries, the fury of her passion, or rather the pressure of her necessities; and, when the male disdains her, or flies from her, she pursues, tears, and, though their embraces are always accompanied with the most acute pain, compels him to comply with her desires. This passionate ardour of the female continues only nine or ten days, and it happens generally twice a year, though often thrice, and even four times. The period of gestation is 55 or 56 days, and four or five are commonly produced at a litter. As the male has an inclination to devour the young, the female carefully conceals them; and, when apprehensive of a discovery, she takes them up, one by one, in her mouth, and hides them in holes, and in inaccessible places. After suckling them a few weeks, she presents them with mice, or young birds, to learn them to eat flesh. But, by an unaccountable caprice, these same, careful, tender, and affectionate mothers, sometimes assume an unnatural species of cruelty, and devour their own offspring.

Young cats are gay, vivacious, frolicksome, and, if nothing was to be apprehended from their claws, would afford excellent amusement to children. But their toying, though always light and agreeable, is never altogether innocent, and is soon converted into habitual malice. As their talents can only be exerted with advantage against small animals, they lie in wait, with great patience and perseverance, to seize birds, mice, and rats, and, without any instruction, become more expert hunters than the best trained dogs. Naturally averse to every kind of restraint, they are incapable of any system of education. It is related, however, that the Greek Monks of the island of Cyprus had trained cats to hunt and destroy serpents, with which that island was much infested. But this hunting must rather be ascribed to their general desire of slaughter, than to any kind of tractibility or obedience; for they delight in watching, attacking, and destroying all weak animals indiscriminately, as birds, young rabbits, hares, rats, mice, bats, moles, frogs, toads, lizards, and serpents. They have not that docility and fineness of scent, for which the dog is so eminently distinguished. They hunt by the eye only: Neither do they properly pursue, but lie in wait, and attack animals by surprise; and, after sporting with them, and tormenting them for a long time, they at last kill them without any necessity, and even when well fed, purely to gratify their sanguinary appetite.

The most obvious physical cause of their watching and catching other animals by surprise, proceeds from the advantage they derive from the peculiar structure of their eyes. In man and most other animals, the pupil is capable of a certain degree of contraction and dilatation. It enlarges a little when the light is faint, and contracts when the light is too splendid. But, in cats and night birds, as owls, &c. the contraction and dilation are so great, that the pupil, which is round in the dark, becomes, when exposed to much light, long and narrow like a line. Hence these animals see better in the night than in the day. The pupil of the cat during the day is perpetually contracted, and it is only by a great effort that he can see with a strong light. But, in the twilight, the pupil resumes its natural roundness, the animal enjoys perfect vision, and takes advantage of this superiority to discover and surprise his prey.

Though cats live in our houses, they are not entirely domestic. Even the tamest cats are not under the smallest subjection, but may rather be said to enjoy perfect liberty; for they act to please themselves only; and it is impossible to retain them a moment after they choose to go off. Besides, most cats are half wild. They know not their masters, and only frequent barns, offices, or kitchens, when pressed with hunger.

Though greater numbers of them are reared than of dogs, as they are seldom seen, their number makes less impression on us. They contract a stronger attachment to our houses than to our persons. When carried to the distance of a league or two, they return of their own accord, probably because they are acquainted with all the retreats of the mice, and all the passages and outlets of the house, and because the labour of returning is less than that which would be necessary to acquire the same knowledge in a new habitation. They have a natural antipathy at water, cold, and bad smells. They are fond of basking in the sun, and of lying in warm places. They are also fond of perfumes, and willingly allow themselves to be taken and caressed by persons who carry aromatic substances. They are so delighted with valerian root, that it seems to throw them into a transport of pleasure. To preserve this plant in our gardens, we are under the necessity of fencing it round with a rail; for the cats smell it at a distance, collect about it in numbers, and, by frequently rubbing, and passing and repassing over it, they soon destroy the plant.

Cats require fifteen or eighteen months before they come to their full growth. In less than a year, they are capable of procreating, and retain this faculty during life, which extends not beyond nine or ten years. They are, however, extremely hardy and vivacious, and are more nervous than other animals which live longer.

Cats eat slowly, and with difficulty: Their teeth are so short and ill-placed, that they can tear, but not grind their food. Hence they always prefer the most tender victuals, as fishes, which they devour either raw or boiled. They drink frequently; their sleep is light; and they often assume the appearance of sleeping, when they are only meditating mischief. They walk softly, and without making any noise. As their hair is always clean and dry, it is easily electrified, and the sparks become visible when it is rubbed across with the hand in the dark. Their eyes also sparkle in the dark like diamonds, and seem to throw out, in the night, the light they imbibe during the day.

The wild cat couples with the domestic kind; and, consequently, they belong to the same species. It is not uncommon to see both males and females quit their houses in the season of love, go to the woods in quest of wild cats, and afterwards return to their former habitations. It is for this reason that some domestic cats so perfectly resemble the wild cat. The only real difference is internal; for the intestines of the domestic cat are commonly much longer than those of the wild cat. The latter, however, is larger and stronger than the domestic kind; his lips are always black; his ears are also stiffer; his tail larger, and his colours more constant. In this climate there is only one species of wild cat; and it appears from the testimony of travellers, that this kind is found in all climates, without being subject to much variety. They existed in America before its discovery by the Europeans. A hunter brought one of them to Christopher Columbus, which was of an ordinary size, of a brownish gray colour, and having a very long and strong tail. They were likewise found in Peru, though not in a domestic state, and also in Canada, in the country of the Illinois, &c. They have been seen in many places of Africa, as in Guiney, and the Gold Coast; at Madagascar, where the natives keep them in a domestic state; and at the Cape of Good Hope, where M. Kolbe says there is likewise a wild kind, of a blue colour; but they are not numerous. These blue, or rather slate-colored cats, are also found in Asia. "In Persia," says Pietro della Valle, "there is a species of cats which properly belong to the province of Chorazan. Their figure and size are the same with those of the common cat. Their beauty consists in the colour of their hair, which is gray, and uniformly the same over the whole body, except that it is darker on the back and head, and clearer on the breast and belly, where it approaches to whiteness, with that agreeable mixture of clare-obscure, to use the language of painters, which has always a wonderful effect. Besides, the hair is fine, shining, soft as silk, and so long, that, though not frizled, it forms ringlets in some parts, and particularly under the throat. These cats are among other cats, what the water-dog is among other dogs. The most beautiful part of the body is the tail, which is very long, and covered with hair five or six inches in length. They extend and turn it upon their backs, like the squirrel, the point resembling a plume of feathers. They are very tame; and the Portuguese have brought them from Persia into India." The same author adds, that he had four couple of these cats, which he intended to bring to Italy. From this description it appears, that the Persian cats resemble, in colour, those we call Chartreux cats, and that, except in colour, they have a perfect resemblance to the cat of Angora. It is probable, therefore, that the cat of Chorazan in Persia, the cat of Angora in Syria, and the Chartreux cat, constitute but one race, whose beauty proceeds from the particular influence of the climate, as the Spanish cats, which are red, black, and white, owe their beauty to the climate of Spain. It may be remarked in general, that, of all climates on the habitable parts of the globe, those of Spain and Syria are most favourable to the production of beautiful varieties in natural objects. In Spain and Syria, the sheep, the goats, the dogs, the cats, the rabbits, &c. have the finest wool, the most beautiful and longest hair, and the most agreeable and variegated colours. These climates, it should appear, soften Nature, and embellish the form of all animals.

The wild cat, like most other animals in a savage state, has coarse colours, and hard hair. But, when rendered domestic, the hair softens, the colours vary; and, in favourable climates like Chorazan and Syria, the hair grows long, fine, and bushy; all the colours become more delicate; the black and red change into a shining brown, and the grayish brown is converted into an ash-coloured gray. By comparing the wild cat with the Chartreux cat, it will be found, that they differ only in this degradation in the shades of colour. As these animals have always more or less whiteness on their sides and belly, it is apparent, that, to produce cats entirely white and with long hair, like the cats of Angora, nothing farther is requisite, than to join those who have the greatest quantity of white, as has been done to procure white rabbits, dogs, goats, stags, &c. In the Spanish cat, which is only another variety of the wild kind, the colours, instead of being weakened by uniform shades, as in the cat of

Syria, are exalted, and have become more lively and brilliant; the yellow is changed into red, the brown into black, and the gray into white. These cats, though transported into America, have not degenerated, but preserve their beautiful colours. "In the Antilles," says Father Tertre, "there are a number of cats, which have probably been brought from Spain. They are mostly marked with red, white, and black. Several of our countrymen, after eating the flesh, carry the skins of these cats into France. When we first arrived at Guadaloupe, the cats were so accustomed to feed on partridges, pigeons, thrushes, and other small birds, that they disdained the rats; but, when the game was much diminished, they attacked the rats with great fury," &c. In general, cats are not subject, like dogs, to degeneration, when transported into warm climates. "The European cats," Bosman remarks, "when carried to Guiney, change not, like the dogs, but preserve their original figure," &c. Their nature is indeed more constant; and, as their domestic state is neither so complete, so universal, nor, perhaps, so ancient as that of the dog, it is not surprising that they are also less variegated. Our domestic cats, though they differ in colour, form no distinct races. The climates of Spain and Syria have alone produced permanent varieties; To these may be added the climate of Pe-chi-ly in China, where the cats have long hair and pendulous ears, and are the favourites of the ladies. These domestic cats with pendulous ears, of which we have full descriptions, are still farther removed from the wild and primitive race, than those whose ears are erect . . .

Supplement

By mistaking some of my expressions in the above history of the cat, I find it has been imagined that I had denied him altogether the power of sleeping. I always knew that cats slept, but not so profoundly as I now find they sometimes do. On this subject M. Pasumot, of the academy of Dijon, an able naturalist, communicated to me a letter, of which the following is an extract.

"Permit me, Sir, to remark, that, in your work, you seem to deny the cat the power of sleeping. I assure you, that, though he sleeps seldom, his sleep is so profound, that it is a species of lethargy, which I have observed at least ten times in different cats. When young, a favourite cat lay every night in bed at my feet. One night, I pushed him from me; but I was surprised to find him so heavy, and at the same time so immoveable, that I believed him to be dead. I pulled him smartly with my hand; but I felt no motion. I then tossed him about, and, by the force of the agitation, he began slowly to awake. This profound sleep, and difficulty of wakening, I have frequently observed. It generally happened in the night, having only once observed it in the day; and this was after perusing what you have said concerning the sleep of these animals. I know another gentleman who has likewise often seen cats sleeping in this profound manner. He tells me, that, when cats sleep during the day, it is always at the time of greatest heat, and particularly before the approach of stormy weather."

M. de Lestrée, a merchant of Chalons in Champagne, who is accustomed to allow cats to lie in his bed, remarks:

1. "That, when these animals purr, when they are tranquil, and appear to be sleeping, they sometimes make a long inspiration, which is followed by a strong expiration; and that, at this period, their breath has an odour which greatly resembles that of musk.

2. "That, when surprised by a dog, or any other object which suddenly alarms them, they make a kind of hissing noise, which is accompanied by the same odour. This is not peculiar to the males; for I have remarked the same thing of both sexes, and of cats of all ages and colours."

From these facts, M. de Lestrée seems to think, that, in the breast or stomach of the cat, there are some vessels filled with an aromatic substance, the perfume of which issues from the mouth. But we discover nothing of this kind from anatomy.

I formerly remarked, that, in China, there were cats with pendulous ears. This variety is not found anywhere else, and perhaps it is an animal of a different species; for travellers, when mentioning an animal called *Sumxu,* which is entirely domestic, say, that they can compare it to nothing but the cat, with which it has a great resemblance. Its colour is black or yellow, and its hair very bright and glittering. The Chinese put silver collars about the necks of these animals, and render them extremely familiar. As they are not common, they give a high price, both on account of their beauty, and because they destroy rats.

At Madagascar there are also wild cats rendered domestic. Most of them have twisted tails; and they are called *Saca* by the natives. But these wild cats are of the same species with the domestic kind; for they intermix and produce.

Another variety has been observed. In our own climate, cats are sometimes produced with pencils of hair at the points of their ears. M. de Seve writes me (Nov. 16, 1773), that a young cat was brought forth in this house at Paris, of the same race with that we have called the *Spanish cat,* with pencils at the points of its ears, though neither of the parents had any pencils. In a few months the pencils of this cat were as large in proportion to its size, as those of the Canadian lynx.

The skin of an animal, which greatly resembles that of our wild cat, has been lately sent me from Cayenne. It is called *Haïra* in Guiana, where they eat its flesh, which is white and good; and hence we may presume, that, however similar to the cat, it belongs to a different species. But, perhaps, the name *haïra* is improperly applied; for it is probably the same with *taïra,* which is not a cat, but a small marten . . .
[*Natural History, General and Particular,* by the Count de Buffon; translated into English, . . . by William Smellie. 3rd ed. London, 1791. (French edition: *Histoire Naturelle, Génerale, et Particulière,* 1749–1767)]

NATURAL HISTORY OF THE CAT

[This anonymous piece, published in vol. 45 of "The Universal Magazine of Knowledge and Pleasure . . . ," 1796, is merely a translation of Buffon except for the last part reprinted below which continues where he left off.]

Such of those cats [Angora] as are met with in Europe have been brought from Angora in Syria; they seem much larger than other domestic cats, and even than the wild cat, their hair being much longer. They are for the most part white; but there are some which are of a fallow colour, and striped with brown . . . The cat, represented in the annexed plate, was fallow. His legs were so short, and his hair so long, that the hair of his belly reached down to the ground; yet his longest hair formed a sort of ruff on the sides of the head and neck, and under the lower jaw-bone, and fore part of the neck, it was four inches long; but the hair of his lips, nose, forehead, fore and hind feet, was short as in other cats. Under each of his eyes were two arches of a reddish fallow colour, and the tip of the nose was of the same colour. The fore legs and tail were encircled with rings of a deep fallow colour; the head, back, sides of the body, flanks and legs were also of a deep fallow colour, which was lighter on the rest of the body.

This cat has a round head, the ears erect, the forehead well proportioned, the eyes large and little distant from one another, the nose with a spring or bearing out, the snout short, the mouth small, and the chin appearing but little. The assemblage of those features gives it an air of softness, which proceeds particularly from the eyes being large, and the snout very short. The proximity of the eyes to each other, and to the mouth and nostrils, with their forward position, seem to express an air of fineness, which is still heightened by the form of the forehead and intire head, and the position of the ears. This mild and fine face changes in a very remarkable manner when the cat is agitated by some violent passion; he opens his mouth and his eyes flash with fire; he turns about his ears and lets them fall; he shews his teeth; his hairs stand on end, and he assumes a furious look, accompanied with quick and vigorous motions of the body, and some lamentable and frightful cries. His tufted hair covers the figure of his body, so as to keep the proportions from being distinguished; all that is seen is, that his body is long and legs very short, but his motions indicate the suppleness and agility of his limbs.

Almost all animals have on each side of the snout some long, straight, and stiff hairs like hog's bristles. These hairs are very apparent in the cat, so assembled and situate as to receive commonly the name of whiskers. There are also others on each side of the forehead over the fore angle of the eye, and on each side of the head beyond the corners of the mouth; they are for the most part white, and the longest are about three inches. There is in the fold of the cat's fore leg a tubercle of a conic figure, which seems formed as that of the dog, by the friction of the third bone of the first row of the carpus.

It will not be amiss to observe in regard to some domestic cats, which, like wild cats, have black lips, and the soles of their feet black, that they generally are the best mousers, and most diligent in attacking their prey of any kind. These have black bands or stripes on the body, and rings of the same colour on the tail and legs, as wild cats, but they have less of the fallow colour, and grey seems to be the predominant colour of their hair. There is reason, however, to believe that they have less degenerated from the original race than others, because they have black lips and the soles of the feet black, and it is therefore they are distinguished from other domestic cats; but their hair is shorter than that of the wild cat, and consequently the head, body, and especially the tail, appear less large.

Cats with red lips are different from the foregoing, and are of one colour, white or black, or of a colour mixed with white, grey, brown, black, and fallow. There are often several of those colours on each hair, and they are also distributed by spots, waves, stripes, and so various that there are not two cats on which the mixture is alike.

The bright and deep red colour is the principal, and perhaps only character that distinguishes the cats of the Spanish breed. These, however, are not all indiscriminately of that colour, some of the females having white and black spots, distributed and mixed irregularly with the red spots, and differently in each individual. It is pretended that none of the male have three colours, having only white or black with the red; so that, when one has a mind to have a fine Spanish cat, a female is generally chosen, because she has a colour more than the males.

The domestic cats of an ash-colour are called by the French Carthusian cats. Some pretend that these cats are blue, but they have not the least tint of that colour. Their hair is of an ash-grey in the greatest part of its length and at the point, and there is a blackish brown under the extremity. The hairs being thick and lying upon one another, the grey colour of the point and the brown underneath are not seen. This mixture of grey and brown is not distinguished but when closely inspected; they seem at a distance as tinged with a glossy grey-brown, and the grey or brown is more or less apparent in different points of view. About the eyes and mouth, the chest and lower part of the legs, there is more grey than brown; the ears are unfurnished of hair, at least on the edges; and of a blackish colour, as are the lips and soles of the feet. These cats are likewise more or less grey at different ages; some are remarkable for a black stripe on the back, and rings of the same colour on the legs, yet very slightly marked.

The cat, being at best but half tame, forms a shadowing, or rather stands in a medium between domestic and wild animals; for we should not place in the number or rank of domestic any of our troublesome neighbours, such as mice, rats, moles, which though inhabitants of our houses or gardens, are not therefore less free and wild, because, instead of being attached and subject to man, they fly from him, and in their obscure retreats, retain their manners, habits, and liberty quite intire.

Education, shelter, care, and the hand of man, have a great influence over the natural disposition, manners, and even the form of animals. These causes, acting conjointly with the influence of climate, modify, alter, and change the species so as to be different from what they were originally, and render also the individuals so different among themselves, at the same time and in the same species that we might have reason to regard them as different animals, if they did not retain the faculty of producing together fruitful individuals, which constitutes the essential and only character of the species. The different races of domestic animals follow in different climates the same order nearly of the human race. As mankind, they are stronger, larger, and more courageous in cold countries; more civilized, more gentle in the temperate climates; more timid, more feeble, and more ugly in too hot climates. It is likewise in temperate climates, and among the people that are best policed, that the greatest diversity is found, the greatest mixture, and the greatest variety in each species; and what is not less worthy of observation is, that there are in animals several evident signs of the long existence of their slavery: Hanging ears, various colours, long and fine hairs, are so many effects produced by time, or rather by the long duration of their domesticity. Most animals that are free and wild have erect ears; the wild boar has them erect and stiff, the tame hog inclined and half hanging. Among the Laplanders, the savages of America, the Hottentots, the negroes, and other unpoliced people, all the dogs have erect ears; whereas in Spain, France, England, Turkey, Persia, China, and all civilised countries, the far greater number have them soft and hanging. Domestic cats have not such stiff ears as the wild, and at China, which is an empire very anciently policed, and where the climate is very mild, domestic cats may be seen with hanging ears . . .

THOMAS PENNANT (1776)

This animal is so well known as to make a description of it unnecessary. It is an useful, but deceitful domestic; active, neat, sedate, intent on its prey. When pleased purres and moves its tail; when angry spits, hisses, and strikes with its foot; when walking, it draws in its claws. It drinks little; is fond of fish; washes its face with its fore-foot, (*Linnaeus* says at the approach of a storm). The female is remarkably salacious; a piteous, squalling, jarring lover. Its eyes shine in the night; its hair when rubbed in the dark emits fire; it is even proverbially tenacious of life; always lights on its feet; is fond of perfumes; *Marum, Catmint, Valerian,* &c.

THOMAS BEWICK (1792)

The domestic Cat differs from the Wild-cat, in being somewhat less; and, instead of being uniformly the same, is distinguished by a great variety of shades and colouring . . .

The cry of the Cat is loud, piercing, and clamorous; and whether expressive of anger or love, is equally violent and hideous.—Its call may be heard at a great distance; and is so well known to the whole fraternity, that on some occasions several hundred cats have been brought together from different parts. Invited by the piercing cries of distress from a suffering fellow-creature, they assemble in crowds; and, with loud squalls and yells, express their horrid sympathies. They frequently tear the miserable object to pieces; and, with the most blind and furious rage, fall upon each other, killing and wounding indiscriminately, till there is scarcely one left. These terrible conflicts happen only in the night; and, though rare, instances of very furious engagements are well authenticated.

Though extremely useful in destroying the vermin that infest our houses, the Cat seems little attached to the persons of those that afford it protection. It seems to be under no subjection, and acts only for itself. All its views are confined to the place where it has been brought up; if carried elsewhere, it seems lost and bewildered: Neither caresses nor attention can reconcile it to its new situation; and it frequently takes the first opportunity of escaping to its former haunts.—Frequent instances are in our recollection of Cats having returned to the place from whence they had been carried, though at many miles distance, and even across rivers, when they could not possibly have any knowledge of the road or situation that would apparently lead them to it.—This extraordinary faculty is, however, possessed in a much greater degree by Dogs; yet it is in both animals equally wonderful and unaccountable.

A General History of Quadrupeds 3rd edition

HENRY JAMES PYE (1807)

CAT, is a beast of prey, even the tame one . . . The tame or domestic cat is diversified with an almost infinite variety of colours and streaks; but the natural colour, in the wild state, is a brown tawney, variegated with streaks of a whitish colour. In France, the cats are of a blueish lead colour, and in the north they are all over white.

All which are of one nature, pretty much of the same shape, but differ in size; the wild cat being much larger than the tame . . .

The tame cat is a creature subtle and watchful, very familiar and loving to mankind, and an enemy to rats, mice, &c. which it seizes on as its prey.

These animals usually generate in the winter season, making a great yawling or crying; go fifty-six days, or eight weeks, with young; bring forth several at a time; they cover their excrements, and love to keep their old habitations.

The Sportsman's Dictionary 5th edition

REV. W. BINGLEY (1813)

The colours of the DOMESTIC CAT are very various, and its manners and disposition seem to be entirely changed by education; and although it does not exhibit the affectionate attachment of the Dog, yet it is not destitute either of gentleness or gratitude . . .

Few animals exhibit more maternal tenderness, or shew a greater attachment to their young, than the Cat; the assiduity with which she attends them, and the pleasure which she seems to take in all their playful tricks, afford a most grateful entertainment to every observer of nature. She has also been known not only to nurse with tenderness the young of different individuals, but even the young of other kinds of animals . . .

To preserve their fur clean, and especially their whiskers, cats wash their faces, and generally quite behind their ears, every time they eat. As they cannot lick those places with their tongues, they first wet the inside of the leg with the saliva, and then repeatedly rub their faces with it. This Dr. Darwin esteems an act of reasoning, because, he says, a means is used to produce an effect, which means seems to be acquired by imitation, like the greatest part of human arts.

A friend of the Doctor saw a Cat catch a Trout, by darting upon it in a deep clear water at the mill, at Weaford, near Litchfield. The Cat belonged to Mr. Stanley, who had often seen her catch fish in the same manner in the summer, when the millpool was drawn so low that the fish could be seen. Other Cats have been known to take fish in shallow water, as they stood on the bank. This he thinks a natural art of taking prey, which their acquired delicacy by domestication, has, in general, prevented them from using, though their desire of eating fish continues in its original strength.

These animals seem to possess something like an additional sense, by means of their whiskers, which have perhaps some analogy to the antennae of Moths and Butterflies. The whiskers of Cats consist not only of long hairs on their upper lips, but they have also four or five long hairs standing up from each eyebrow, and also two or three on each cheek; all which, when the animal erects them, make with their points so many parts of the periphery of a circle, of an extent at least equal to the circumference of any part of their own bodies. With this instrument, it is supposed that, by a little experience, they can at once determine whether any aperture amongst hedges and shrubs, in which animals of this genus live in their wild state, is large enough to admit their bodies; which to them is a matter of the greatest consequence, whether pursuing or pursued. They have likewise a power of erecting and bringing forward the whiskers on their lips; which probably is for the purpose of feeling, whether a dark hole be farther permeable.

Cats are very seldom, like the Dog, attached to our persons, all their attachment seems to be confined to the houses where they have been brought up. Instances are very common of Cats returning of their own accord to the place from whence they have been carried, though at the distance of many miles, and even across rivers where they could not possibly have had any knowledge either of the road or the direction that would lead them to it. This may perhaps arise from their being acquainted there with all the retreats of the Mice, and all the passages and outlets of the house, and from their dislike to acquire the knowledge of these conveniences in their new habitation.

No experiment can be more beautiful than that of setting a kitten for the first time before a looking-glass. The animal appears surprised and pleased with the resemblance, and makes several attempts at touching its new acquaintance; and, at length, finding its efforts fruitless, it looks behind the glass, and appears highly surprised at the absence of the figure: it again views itself; tries to touch it with its foot; suddenly looking at intervals behind the glass, it then becomes more accurate in its observations, and begins, as it were, to make experiments, by stretching out its paw in different directions; and when it finds that these motions are answered in every respect by the figure in the glass, it seems, at length, to be convinced of the real nature of the image. The same is the case with the Dog at an early age.

The sleep of the Cat, though generally very light, is, however, sometimes so profound, that the animal requires to be shaken pretty briskly before it can be awakened. This particularity takes place chiefly in the depth of winter, and especially on the approach of snowy weather. At such periods also, as well as some others, the animal diffuses a fragrant smell somewhat like that of cloves.

It is generally remarked, that Cats can see in the dark; but, though this is not absolutely the case, it is certain that they can see with much less light than most other animals, owing to the peculiar structure of their eyes, the pupils of which are capable of being contracted or dilated, in proportion to the degree of light by which they are affected. In the day-time, the pupil of the Cat is perpetually contracted, and sometimes into a mere line; for it is with difficulty that it can see by a strong light: but in the twilight the pupil resumes its natural roundness, and the animal enjoys perfect vision. It appears somewhat singular, that, on plunging the head of a Cat into water, although the animal be exposed to a very bright light, the pupil should become immediately expanded to all its width. This, however, is to be accounted for upon optical principles.

It has been remarked, that the eyes of Cats always shine with a bright light when they are in the dark . . . [The possible reasons for this phenomenon are then discussed.]

The fur of the Cat, being generally clean and dry, readily yields electric sparks when rubbed: and, if a clean and perfectly dry domestic Cat be placed, in frosty weather, on a stool with glass feet, or insulated by any other means, and rubbed for a little time, in contact with the wire of a coated vial, the vial, by this means, becomes effectually charged . . .

The patience, craft, vigilance, utility, and cleanliness of the Cat have also obtained for it the highest degree of protection in the Eastern mythology, so far indeed as to have it esteemed the noblest species of its genus.

The following curious fact in the natural history of the Cat, is related by Dr. Anderson, in his entertaining work, the Recreations in Agriculture:—A Cat belonging to Dr. Coventry, the ingenious Professor of Agriculture in Edinburgh, which had no blemish at its birth, lost its tail by accident when it was young. It had many litters of kittens, and in every one of these there was one or more that wanted the tail, either in whole or in part . . .

Animal Biography

BARON CUVIER (1769–1832)

(The Domestic Cat). Is originally from the forests of Europe. In its wild state it is of a greyish brown, with darker-transverse undulations; below pale; the insides of the thighs and of all the feet, yellowish; three bands on the tail, its inferior third blackish. In a domestic state it varies, as is well known, in colours, in the length and fineness of the hair, but infinitely less so than the dog; it is also much less submissive and affectionate.

The Animal Kingdom

William Rhind (1834)

In treating of the moral qualities of the Cat, we are aware that we are touching on debatable ground. While some bestow upon poor Puss all the epithets of treachery, cruelty, and ingratitude, others, finding in its disposition, kindness, gentleness, and playfulness, are warm in eulogies of their favourite. In fact, the character of the Cat is judged of too much by comparison, and thus, like many persons in the world, its stock of really good qualities are thrown into the back ground, and all its bad propensities magnified. That the Cat has not the sagacity, approaching almost to human reason, of the Dog—that it has not his devotedness of affection, his entire self-control and patient submissiveness under the rebuke of his master,—is not to be denied, nor, from its natural inherent habits, is it to be expected that it should have these qualities to the same extent. Neither can it be affirmed, that the Cat is in disposition to be estimated like the noble and patient Horse, another of the chief and favourite companions of man. Yet Puss is not only the affectionate sharer of the clean and quiet hearth of the lonely widow; but it will be found quietly reposing on the silken covered cushion in the boudoir of the more wealthy; and from the palace to the cottage it everywhere finds its patrons, to whom its gambols and its fawnings, the beauty and symmetry of its elegant figure, and its graceful motions, are all circumstances of recommendation. In fact, it is bad usage alone that calls forth the savage propensities of this Feline domestic; with gentle and kind treatment, it can be as gentle, and kind, and insinuating as any other animal. It is true, even in its most domestic state, it exhibits a native propensity for prey, and hence is derived its usefulness; though fed with the most delicate dainties, it will still prefer as a peculiar delicacy a Mouse, caught by its own prowess and cunning, and it will revel in the quivering flesh of the yet gasping victim. Still nothing can exceed the affection of the Cat to those who treat it kindly. This affection it expresses by rubbing its body close on the individual, and by the loud purring noise indicative of its satisfaction. It will not, however, bear to be crossed, and though it returns kindness by every expression in its power, it is also prompt to retaliate on the slightest opposition. Neither has it the perception of the Dog, in desisting from any action when commanded to do so; it will persist in clawing food off one's plate, and has no hesitation in stealing whenever it can. Although the Cat can be made to perform some action at the command of its master, such as leaping, and other tricks, yet it does so always with reluctance, and has by no means the teachable and persevering disposition of the Dog.

The Cat, however, shews many instances of a species of reasoning powers, which . . . almost surpass what can strictly be termed instinctive . . ."

The Natural History of the Feline Species

AN 1830 JUVENILE

All animals of the cat kind have sharp and strong claws, round heads, and whiskers; are naturally sullen, cruel, and treacherous; and cannot, like obstinate children, be persuaded or forced to do anything, even for their own good. This cat (a crude illustration shown) was the terror of all mice and birds, but while she watched these pretty nibblers, she stole by wholesale herself. Indeed she was kept very sharp, and the children often teased her.

Short Stories, or Treasures of Truth . . .

THOMAS HUXLEY (1825–1895)

A long series of cats has reigned over my household for the last forty years or thereabouts. The present occupant of the throne is a large, young, grey Tabby,—Oliver by name. Not that he is in any sense a Protector, for I doubt whether he has the heart to kill a mouse. However, I saw him catch and eat the first butterfly of the season, and trust that the germ of courage, thus manifested, may develop with age into efficient mousing.

As to sagacity, I should say that his judgment respecting the warmest place and the softest cushion in a room is infallible, his punctuality at meal times is admirable, and his pertinacity in jumping on people's shoulders till they give him some of the best of what is going, indicates great firmness.

from a letter to J. G. Kitton

ANDREW LANG (1844–1912)

From the dawn of creation the cat has known his place, and he has kept it, practically untamed and unspoiled by man. He has *retenue*. Of all animals, he alone attains to the Contemplative Life. He regards the wheel of existence from without, like the Buddha. There is no pretence of sympathy about the cat. He lives alone, aloft, sublime, in a wise passiveness. He is excessively proud; and, when he is made the subject of conversation, will cast one glance of scorn, and leave the room in which personalities are bandied. All expressions of emotion he scouts as frivolous and insincere, except, indeed, in the ambrosial night, when, free from the society of mankind, he pours forth his soul in strains of unpremeditated art. The paltry pay and paltry praise of humanity he despises, like Edgar Poe. He does not exhibit the pageant of his bleeding heart; he does not howl when people die, nor explode in cries of delight when his master returns from a journey. With quiet courtesy, he remains in his proper and comfortable place, only venturing into view when something he approves of, such as fish or game, makes its appearance. On the rights of property he is firm. If a strange cat enters his domain, he is up in claws to resist invasion. It was for these qualities, probably, that the cat was worshipped by the ancient Egyptians.

quoted in Agnes Repplier, *The Fireside Sphinx*

ALAN DEVOE (1937)

Concerning Cats

We tie bright ribbons around their necks, and occasionally little tinkling bells, and we affect to think that they are as sweet and vapid as the coy name "kitty" by which we call them would imply. It is a curious illusion. For, purring beside our fireplaces and pattering along our back fences, we have got a wild beast as uncowed and uncorrupted as any under heaven.

It is five millenniums since we snared the wild horse and broke his spirit to our whim, and for centuries beyond counting we have been able to persuade the once-free dog to fawn and cringe and lick our hands. But a man must be singularly blind with vanity to fancy that in the three—ten?—thousand years during which we have harbored cats beneath our roof-trees, we have succeeded in reducing them to any such insipid estate. It is not a "pet" (that most degraded of creatures) that we have got in our house, whatever we may like to think. It is a wild beast; and there adheres to its sleek fur no smallest hint of the odor of humanity.

It would be a salutory thing if those who write our simpering verses and tales about "tabby-sit-by-the-fire" could bring themselves to see her honesty, to look into her life with eyes unblurred by wishful sentiment.

It would be a good thing—to start at the beginning—to follow her abroad into the moonlight on one of those raw spring evenings when the first skunk-cabbages are thrusting their veined tips through the melting snow and when the loins of catdom are hot with lust.

The love-play of domestic creatures is mostly a rather comic thing, and loud are the superior guffaws of rustic humans to see the clumsy, fumbling antics that take place in the kennels and the stockpen. But the man had better not laugh who sees cats in their rut. He is looking upon something very like aboriginal passion, untainted by any of the overlaid refinements, suppressions, and modifications that have been acquired by most of mankind's beasts. The mating of cats has neither the pathetic clumsiness of dogs' or the lumbering ponderousness of cattle's, but—conducted in a lonely secret place, away from human view—is marked by a quick concentrated intensity of lust that lies not far from the borderline of agony. The female, in the tense moment of the prelude, tears with her teeth at her mate's throat, and, as the climax of the creatures' frenzy comes, the lean, silky-furred flanks quiver vibrantly as a taut wire. Then quietly, in the spring night, the two beasts go their ways.

It will be usually May before the kittens come, and that episode, too, will take place secretly, in its ancient feline fashion, where no maudlin human eye may see. Great is the pique in many a house when "pussy," with dragging belly and distended dugs, disappears one night—scorning the cushioned maternity-bed that has been prepared for her—and creeps on silent feet to the dankest cranny of the cellar, there in decent aloneness to void her blood and babies. She does not care, any more than a lynx does, or a puma, to be pried upon while she licks the birth-hoods from her squirming progeny and cleans away the membrane with her rough pink tongue.

A kitten is not a pretty thing at birth. For many days it is a wriggling mite of lumpy flesh and sinew, blind and unaware, making soft sucking noises with its wet, toothless mouth, and smelling of milk. Daily, hourly, the rough tongue of the tabby ministers to it in its helplessness, glossing the baby-fur with viscid spittle, licking away the uncontrolled dung, cleaning away the crumbly pellet of dried blood from its pointed ears. By that tenth or fourteenth day when its eyes wholly unseal, blue and weak in their newness, the infant cat is clean to immaculateness, and an inalienable fastidiousness is deep-lodged in its spirit.

It is now—when the kitten makes its first rushes and sallies from its birthplace, and, with extraordinary gymnastics of its chubby body, encounters chair-legs and human feet and other curious phenomena—that it elicits from man those particular expressions of gurgling delight which we reserve for very tiny fluffy creatures who act very comically. But the infant cat has no coy intent to be amusing. If he is comic, it is only because of the incongruity of so demure a look and so wild a heart. For in that furry head of his, grim and ancient urges are already dictating.

Hardly larger than a powder-puff, he crouches on the rug, and watches a fleck of lint. His little blue eyes are bright, and presently his haunches tense and tremble. The tiny body shivers in an ague of excitement. He pounces, a little clumsily perhaps, and pinions the fleeting lint-fleck with his paws. In the fractional second of that lunge, the ten small needles of his claws have shot from their sheaths of flesh and muscle. It is a good game; but it is not an idle one. It is the kitten's introduction into the ancient ritual of the kill. Those queer little stiff-legged rushes and prancings are the heritage of an old death-dance, and those jerkings of his hind legs, as he rolls on his back, are the preparation for that day when—in desperate conflict with a bigger beast than himself—he will win the fight by the time-old feline technique of disembowelment. Even now, in his early infancy, he is wholly and inalienably a cat.

While he is still young he has already formulated his attitude toward the human race into whose midst he has been born. It is an attitude not easily described, but compounded of a great pride, a great reserve, a towering integrity. It is even to be fancied that there is something in it of a sort of bleak contempt. Solemnly the cat watches these great hulking two-legged creatures into whose strange tribe he has unaccountably been born—and who are so clumsy, so noisy, so vexing to his quiet spirit—and in his feline heart is neither love nor gratitude. He learns to take the food which they give him, to relish the warmth and the comfort and the caresses which they can offer, but these profferments do not persuade his wild mistrustful heart to surrender itself. He will not sell himself, as a dog will, for a scrap of meat; he will not enter into an allegiance. He is unchangeably and incorruptably a cat, and he will accommodate himself to the ways and spirit of mankind no more than the stern necessity of his unnatural environment requires.

Quietly he dozes by the fire or on a lap, and purrs in his happiness because he loves the heat. But let him choose to move, and if any human hand tries to restrain him for more than a moment he will struggle and unsheath his claws and lash out with a furious hate. Let a whip touch him and he will slink off in a sullen fury, uncowed and outraged and unrepenting. For the things which man gives to him are not so precious or essential that he will trade them for his birth-right, which is the right to be himself—a furred fourfooted being of ancient lineage, loving silence and aloneness and the night, and esteeming the smell of rat's blood above any possible human excellence.

He may live for perhaps ten years; occasionally even for twenty. Year after year he drinks the daily milk that is put faithfully before him, dozes in laps whose contours please him, accepts with casual pleasure the rubbing of human fingers under his chin—and withdraws, in every significant hour of his life, as far away from human society as he is able. Far from the house, in a meadow or a woods if he can find one, he crouches immobile for hours, his lithe body flattened concealingly in the grass or ferns, and waits for prey.

With a single pounce he can break a rabbit's spine as though it were a brittle twig. When he has caught a tawny meadow-mouse or a mole, he has, too, the ancient cat-ecstasy of toying and playing with it, letting it die slowly, in a long agony, for his amusement. Sometimes, in a dim remembrance from the remote past of his race, he may bring home his kill; but mostly he returns to the house as neat and demure as when he left, with his chops licked clean of blood.

Immaculate, inobtrusive, deep withdrawn into himself, he passes through the long years of his enforced companionship with humanity. He takes from his masters (how absurd a word it is) however much they may care to give him; of himself he surrenders nothing. However often he be decked with ribbons and cuddled and petted and made much over, his cold pride never grows less, and his grave calm gaze—tinged perhaps with a gentle distaste—is never lighted by adoration. To the end he adores only his own gods, the gods of mating, of hunting, and of the lonely darkness.

One day, often with no forewarning whatever, he is gone from the house and never returns. He has felt the presaging shadow of death, and he goes to meet it in the old unchanging way of the wild—alone. A cat does not want to die with the smell of humanity in his nostrils and the noise of humanity in his delicate peaked ears. Unless death strikes very quickly and suddenly, he creeps away to where it is proper that a proud wild beast should die—not on one of man's rags or cushions, but in a lonely quiet place, with his muzzle pressed against the cold earth.

GUSTAV ECKSTEIN (1932)

Seven Cats

A cat had followed Joe up the path and round the road and to the back of the building, and Joe fed her and drove her away. Next day she followed again, was fed again, was driven again, was harder to drive, and harder still on the day after that. It worried Joe. A medical college is no place for a cat. So he took to walking to the other side of the dump to feed her there, but she followed just the same. He tried chasing her with his dog, the dog having plain directions to chase the cat but not to harm her—and the cat understood the directions. Finally, exasperated, he came to me, and the upshot was that I had the cat. She was the alley kind, gaunt, young, looking middle-aged.

I had her, but could not make her eat. I thought it hurt feelings, but Joe thought her ill, and it went so a number of days. She still had no fever and the whites of her eyes were clear, yet by the end of the week I could not doubt that something serious was the matter with her, and by the end of another week I knew I must help her die.

On the top of the radiator is a marble slab. It is warm on the slab, so I laid her on it, then sat myself in front of her and watched her. Her chin, her neck, her belly, the whole of her flat body seemed sunk into the marble. Her respirations also had changed, had taken the rhythm of death. Mr. Kupka came into the laboratory. He knows animals, and I asked him if he thought I ought to chloroform her. He thought not, though she had only the slimmest chance, but need not die immediately.

He went, and maybe I dozed, because it was with a shock I realized that some queer change had passed over that cat. Something seemed to have run out into that limp left front leg and made it rigid, and she drew back the leg and planted the paw squarely on the marble. But, what was more queer, she opened the left eye, though she kept the right tight shut. It was an unnatural, a fantastic, almost a frightful behavior. That left eye appeared not looking at me, but beyond me, appeared to be seeing something I could not, something possibly not even materially in the room. At the thought of that I leaped quickly up and looked quickly behind me, and there, leisurely crossing my desk on her way to her drawer, went mother rat. It was mother rat the dying cat had seen, had imagined, no doubt, she was in heaven already where rats disport at random. Anyway, something remarkable happened to her, touched her soul or her psyche, or a doctor might say her secretions, because when I brought her milk she drank, and in a few days was her own old self.

I took her to the house, and soon she was staying out nights and I knew she had a lover. There were others, admirers, and my neighbor said they were killing the chickens. Funny eyes my neighbor has—the kind of man likes to finger a gun, would have made a great huntsman or a great soldier, but danger in those professions, and shooting cats has its interest too. He would open his window, settle in his chair, and every time he hit he laughed. You would hear the shot, then the laugh. A mad laugh. More than the eyes of my neighbor was mad. He killed those admirers one by one and after each laughed. Mine took hers up the windowless side of the house to the roof. Nights you could hear the two discussing.

A little after dark I would see the lover come from behind his barrel, and he looked hungry, yet when I tried to feed him fled. He was afraid of the window, but afraid also of her, who did not allow him near the house, preferred to go out to her friends, did not like this hanging about of males. Nevertheless, one evening as I came in through the lower door I stumbled over him, talked to him, which he did not like, but in spite of that began with me to mount the steps. We were about half way up when I saw a head push out above through the open door. And he saw the head. And the head saw him. It was as two antique swordsmen see each other through the tear in an arras, and the instant that followed had also that speed. Not that she moved, but there was such movement in the way she did not. And he, he went at one bound back to the bottom, then wanted to go straight on through the door, beat his head into it again and again, and when I opened it rushed into the night.

One small matter more was hard on my neighbor. At 3 P.M. she would go to her sand, would go at other times, too. but always at 3 P.M., and the sand was just under the window, and there she would sit, aware of where she sat, and of who sat, and of the divine right of who sat to sit where she sat.

In July she and I drove to Elkhart. She was used to driving, but on this trip was nervous from the start. We slept the first night in Connersville, then next morning went up through the sandier parts of In-diana. To me sand is sand, but to her there are distinctions, and I could get no interest for any sand I showed her. Then in the restaurants they began not to want her, and that made me apologetic, and then they wanted her less. Then I began letting her eat on the seat of the automobile, but a dog barked, and after that she was forever prowling on the floor.

By the second night we entered Chicago. I stuck her under my coat, registered at the Palmer House, and no one found us out, but it was not a happy night. The room was long, with expensive carpet and a low bed, and she was perpetually going about under the bed and making me uneasy for what she might do, especially as she liked the carpet in exactly the same way that she did not like the sand, kept pressing her paws rhythmically in and out, as a cat does, a female cat particularly, and more at one period of her life than at any other. Unexpectedly her purr would swell through the night and she would seem in an orgy of content.

At Elkhart she showed something new. She never had hunted beetles or mice or other living things, but at Elkhart one afternoon I caught her watching a frog. The frog was playing dead. She tapped him. He went on playing dead. She tapped him more energetically, and he leaped, and instantly she was on him and I on her. I scolded her and took her in. Half an hour afterward she was out again, and I scolded her and took her in. But the huntress was roused, and late that day when I saw him he was dead.

She and I got back from Elkhart in September. Her nervousness was gone and she was quite at the other extreme. Whatever I did for her she thanked me disproportionately, then toward seven o'clock one evening I knew the hour had arrived, so got a rag-lined basket and went with her round the room to find what would be the most suitable place. I hoped it might not be the clothes-closet, and kept that shut and did not refer to it, but there she stood and stuck. It was a first labor and hard. She knew just what to do—bit off the cords, licked away the blood, licked the bodies, and all the while pressed her paws rhythmically into the rags as she had into the carpet at the Palmer House, and at each accomplished birth was more tired till, with the last, the third, I helped her. She rubbed my leg and purred when I changed the soiled rags.

By noon the next day she was asking for a woolen blanket—the room had got cold. And all that day she warmed the three with the blanket and with her body, and all the next day, but on the evening of the third day disappeared. I found her far from the house, tripping along like an irresponsible kitten, and the lover I saw slipping behind his barrel. I snatched her up and carried her home and pointed severely to her three, and as soon as she saw them she was wholly absorbed in them again. That night she brought them into my bed. She herself always liked to lie in the hollow between my feet and the wall, but now it was she and three, so I lugged them back to the basket. Each time I waked they were in the bed again. She simply waited till I slept.

On the tenth day she brought a rat, and in the following days all species of living things, but when she began with birds I strung a bell round her neck. Any sudden move must warn every bird for a quarter of a mile. Consequently there were no sudden moves. She would put out one paw, then one paw, then one paw, infinitely cautiously approach a tree, infinitely cautiously climb the trunk, creep out a branch, and when she was at the end of the branch turn round, and all without once ringing the bell. And she would stay there hours, seemed to expect a bird to fly precisely into her mouth, which, to judge by the quiet of her, may sometimes have occurred. Once, however, she was in that tree for a different reason—was chased there by a dog who made himself comfortable below, and had to wait till a policeman came and got her down.

On a Sunday—she in the tree—I left the room at four o'clock, and when I got back at five o'clock two of the kittens were gone. Two were gone and the third crouched in a corner and could not be made to come out. I looked everywhere. Everybody looked. The policeman, a big-bodied, healthy man, was so simply concerned when I told him, also looked. I knew it was no use. How the two had been done away with I did not know, but done away with they were. Of course they could not have been shot from the window, because it was a quiet Sunday and people would have heard. And they were not out-of-doors where they could have been shot. They were in the closed room.

The third, who crouched in the corner and could not be made to come out, was so tiny when he was born that it was hard to see how he could live. Hence his name, Tiny. But so soon as he had his name, so soon as the baptism was over, he began to grow, and grew and grew and grew, prodigiously, till in a few months he was twice as big as Mother, and more beautiful than any other kitten I have ever known.

He never would go down into the dump, but would sit poised in the window, and from the window watch most carefully everything that went on in the dump and in the street beyond the dump. One afternoon there was a crowd in the street. He would like to have known what drew that crowd. The wish got him restless, and I heard the thud as he dropped to the floor, then his complaint that the outer door was locked. I got up and unlocked the outer door. He proceeded down the steps and round the road and to the edge of the crowd, then went round the crowd, wary of the feet, saw what he went to see, which was all there was to see, merely a wreck, and immediately came back round the road and up the steps, returned to his window, and at his leisure followed what further unfolded below.

With evening he deserted his window for the shadow at the end of the room. He did that every evening. He moved to and fro in the shadow. One sometimes wonders what an old cat thinks when he blinks that way, but it is more a question what a young cat thinks, for an old cat, after all, has his past. Tiny in the blue-black on this particular evening was like a figure on a basalt etching, and it may be he was thinking of Egypt and ancestors. At least it was far he came to be aware for the first time of the music. With one spring he was up beside me on the piano bench, and with a second on the books at the end of the piano, was peering in on the hammers, his imagination caught by some problem of the mechanism, his head darting back and forth as the hammers leaped up here and there. With a shrewd quiet he glided now to where he could look instead at the keys. I struck the keys slowly. He glided once more, back a little to where he could at one time see both hammers and keys, and in the next moment it was plain in his face that he had grasped the principle and was staying only long enough to establish experimentally how tone is made. With a shrug he deserted the books and went again to blink in the shadow.

April came and with it three more, two gray, and the third the boy who does the chores named Little Black. And Little Black is what her name just had to be. Again the difficulty about the bed, but no curing Little Black. I would burst from sleep because some villain was choking me. Paws! But impossible to be angry with Little Black.

It was Little Black too [who] tried to undermine the laws of the high-chair, despite the high-chair was an old institution. I had bought it when Mother was the only one, my idea being to lift her where she could be part of the room's principal activities—dinners, table conversations, newspapers. When Tiny was weaned, Mother gave him the seat of the chair, took for herself the board where I up to then had set her warmed plates. This was not for comfort, but for justice. It raised her above Tiny. It placed her in front of Tiny. It brought Tiny's food a measurable interval late. In short, it put rank where you could see it, and every distinction was minutely kept up. When the new kittens came and were weaned, Mother ruled there was no more free space on the chair, and the two gray ones obeyed. But Little Black simply couldn't. She simply had to climb up now and then where Tiny was, Tiny always moving over and giving her room, but Mother always ordering her down. Some kind of discipline Mother must maintain, with Tiny getting so big and the kittens every day growing. It was all the happy time of kitten life, a gloss over everything that spring. Tiny so beautiful, Mother so wise, Little Black so quaint, the gray ones so snub-nosed and dear.

As for the meat, the first piece went to Mother, the second to Tiny, the third to Little Black, the fourth to the one gray one, the fifth to the other gray one, each in turn raising a paw. This was Tiny's idea. He thought he ought to take his food like a human being, ought to take it in his paw, and ought to sit. For this he was much praised, and therefore, when hunger was not too pressing, the others tried it too, and they were much praised, and soon all were doing it regularly. After meat came milk, which was preferred warm but not hot, and if hot, was fanned cool with paws.

Then on a Tuesday night when I came to feed them Tiny would not eat. He seemed so quiet. And perhaps he glistened more than otherwise. After a while we all went to bed, he under the piano bench, Mother and the kittens in the corner by the book-closet.

I had slept an hour when I waked with the feeling that someone had waked me, but there was utter quiet. I got right up and went to find Tiny. He was not asleep. He was under the bench just where I had left him, sitting, and the fact that he was sitting was somehow appalling. He was like a huge, beautiful woman with a fever, but when I touched him he was cold. I was stricken with fear at that touch, and lifted him quickly into my arms and hurried with him to the radiator. His eyes shone so. I knew what it meant, and yet it was not like death, but more like the end of some sublime imagined thing. He took one long quiet breath, and that was all.

A terrible night, Tiny dead, something plainly wrong with Mother, something plainly wrong with the kittens. About dawn I went for a few moments into the air, and when I came back through the lower door I saw Little Black above me on the steps. She was wanting to greet me as she always had when she heard my keys, but her legs were too weak, and down she rolled, catching herself and falling to catch herself, like an awkward bag. Before I got her to the room she was dead. Then the one gray one died. Then the other. Then Mother. Mother I helped a bit. She did not want me to, poor Mother. Poison. May God understand it. I do not.

PART TWO

BIOLOGY

VII
Cats and Humans—All the Same

Of all the beasts that live, we must,
I guess, call Cats the humanust;
For jest like folks, you'll find that these
Has no end to their qualities.
For some is fat and some is lean,
Some very dirty and some clean,—
Some's always licken at their fur
And some's not so particular.
Some Cats take jest fresh milk and meat,
Some takes all that they're gave to eat.
Some Cats they cough, and some they wheeze,
And some's afflicted by disease;
Some Cats is blind, and stone-deaf some,
But aint no Cat wuz ever dumb.
Some Cats will monkey round and fool,
And play for hours with jest a spool,
While some jest sit and blink their eyes,
Preferrin to philosophize.
Some Cats like most folks pretty fine,
But some takes care to draw the line.
Some comes and rubs against you which,
Means will you scratch them where they itch,—
While others is so mean all through
They like lots better scratchin you.
And so you see the marvellous
Way Felines does resemble us,
Cats and Humans—all the same,
Jest sort of diff'rin in the name.

ANTHONY EUWER

CATS are similar to humans in many more ways—both physiologically and anatomically—than Mr. Euwer mentioned, and for this reason they are used extensively in experimentation, particularly in experiments on the brain. More is known about the cat brain than that of any other animal.

Despite the close similarities, however, a cat far excels man, and for that matter all mammals, structurally speaking. As Mivart pointed out "its organization, considered absolutely in itself, is one of singular perfection, and the adaptation of means to ends which it displays is truly admirable." It is the superb synchronization of anatomy, physiology and mentality that gives the cat a high survival value and provides some of its proverbial nine lives.

This magnificent equipment for its particular role in life has resulted in one bad restriction. With an anatomy geared for agility and huge bursts of power, it has little sustaining power. A cat's lifetime fluctuates between periods of complete repose and intense activity, but the periods of activity can't be maintained very long without producing exhaustion. Konrad Lorenz observed that a strong healthy adult cat can't take even a half hour stroll with a person without showing signs of fatigue.

To what does a cat owe its abilities and inabilities? First, it is a muscular masterpiece with perfect control of its powerful voluntary muscles of which there are over 500. These, combined with an extremely flexible skeleton, give the animal its graceful agility and fluid motion. A. S. J. Tessimond describes this feline characteristic:

> Cats, no less liquid than their shadows,
> Offer no angle to the wind.
> They slip, diminished, neat, through loopholes
> Less than themselves . . .

The muscles are capable of great endurance; it is other parts of the animal that aren't. A cat's chest cavity is small for its relative size and so, necessarily, are its lungs and heart; and it is the potentialities of these two organs that determine an animal's capability for sustained action. The space saved by small lungs and small heart is occupied by the digestive organs which are large, to accommodate alternate periods of stuffing and fasting.

A discussion of the cat's general physiology and anatomy, however, is beyond the scope of this book, especially since they parallel those of man, and can be found in any number of textbooks.*

As a matter of historical interest only, an account of a physiological experiment performed in the middle of the 18th century follows. At that time it had already been observed that cats did little drinking, which of course is natural for a carnivore whose food is 67–73% water. But, as happens so frequently today, merely from curiosity and with no thought about the animal's discomfort, a cat was forced to endure unnecessary hardship.

AN ACCOUNT OF A CAT THAT LIVED TWENTY-SIX MONTHS WITHOUT DRINKING

Monsieur l'Abbe de Fontenu of the royal academy of inscriptions and belles-lettres, to whom the academy is indebted for several curious observations, was pleased to communicate this year a very singular one. Having remarked how cats often habituate themselves, and oftener than one could wish, to dry warrens, where they certainly cannot find drink but very seldom, he fancied that these animals could do for a very long time without drinking. To see whether his notions were well grounded, he made an experiment on a very large and fat castrated cat he had at his disposal. He began by retrenching by little and little his drink, and, at last, debarred him of it entirely, yet fed him as usual with boiled meat. The cat had not drunk for seven months, when this observation was communicated to the academy, and has since passed nineteen without drinking. The animal was not less well in health, nor less fat; it only seemed that it ate less than before, probably because digestion was somewhat slower. The excrements were more firm and dry, which were not evacuated but every second day, though urine came forth six or seven times during the same time. The cat appeared to have an ardent desire to drink, and used his best endeavours to testify the same to M. Fontenu, especially when he saw a pot of water in his hand. He licked

* But mention should be made that other animals besides man and cat possess Cowper's glands. The misstatement that they alone have them is being copied from one book to another and should be stopped.

greedily the mug, the glass, iron; in short every thing that could procure for his tongue the sensation of coolness; but it does not appear in the least, that his health suffered any alteration by so severe and so long a want of all sorts of drink. It may be inferred from hence, that cats may support thirst for a considerable time, without risk of madness, or any other fatal accident. According to M. de Fontenu's remark, these, perhaps, are not the only animals that enjoy this faculty, and this observation might lead, perhaps, to more important objects.

VIII
Cat Facts at a Glance

Temperature

Body Temperature: 101.5° F ± 1.0°

Rectal Temperature: 99–102° F

Critical Air Temperature (that at which the first indication of rectal change occurs): 90° F

Thermo-neutrality Zone (that in which the metabolic rate is lowest and constant): 50–86° F

Temperature Regulating Mechanisms: Shivering, panting, sweating

Temperature Tolerance: 100% survival up to seven hours with the air temperature 105.8–109.4° F and the humidity 35–65%

Water

Total Body Water: 580 ml/kg; similar to man

On the average the adult cat is 73% water (fat-free body weight); the kitten at birth is 83% water.

Water Intake: decreases as age increases. For example, the intake of a

6–8 months old cat is 76.9 g/kg body weight; that of a 15–17 months old cat is 57.1 g/kg.

Spontaneous Motor Activity

Normal cats never exceed 50 movements per hour. The range is from 0.4 to 48.0 movements. Time of year, season, sex and age do not affect the number.

Length

Male Average: 21 inches. *Female Average:* 18 inches.

Weights

At Birth: 3½ oz.; doubles in a week
Adult Male: 6.7 lb. average; range usually between 3.1–10.2 lb.
Adult Female: 5.8 lb. average; range usually between 3.1–7.7 lb.
Kittens: 8 week male: 1.6 lb. 12 week male: 2.9 lb.
8 week female: 1.5 lb. 12 week female: 2.2 lb.
Brain in g/100 g: 0.77 compared to man's ca. 2.0 and chipmunk's 3.0, illustrating that weight has nothing to do with intelligence.
A lion is 60 times heavier than a cat, a man 20 times.

Age

Average: 13-17 years
Maximum: around 30 years compared to a terrier's 18-20 years and a rabbit's 15-18 years. Not only is the cat the longest-lived of the smaller domestic animals but the highest age range is more commonly reached by them than by other pets.
Age and Physical Fitness: much better preserved in old age than other pets. Males continue to mate throughout their life span and females getting kittens in their 20's are not uncommon.

Respiration

Breaths/minute at rest: 26 as compared to 11.7 in man

Nutrition

High protein, high fat diet. Actual needs in the way of vitamins, minerals, etc. not yet determined or agreed upon. See veterinary journals for most recent information.

Ears

Hearing Threshold for Pure Tones:

Sound Wave Frequency

CYCLES/SECOND	DECIBELS
100	38
200	24
400	9
500	6
1,000	− 1
2,000	− 2
3,000	− 7
4,000	− 6
5,000	− 8
8,000	− 7
10,000	− 7
14,000	− 9
16,000	− 4

(Negative values indicate that less energy is required to make the sound audible than is required for a tone of 1000 cycles/second)

Range of Hearing: Frequency 30–45,000 cycles/second. This does not necessarily represent the capacities of the *entire* auditory system.

Eyes

Weight in g/100 g of cat: 0.32
Volume in ml: 3.9 compared to man's 5.4 (This measurement and the one above show how relatively large a cat's eyes are in respect to itself and to man)
Wavelength of Maximal Sensitivity: 560 $m\mu$ in cat and man
Critical Flicker Frequencies: 50 cycles/second, cones
Ratio of Rods to Cones: around 20–25 to 1

Reproduction

Chromosomes: 38 in number; sex type x-y male
Age at Puberty: 6–15 months
Oestrous Type: polyoestrous
Gestation: 63 days average; range 52–69 days
Young Per Litter: 4 average; range 1–6 or more, correlated with weight of female

Oestrous: 4 days duration with presence of male; 9–10 days in absence of male. Return to oestrous cycle, post partum, 2–3 weeks after weaning.

Ovum: size 0.120–0.130 mm; 4–6 on average released at one time; transport, tube to uterus, 4–8 days; implantation or attachment 13–14 days.

Ovulation: 24–56 hours after mating

Copulation: duration usually 1–2 hours from preliminaries to final act; female most receptive on third day

Fertilization: time, 2 days after mating; site, oviduct; transit of sperm from cervix to ovarian end of oviduct (Fallopian tube) 100 min.

Reproduction Interval—Optimum Breeding Period: Variable and geographically influenced; may be continual.

Gestation: assuming it to be 66 days

1) earliest spontaneous activity: 36% of total time elapsed
2) sucking: 74%
3) phonation: 74%
4) tail movement and most other trunk movements: 42–47%
5) head movement 36–42%

Blood

Average red blood cell count: 8,000,000/cu. mm.

Average white blood cell count: 16,000/cu. mm.

Blood variation due to age and sex:

1) The RBC's and hemoglobin in males are higher than in females, each RBC of the male also having a higher concentration of hemoglobin than in the female.
2) Male and adult cats have lower white blood cell counts than females and kittens.
3) The sedimentation rate is slower in the male than in the female.

Specific Gravity: 1.051

Relative viscosity at body temperature: 4.2–4.7

pH: 7.35 for whole blood

Pressure (arterial): systolic 155, diastolic 100; at birth 25–30

Blood Groups: present

Circulation

Heart rate: 120/minute average; range 110–240; in kittens 168–300, averaging closer to 300

Time required for one complete circuit: approximately 10.8 seconds

Urine

22–30 cc (average 26 cc)/kg body weight
acid with pH from 5.0 to less than 7.0
Specific gravity: 1.018–1.040

IX
Ears

The cat has a nervous ear
That turns this way and that.
And what the cat may hear
Is known but to the cat.
DAVID MORTON

For a good many years science has been trying to do something about this fact—to make the cat reveal what it can and can't hear. Of course, tests aren't necessary to prove that the cat hears things that we don't. Often when our ears register complete silence the cat will suddenly spring up from its nap in tense alertness, its flexible ears probing the air for the noise that awoke it.

Limits of Hearing. Early tests, however, didn't show that the cat heard particularly more or better than we did. Only since cat psychology has been taken into consideration have tests become adequate enough to produce results more in keeping with casual observation. It is now agreed that the cat's range of hearing is from 30 to 45,000 cycles per second, 25,000 cycles higher than the high notes of a violin which are about the limit of human hearing.

From 62.5 to 2000 cycles per second, human hearing compares favorably with the cat's, but over 2000 cycles the cat far excels us even though our best hearing range is between 2000 and 4000 and the cat's around 8000. Past 8000 cycles its hearing continues to be good until 40,000 cycles are reached. There it begins to taper off. The absolute limit of audibility, which few cats attain, is somewhere close to 60,000 cycles.

Low frequency comparisons are difficult to make because these frequencies are felt as well as heard. The indication that we exceed the cat somewhat in lower ranges may be due to our inability to devise adequate tests for such measurements. Comparison of intensity of sound with sound wave frequency in the cat (see section of Chapter 8 on ears) gives further evidence of its acute hearing abilities in contrast to ours.

Not much is written about hearing in cats, possibly because it is not dissimilar to but merely better than that of other animals. It surpasses that of the dog not only in range but in localization; cats can accurately and effortlessly ascertain the direction and depth of a noise above or immediately behind them. They can easily differentiate closely similar sounds even when these are 60 feet distant and only 18 inches apart. The limit of their loudness discrimination is under 4 decibels, and they can distinguish half tones to which many animals are deaf.

External Ear. Built to augment the mechanics of hearing as much as possible, the cat's external ears are large, erect and pointed, roughly half cones in shape with the openings directed forward and out. They are well equipped with muscles which can move them forward, backward and down to facilitate picking up sounds. This, combined with the extreme flexibility of the neck which can rotate the head almost 180° and move it up, down, and sideways, explains in part why the cat experiences no difficulty in tracing sounds to their source.

The fur on the outside of the ears is short and sparse. The inside ear is naked except for numerous long hairs which protect the inner ear by straining out foreign bodies that come in contact with them. There may or may not be tufts of fur on the ears' tips, similar to but not as pronounced as those of the bobcat or lynx.

A variety of ridges on the inner and lower ear walls helps to gather and concentrate sound waves. The small purse-like flap of skin on the posterior and lower edge is also credited with increasing sensitivity to sound, but whether this flap actually has a function is questionable.

Size of the outer ear varies not only in breeds but in individuals; but the shape is always similar. A race of cats with duplicated ears combined with reduced eye diameter is being perpetuated in genetics laboratories, but there never existed a race of cats with hanging ears. This is another of those myths which cats have an affinity for inspiring.

In 1896 a seaman brought a cat with hanging ears back from China. He said that it was one of a breed raised there for eating purposes. Scientists agreed that the stock must be very old; drooping ears are never found in the wild state, but only in animals that have been domesticated a long time.

Anxious to uncover the history behind these cats, zoologists attempted to locate more specimens and discovered that they could find no trace of them. Nevertheless, when breeds of cats were listed in literature, Chinese cats with hanging ears were always mentioned. People wanted to believe in them. A prize was offered for anyone rediscovering the breed.

In 1938 a second cat with hanging ears was finally located and the characteristic was proved to be a very rare mutation apparently restricted to white long-haired cats. Science had unmasked another exciting legend.

The ordinary-shaped ear is far more expressive than a hanging ear could ever be, and it indicates many of the cat's moods. Laid back close to the head and accompanied by a fierce facial expression like that of the wild cat, it signals attack. The same position is also assumed in order to protect the inner ear from intense sounds or to avoid contact with an object. A slight folding back takes place when the cat is anticipating something unpleasant—a swat from another cat or human or something as innocuous as a scolding. The ears are plastered especially close to the head when a fight is in progress, but despite this safeguard most tomcats' ears eventually show signs of battle.

Pricked forward, ears signal attentiveness and joy. Directed downward to the point where they look like outstretched wings they signal a wary suspiciousness. These are generalizations; each individual cat has its own ear signals and only by living with it can you learn their meanings.

Middle and Inner Ear. A description of these two parts of the cat's ear would serve no purpose, approximating as they do the human ear both in structure and function. The cat's labyrinth or inner ear, including both the apparatus of equilibrium and the organ of hearing, receives the most attention from physiologists. It differs from other sense organs in that its sensory cells send out a continuous stream of impulses to the nervous system whether they are receiving stimuli from the outside or not.

In their studies on equilibrium physiologists remove or plug the cat's individual semicircular canals and after each operation test and retest the cat for performance. From such experiments a partial explanation has been obtained for the cat's ability to fall and land feet first, which accomplishment is discussed in the next section. No information has been obtained as to how the cat's canals differ from those of man and dog to keep it practically immune to seasickness or carsickness, an ailment that torments a good percentage of people and canines.

Chosen at random, a few further findings on the functioning of the cat's ears are:

1 Neural pathways connect one ear with the other so that a stimulus in one is shared with the other.

2 There is a high safety factor in the cat's auditory system. Complete destruction of the cochlea in one ear results in a hearing loss of from only 3 to 5 decibels.

3 Body movement and vocalization as well as sound produce activity in the middle ear muscles.

4 With all 6 semicircular canals nonfunctional cats lack all sensitivity to angular acceleration but retain normal response to linear acceleration. They are unable to retain an upright position when the horizontal surface on which they are walking is rapidly tilted 45°.

5 The vertical semicircular canals initiate corrections for fast, and the otoliths for slow angular displacements about horizontal axes.

6 Both horizontal semicircular canals contribute equally to the reception of angular acceleration in both directions.

7 Pathological changes in the cochlea are the cause of deafness in blue-eyed white cats. This in no way affects the organs of equilibrium. Extreme sensitivity to vibrations in these cats compensates for their lack of hearing.

SORTING SOUNDS. Juno and Alpheus, two of my cats, were with me in an upstairs room, sound asleep. Simultaneously both lifted their heads, leaped to their feet and vanished. Up the carpeted stairs finally appeared the tyrant of the household, a stray tom who walked through the cat door not long ago and decided that he liked what he found well enough to stay. Not only were his footsteps heard by Juno and Alpheus *before* he started climbing the stairs, but they were recognized. Neither cat would have deigned to move if his ears had registered the footsteps of any other cat than Omega.

Cats not only recognize footsteps—they interpret the mood behind them. My cats' responses to my approach can tell me my mood before I'm aware of it myself. If my walk indicates irritability I see no cats where I know they were moments before. If it tells them I'm feeling good they approach for a tickle or a little panhandling. When I'm normal I'm ignored.

In the 1940s C. N. Winslow and other workers carried out a sound sorting experiment with four cats. They first conditioned them to the chord C-major. Next they tested their response to the chord's components, C, G, and E, alone and paired. The results indicated that conditioning to the part or parts of the chord had not taken place along with the chord conditioning.

When other chords were presented to the cats it was found that no general transposition of the conditioned response to the C-major chord had occurred. Some transposition to the B-major chord did occur, presumably because it contains two of the same notes as the C-major chord. Summing up, the two similar notes of these two chords, E and G, did not elicit as much response in the C-major conditioned cats as the B-major chord itself.

From these results it was concluded that in the cat, conditioning to patterns (in this case the chords) is as rapid as conditioning to single, discrete stimuli. This is to be expected. The cat is confronted with patterns of sound in its natural environment more often than with single tones and its hearing is geared to its environment as magnificently as every other part of its body.

The family car, the refrigerator door, kitchen utensils, doors, all the familiar everyday sounds the household cat learns almost immediately. But it is its recognition of human words that is truly amazing. With all the strays that continue to appear where I live, I have an average of 10 to 12 cats at a time. Each learns not only his name but that of all the other cats, usually within a week, besides picking up human-to-cat conversation. At present there are 6 black cats living with me and 3 are very similar in body conformation. Unless I see their faces I often mistake one for another, and their disgust and amazement at my stupidity is amusing. Considering the number of mistakes I make, I don't know how they managed to learn their own names in the first place.

Other laboratory experiments on the cat's ability to discriminate between tones of different frequencies have come up with an interesting find: the ability improves when the cat passes from a wakeful state to catnapping. Observation certainly bears this out. Seldom is a cat "caught napping" and, on the other hand, seldom is it roused by insignificant noise. The following letters written to the periodical *Science* by, I would say, cat-owning "catty" critics discuss this aspect in a humorous vein.

The Imperturbable Feline. The "report on learning-set formation in various mammals reminds me of a paper prepared for *Science* . . . on learning in cats. The paper was never submitted because . . . it might have been misconstrued as trivial.

"Three cats were observed for twelve months in three widely separate areas of Los Angeles. The cats were two American short-hairs and a cross-eyed pedigreed Siamese. Specifically, ear-twitching was observed while the cats were dozing. Sounds which did or, more important, did *not* cause ear-twitching were noted. None of the three cats ever twitched to the following sounds: (i) wife shouting in kitchen, (ii) champagne bottle popping, (iii) people falling into swimming pool, and (iv) approaching police sirens.

"I have been unable to persuade my co-authors that we were walking in the steps of Pavlov." H. P.

More on the Stoical Cat. "H. P.'s cats were not imperturbable . . . but merely unperturbed. Domesticated cats do not twitch at familiar sounds, from which I infer that his subjects lived in very interesting households.

"But let him invent a new sound, and he will spot a twitch. Or, of course, an old sound that means danger or food." A. B.

Music. "She also had a taste for music. Nestling upon a pile of scores, she would listen attentively and with every mark of satisfaction to the singers who came to perform at the critic's piano. But high notes made her nervous, and she never failed to close the singer's mouth with her paw if the lady sang the high A. We used to try the experiment for the fun of the thing, and it never failed once. It was quite impossible to fool my dilettante cat on that note." Theophile Gautier

We are always told that cats prefer low notes to the high which appear to upset them. Why should notes in the middle of their hearing range, that is, around 20,000 cycles per second, disturb them? In 1932 Bachrach and Morin reported that certain sharp sounds, in particular *mi* of the fourth octave, acted as a powerful genital excitant for cats. The same sound, they said, served to fix a conditioned reflex of defecation in the sub-adult cat which after puberty was superseded by the sexual one. Reasons just as obscure may produce the response that people describe as extreme agitation in their cats when subjected to high notes, and further investigation on the subject might turn up interesting facts.

Judging from the anecdotes about cats and music, cats have as varied musical tastes as their owners, and like people, no cat seems to be an all-around music lover. Their preference may be classical or modern, or a particular period or type, like Baroque or Rock-and-Roll. Some are supposed to enjoy only one particular composer or instrument and to be seldom mistaken in their judgment. If true, this can be interpreted as an extreme example of sound-sorting.

The cat that sets itself up as a music critic like Gautier's pet is frequent, and so is the cat that dislikes music in any form. C. C. Pierquin de Gembloux wrote of one cat's abhorrence of it.

"I have frequently had an opportunity of observing a cat's antipathy to music carried to the extent of convulsions. Every time that a certain series of sounds was produced on the piano or by the voice, the animal in question became convulsed, while another cat, its companion, would sit on the instrument listening to the choicest airs of French opera, and enjoying the vibrations of the sonorous chords."

This is easy to believe. Why should the cat think our idea of music is any better than the noise of a vacuum cleaner which few cats can tolerate for long? After all, very few of us can tolerate *their* music for even a few seconds.

HEARING IN CATS

FRANCIS GALTON

Of all creatures, I have found none superior to cats in the power of hearing shrill sounds; it is perfectly remarkable what a faculty they have in this way. Cats, of course, have to deal in the dark with mice, and to find them out by their squealing. Many people cannot hear the shrill squeal of a mouse. Some time ago, singing mice were exhibited in London, and of the people who went to hear them, some could hear nothing, whilst others could hear a little, and others again could hear much. Cats are differentiated by natural selection until they have a power of hearing all the high notes made by mice and other little creatures that they have to catch. A cat that is at a very considerable distance, can be made to turn its ear round by sounding a note that is too shrill to be audible by almost any human ear.

Inquiries Into Human Faculty and its Development 1883

ON EAR CROPPING

"If the ears of cats be cropped or cut off it makes them keep home the better, because the water (which they cannot abide) will drop into their ears, being open."

THOMAS LUPTON c 1583. *A Thousand Notable Things*

X
On Falling Feet First

"and unneth is hurt when he is thrown down off an high place"
BARTHOLOMEUS ANGLICUS 13th Century

WE all know that the cat is usually unhurt when it falls from a height because it lands on its feet. The Persians have a saying that Ali passed his hand along its back one day to make this possible. *How* it is accomplished is another matter. The physiology and mechanics of this seemingly simple act are intricate and involved and not yet completely understood. It is a superb example of pure reflex; if the cat had to think about what to do next as it dropped through space it would never survive its first fall.

Cats need this safeguard, and they seem to rely on it far too much. Agile and quick-witted though they are, they fall from windows, trees and other heights with predictable regularity and for no apparent reason other than carelessness or excitement. While in precarious positions they overestimate their reaching capacity in their eagerness to grasp something, and they insist on rolling in happy abandon on the brink of small and great drops. They do any number of thoughtless things such as these which are entirely inconsistent with their cautious nature and which frequently result in a fall. Scratches on cat owners' thighs and furniture, the result of last minute attempts on the cat's part to save itself, are ample evidence of their folly. Yet, on landing from a fall a cat will often go back to its original location to continue from where it was interrupted unless, realizing that its mistake has been observed, it stalks off with as much dignity as it can summon. Woe to those who laugh at it under these circumstances.

According to Moncrif in his *Les Chats,* a description of the cat's righting reflex was published in the *Mémoires de l'Académie des Sciences* in 1700. Almost 200 years later, in 1894, the academy published another article on the subject, this time an analysis of photographs that show a cat performing the act. Numerous articles, both popular and scientific, have subsequently been published in English.

Through physiological experimentation it is now known that the labyrinth or inner ear plays the greater part in a cat's feet-first landing. It is already functional in the 54 day old cat foetus, that is in a foetus 6 days before birth. The *body* righting reflex is present almost a week earlier, on the 49th day. This part of the reflex is initiated by the proprioceptive impulses of the muscles and the exteroceptive impulses of the skin.

(*Proprioceptive* means receiving stimulations within the tissues of the body. Besides being present in the labyrinth, proprioceptors are located throughout the body, principally in muscles and tendons. They are sensory nerve terminals which give an animal information concerning the movement and position of its body. *Exteroceptors* are those nerve terminals which give information received from the external environment).

The righting reflex is therefore triggered by such signals as: (1) the cat's feet losing contact with something solid, that is losing their normal tactile sensation, (2) the eyes registering an abnormal body position through external stimuli, (3) the muscles etc. registering the same through internal stimuli, and (4) the ear registering an upset equilibrium.

Skin, eyes, ears, muscle proprioceptors—at least four senses act together to produce a reflex act far too rapid for the eye to register. Blindness or inner ear injury do not prevent a perfect landing unless both handicaps exist together. The cat will then land "any which way" as we do when we fall. Even figuratively speaking, very few humans manage to land feet first; the proverb "No matter what happens he always lands on his feet" indicates the relative rarity of such an occurrence.

Other vertebrates like squirrels, monkeys, frogs, dogs and rabbits do share the righting reflex with cats but not to as great a degree. Cats are masters in the art. As Dr. McDonald points out in his excellent article that follows, "the speed and agility with which a cat turns over is truly wonderful."

HOW DOES A CAT FALL ON ITS FEET?

DONALD MCDONALD

The proverbial ability of a cat to fall on its feet even when dropped upside-down tends to obscure the fact that turning over, when falling freely, is a difficult thing to do. The problems it raises are many and their analysis has fascinated both physicists and physiologists.

The first problem, at least in historical and intellectual priority, is how a body in free fall can rotate itself—that is, acquire angular momentum without pushing against anything. Clark Maxwell is said to have interested himself in this, but the first detailed discussion I have come across was in the French Académie des Sciences in 1894, when Marey, a physiologist, showed a sequence of photographs of a cat turning. These were taken at the rate of 60/sec and Marey's invention really preceded the more orthodox ciné-camera. Many physicists, in spite of the film, denied that it could happen and implied that the animal twisted at the time of take-off, rather as a fancy high-diver does. One physicist, Guyou, however, pointed out that if the animal arranged its body and limbs in such a way that the moments of inertia of the front and rear parts were different, then one could be rotated on the other without creating any angular momentum for the whole body.

Only one or two other people have done any serious research on the topic, and I have used a high-speed camera working at 1,500 frames/sec to study the problem anew. Such high speeds of filming are necessary because a cat when dropped upside-down turns over very rapidly—in fact, a cat will turn over within its own standing height. In my experience the time is about ⅛ sec, which at ordinary "slow-motion" camera speeds covers only 8 frames of the film or ½ sec when projected. On my film it takes rather more than 10 sec of projection time, and furthermore each frame is free from blur due to movement, so that analysis is much easier.

The suggestion put forward by M. Guyou in Paris, about twisting one part of the body on the others, is correct, but we can now add more details. Not all cats solve it in the same way, but the commonest method for lithe and agile ones (although it is not easy to describe the movement in words) is roughly as follows:

First, the body is bent to a right angle at the waist and the fore-limbs are held close to the head while the hind-limbs are held out from the trunk. The forepart of the body is then rotated through 180° about its axis. This rotation is offset by a slight counter-rotation of the hind-part of the body; this only amounts to about 5° and fits in with the calculated moments of inertia. The head and fore-part of the body are now facing the ground. The front legs are then moved vertical to the ground and the hind-limbs are put straight out in line with the body. Thus by a reversal of the process the rear end is rotated in line with the front. This movement is rather complicated by the fact that the cat also flexes at the waist at the same time. Therefore it ends the turn with the back arched and all four limbs extended ready to land. The ingenious way in which it does this complete half-turn without involving any change in its total angular momentum is worthy of a well-trained physicist. I ensured that there could be no question of its acquiring any twist from the take-off by starting, in some cases, close to the ground and throwing the cat up some 2–3 feet—the films show clearly that in this case the cat does not begin to turn until it is almost at the top of its "flight" with no solid structure anywhere near it.

The purely physical problems do not end with the completion of the turn, although the rotation is what has worried most people. For if it is difficult to explain the creation of spin—how does the cat stop spinning at the right place? In the case of the front part of the body any residual momentum is "mopped up" by the reaction to the rotation of the hind-part. The rear end is, however, rather heavier and in fact often tends to overswing, sometimes by as much as 30°. Provided that the cat has room to manœuvre any overshoot is always corrected before it lands. I confess that this has puzzled me. In many cases rapid counter-rotation of the tail seemed to be the technique, and this must depend mainly on its air-resistance—in fact, I have proposed that it acts as an "air brake". However, testing out a tailless cat (and I found them hard to come by) showed that it could make a perfectly normal and trim landing. Therefore fine adjustments of posture must be able to be made by contracting various body muscles rather as a trained acrobat does.

I might add that experience undoubtedly improves the skill of a cat. The basic pattern, however, seems to be present from about the age that a kitten can run about nimbly—that is, from 3–4 weeks of age. The use of body-muscles is also seen in more thickset cats, which do not do a full half-turn at the waist but seem to use a sideways bend of the body to bring the hind-limbs around before the front end is fully around. On the other hand, I have records of a fat little guinea-pig twisting through a full 180° at the waist—also rabbits. (Others have reported the same righting behaviour in dogs and apes.)

I have often been asked the question whether human beings can right themselves in this way when falling, but I have no direct evidence owing to lack of volunteers! I am very doubtful if they can. The instinctive posture for a man is the vertical, and the inertial forces required to rotate the body at right angles to its longitudinal axis are very much greater than those of the cat, or any four-footed animal. Certainly a cat cannot do it. One often learns from mistakes, and in some of the experiments when they were tossed in the air they became up-ended through a bad throw. No cat managed to correct itself; it fell with the body vertical in spite of vigorous movements. Once one pair of feet touched the ground it corrected its position immediately, but never while still in the air. Circus acrobats and divers certainly do remarkable gyrations while in mid-air, but most of these are almost certainly due to residual momentum from their take-off.

A further physical problem is raised by the fact that a cat can fall from far greater heights than a man. My own cat has certainly fallen from a window about 12 ft. up without being disturbed in the slightest, but I admit that I have lacked the courage to try the experiment from great heights. The smaller the animal, the greater is the ratio of surface area to body-weight. This is because the weight increases as the cube of the linear dimensions, but the surface area only increases as the square. Now when falling the acceleration due to gravity is opposed by the drag of the air, which is proportional to the velocity and the surface area. Thus a body falling in air reaches a limiting velocity where the resistance balances out the acceleration due to gravity. This terminal velocity for a man is about 120 m.p.h. (e.g., for a parachutist delaying the opening of his 'chute); the corresponding velocity for a cat is probably

40 m.p.h. at the most. Some crude experiments, with a model representing a cat, suggest that it reaches this velocity in about 60 ft. Therefore if it can survive a fall of this height it should be able to manage any height. I have heard of cats falling safely from trees of this height, but if this is so it shows remarkable resilience in landing. This speed represents that of a man falling nearly 50 ft., which would usually be fatal.

The cat has, of course, much less momentum because of its smaller weight; but it has smaller muscles to absorb the shock, although they may be more efficient. We lack sufficient precise knowledge of what the speed of landing is to put this comparison on a quantitative basis, but it looks as if the only human parallel to a normal cat is a highly-trained circus performer. Cats fairly certainly would not survive falls from heights much lower than 60 ft. if they were unable to see; when blindfolded they land clumsily even from a height of 3 ft.

The physiologist is not only concerned with the physical problems of the performance but also the actual mechanisms by which they are carried out. The main problems here are, firstly, what are the sensory organs that the animal uses to register that he is the wrong way up and that he is falling? Secondly, what are the nervous pathways through which the reflex actions are set off? The second of these must be dismissed briefly with a confession of ignorance. There is an explanation current in the textbooks, but the work described above has shown that it must be wrong in detail—without presenting an alternative.

With regard to sense-organs, there is no doubt that in the higher animals the "horizon" registered by the eyes is very important in orientating an animal in space. In addition, there is a complicated organ in the inner ear called the vestibular organ. Actually it consists of two parts; one is a set of three semi-circular canals set in three planes, and the other is called the otolith organ. Both these are concerned with sensing the position and movements of the head. The semicircular canals sense rotational movements, and it is overstimulation of these that gives rise to the feeling that the room is going around after spinning vigorously. The otolith is thought to be a static receptor which tells us the direction in which gravity is working. It consists essentially of a small weight attached to a hair which is bent in whatever direction the force of gravity acts. It is this organ which almost certainly sets off the turning movements of a cat when its eyes are covered. The turn is, however, slower in starting than when the eyes are open, so that it looks as if the eyes are normally predominant in signalling the need to get right way up. Information is also provided, of course, by the pressure on the back, etc., but this seems to be slower still as the following experiment shows.

I was lucky enough to be lent a cat by Professor J. B. S. Haldane; he had had it as a pet since it was born and it was then a mature old lady of fifteen, but it was congenitally deaf. In this condition the whole inner ear is missing so that there is no vestibular organ, in addition to an absence of the cochlea (for hearing). Yet when dropped upside-down this cat turned over in a perfectly normal way. After blindfolding, however, it made no attempt to turn over and fell on its back in the position in which it had been dropped. Lacking both the use of its eyes and its vestibular organ, it failed to perceive that its position was abnormal. Even when it had landed (on a rubber mattress) it turned over only very slowly—the movement had hardly begun when the film ran out ½ sec. later. Pressure sensations on the back are not, therefore, very potent stimuli (and these were also present when it was being held in the air) for setting off righting reactions; nor does the air current on the fur seem to have any effect, as some people have postulated.

In order to test whether one could alter the turning pattern by "confusing" the otolith organ, some other experiments were done. A simple apparatus was made so that a blindfolded cat could be rotated slowly before being dropped. The idea was that there would then be no steady discharge from the otolith while it was being held and so we could see whether it did, in fact, operate during the fall. As the cats appeared to turn over naturally it seemed, at first, that it was operating during the free fall—a somewhat disconcerting finding. Then one cat slipped in the apparatus and fell out feet first—and promptly turned over and fell on its back! The reason for the turn was clearly that the rotation was stimulating the semi-circular canals and causing the cat to turn. At this point I left the pursuit of the research. To have reached a stage where one dropped a cat the right way up and it turned over and fell on its back really seemed to be the logical end!

As can be seen, the turning cat raises a lot of interesting problems, even though their solution may not be of much practical importance—except to other cats. Many details remain to be filled in, especially on the physiological side, but in a research which really needs intact animals the plotting of the nervous pathways and muscles involved will inevitably be very difficult. The general solution to the physical problems, I think, has been attained. The paradox of the apparent creation of angular momentum can be explained, although the precision with which the animal stops turning needs more light on it. The conclusion that the eyes are the most important organs for sensing "upside-downness" is borne out by a lot of evidence in human beings. The otolith organ is an important standby when the eyes cannot function, but it also operates according to the laws of physics and only acts as a gravity sensing organ when the animal is stationary. And the fact remains that the speed and agility with which a cat turns over is truly wonderful.

New Scientist 30 June 1960 7:1647–1649

WHY THE CAT ALWAYS LANDS ON ITS FEET. A LEGEND.

Once upon a time there was a good wizard who did all that he could to help every living thing. Travelling through a great forest one day he stopped at noon to lie down and rest at the foot of a large tree, and soon he fell asleep.

As he slept a large snake happened by and seeing him it began to hiss angrily. "Ah-ha, he's at my mercy now," it said. "If it hadn't been for his interference I'd have had a fine meal of cat last night. Now I'll have my revenge." With that it began to crawl toward the wizard who slept on unmindful of his danger.

It so happened that the cat whose life he had saved was in a tree nearby. She saw what the snake intended to do and knew she must attempt to save the wizard. But how? The snake was very big and bold and she was very small and afraid.

Nevertheless, unmindful of her own danger she leaped upon the snake's back just as it was about to strike the wizard. Digging her claws deep into its flesh she sank her teeth into its neck. Her struggle was long and hard but she was quick and agile. Using tooth and claw to good purpose she finally killed her enemy. Then, completely exhausted, she curled up next to the wizard and slept.

There he found her when he awoke and seeing also the dead snake he knew that he owed his life to the courageous little animal. "Brave little cat," he said, "I must give you something in return for your devotion. You already have eyes that see much and ears that catch the faintest sound. You have feet that carry you swiftly and softly, but this you do not have that I can give. For your sake all cats forthwith shall be able to leap where they will and always land upon their feet. And men shall welcome you as a friend and allow you to live out your days in their homes in peace and contentment."

And as the wizard said, so it happened.

XI
Eyes

A cat as she beholds the light, draws the ball of her eye small and long, being covered over with a green skin, and dilates it at pleasure.
HENRY PEACHAM, early 17th Century

MOST mammals rely on their sense of smell regardless of the excellence of their eyesight. Cats and the primates are the only sight-guided mammals. Probably for this reason cats respond far more often than dogs to motion pictures and television, often becoming highly excited when animals appear on the screen. And, contrary to the findings of experimenters, I know cats who respond to pictures of other cats, especially life-size pictures. I have one framed cat head in particular that excites many cats. They will sit gazing up at it for a long time, then reach up and tentatively pat at it. All cats react to three-dimensional dummy animals and stuffed toys.

GENERAL. A cat's eyes are very large in relation to the size of the skull; they are wide-set and directed forward, the frontal position giving an overlapping of visual fields as in other beasts of prey. Such a placement is of no handicap to the animal since its head is capable of considerable rotation, as was mentioned in the section on the ear, which allows extensive scanning without a change of position. Also, the maximum angle of the visual field for one eye is large, close to 205°, greater than that of the dog.

Stimuli are shared by both eyes in the same way that they are shared by both ears. Visual discriminations learned by one eye are immediately transferred to the other.

Unless a cat is excited or alarmed, which causes the pupils of its eyes to dilate and contract regardless of light conditions, it makes an efficient light meter. Extremely sensitive to light intensity, its eyes respond almost instantaneously to changes in brightness. The size of the pupil ranges from a full round in the dark (which obliterates most of the iris) to an almost invisible vertical slit in bright light. It was due to this great fluctuation of pupil size in response to light intensity that cats were thought to symbolize the sun and be sacred to it. And it is also one of the reasons why a cat was considered an emblem of the moon. According to the ancients its pupils were full at the full moon and contracted as the moon diminished in size. Plutarch spoke of this strange belief, and Marc de Vulson, who died in 1658, wrote:

"As the lion is a solitary animal, so the cat is a moon-struck beast. Its eyes, clear-visioned and glittering in the darkest nights, wax and wane in imitation of the moon; for as the moon, according as she shares in the light of the sun, changes her face every day, so is the cat moved by a similar affection toward the moon, its pupil waxing and waning at the times when that heavenly body is crescent or in its decline. Several naturalists assert that when the moon is at its full, cats have more strength and cunning to make war upon mice than when it is weak."

Anyone watching cats on nights when the moon is full or near full will have to agree that they are moon-struck. It is almost impossible to keep them indoors on these nights, they delight so in the light of the moon. Mine like to climb onto the house roof where they gambol and prance and cavort, sometimes alone and sometimes in unison. On other nights their surrender to their emotions is never so complete.

Besides changing with the moon's phases the size of the pupil in the cat was also thought to conform with the ebb and flow of the tide. The widely open pupil was considered to indicate high water, the closed low. In addition there is that well-known belief that the time of day can be reckoned by pupil size.

Feline eyes are very well developed but this alone doesn't give the cat its excellent eyesight. Buddenbrock in *The Senses* points out that the codfish and the cat, animals of approximately the same size, have eyes similar both in size and structure; yet the codfish is unable to see and distinguish objects as well as the cat. The development of its brain has not kept pace with that of its eyes as has the cat's.

The cat's ability to concentrate its vision for long periods of time without fatigue makes many people uncomfortable in its presence: the prolonged scrutiny with which it may favor them makes them squirm. A need for such concentration is necessary because of the way cats hunt. I have seen mine, perched on their favorite hunting stump or tree, gaze fixedly down into the meadow grass for an hour or more, motionless except for their ears and tail tip. Suddenly, without warning, they pounce, and another mouse is added to their life list.

"He has cat's eyes" is an old expression still in use today. It usually refers to someone's ability to see in poor light, but it also means that a person has good eyesight and is alert and watchful.

Color and Brightness Discrimination. How and what the cat actually sees with its remarkable eyes is not yet known with certainty because of the complications encountered in testing vision. For instance, many people still think that the cat lives in a grey world—that it is completely color-blind—and until recently, experiments indicated that this was so. Scientists, however, were bothered by the results of the tests. Physiological and anatomical evidence indicated that the cat *could* distinguish color. Electro-physiological evidence in particular showed that the cat's visual system was sensitive to different wavelengths.

Testing for color discrimination in cats presents many problems. Brightness discrimination is paramount in the cat's visual world as would be expected in a nocturnal animal; all other elements such as size and form and color are of secondary importance. Color is significant only to diurnal animals. In testing for color discrimination it is difficult to have the test-colors of equal brightness. Consequently early tests indicating that cats could see colors were found to be invalid on the grounds that the discrimination was one of intensity rather than wavelength. More recently, the persistence of the cat's response to cues based on brightness differences was found to account for the failure of other experimenters to show that it can distinguish among wavelengths.

The past few years have produced many experiments overcoming this difficulty, but they have conflicting results. At present, the question is not so much whether a cat can see colors but how many it can distinguish and how well. One experiment demonstrated only red-green discrimination. Others have found cats able to distinguish between red and blue and red and yellow as well as red and green; and a more extensive test done in 1966 on paired comparisons of red, green, blue, yellow and grey, found that cats could distinguish all except yellow and green and yellow and red. From this it is easy to see that many more tests must be made before what cats actually see is known. Experimental results with ultraviolet agree that their sensitivity to it far exceeds ours.

Anecdotes about cats preferring one color to all others are indicative that they perceive color. One of the reasons that they were considered evil beasts linked with the devil was their supposed hatred of the color blue, the color of heaven and the Virgin's dress. A summary of individual findings, however, shows no one color preferred or disliked over all others by the majority.

An interesting report on color and taste preferences is that of a cat who enjoyed pink sweetpeas. From vases of flowers she would select only pink sweetpeas to nibble, never touching any other kind of flower, pink or not. In the garden where pink sweetpeas grew among those of other colors she again would choose to eat only the pink. If there were none of these available she would eat others but only those that were light-colored.

Summing up, the cat is no longer considered to be color-blind but its color perception is considered to be relatively poor. It is this that explains its poor performance in some tests attempting to measure other abilities like object learning. That its color sense can't be too effective is borne out by the small number of retinal cones it has compared to rods.

NIGHT SIGHT. Cones register color and rods register light intensity. Cats' eyes average about one cone for very 20–25 rods while humans average about one for every 4, the difference indicating a nocturnal versus a diurnal animal. Rods contain rhodopsin, or visual purple, a photosensitive purple chromoprotein that bleaches to yellow on exposure to light. The color change stimulates sensory nerve endings in the retina and in so doing gives an animal the sensation of light.

The abundance of rods in a cat's eyes therefore aids in giving the animal excellent night vision. Night vision does not mean that the cat is able to see in total darkness. A cat's ears and whiskers make this feat possible. It "sees" by locating objects through the sound and feel of reflected air waves, its whiskers guiding it through contact stimuli as well.

Infrared radiations do not account in any way for the cat's night sight. Experiments indicate that infrared rays produce no visual stimulus and are therefore equal to darkness for the cat. The structure of its eyes is such, however, that it can pick up the faintest rays of light and intensify them. This intensification, accomplished by the tapetum lucidum, helps to make the amount of light that a cat detects in absolute darkness, that is, its brightness discrimination, seven times better than ours. Long after our eyes register complete darkness the cat can distinguish light. In this it surpasses not only us but the dog, rat and monkey.

THE TAPETUM LUCIDUM. The tapetum lucidum acts like a mirror, the light that falls on it being reflected back to the retinal cells. In this way any light that is not absorbed by the cells during its initial passage into the eye can restimulate them as it passes over them a second time from the reflection. Not a mere accessory to the sense of sight, the tapetum is essential for visual function; its degeneration causes blindness.

Triangular in shape, it is located in the upper half of the eye. Retinal cells in the area contain no pigment and are backed by layers of large flat cells filled with crystals which are a complex of zinc with the sulphur-containing amino acid cysteine. Free riboflavin is said to produce the eyeshine that emanates from the tapetum. This fluorescence is usually green in color, ranging from a blue- to a yellow-green, but it can also be red as in the blue-eyed Siamese.

Early references to eyeshine in the cat generally refer to it as being red which is strange considering that the prevailing color in today's cats is green. In *Pericles* for example Shakespeare speaks of "the cat, with eyne of burning coal" crouching before the mouse's hole, and in *Grammer Gurton's Needle,* a mid-sixteenth century comedy, the plot revolves around Gyb the cat, also with red eyeshine. A serving man mistakes her eyes for sparks in a dead fire where she has retreated unknown to him. (But the sparks)

"were indeed nought else but Gyb our cat's two eyes.
'Puff!' quoth Hodge, thinking thereby to have fire without doubt:
With that Gyb shut her two eyes and so the fire was out,
And by and by them opened, even as they were before.

With that the sparks appeared even as they had done of yore
And even as Hodge blew the fire, as he did think,
Gyb as she felt the blast straightway began to wink,
Till Hodge fell to swearing, as came best to his turn,
The fire was sure bewitched and therefore would not burn."

Hodge remains skeptical when told that a cat's eyes have deceived him, that "they shine as like fire as ever man did see."

VISUAL DISCRIMINATION AND ACUITY. Like brightness discrimination, visual movement discrimination in the cat is highly developed: in large part its prey is located through movement. Discrimination of form is consequently secondary to that of movement, just as color is secondary to brightness. It remains a relatively undeveloped sense because it isn't vital to the cat's existence. Tests show, however, that once a cat begins to discriminate among shapes, its sense of form improves from trial to trial and from problem to problem. The cat becomes very adept at selecting an odd object from a group of identical objects, even when the odd object and the identical ones are changed from trial to trial. In some tests, for example the discrimination of oblique rectangles, it even excels other animals including young children. A sense of size constancy and depth discrimination also exists but these, too, are brought out only through training.

Visual acuity was long thought to be poor in the cat. Only those animals that have a well-developed fovea in the eye are able to see sharp images. The cat has a fovea, but it isn't as clearly differentiated as that of primates. Nevertheless, through photographs taken of retinal images in the cat's eye it has been discovered that cats see their environment sharply and clearly.

C. H. Lane in *Rabbits, Cats and Cavies* (1903) tells of a cat who was fitted for glasses because of poor vision. "*The Deoptic and Ophthalmometric Review*, certainly not a likely source for fairy tales or throwing the hatchet, is responsible for the following, and as the periodical referred to is the organ of the British Optical Association, it may be taken as thoroughly reliable:—

" 'A well-known lady who possesses a pet Maltese cat recently found her cat's eyesight begin to fail, so she took him to an oculist.

" 'By means of a modelled representation of a mouse, the oculist carefully ascertained what was the matter, and was able to fit his interesting patient with suitable glasses, the lenses were set in gold frames specially made for the purpose, and the result was so satisfactory that the eyesight of the cat became as good, or better, than before.' "

If this account is actual fact, the patient was an unusual cat since feline vision is seldom poor and changes little with age. Eye accommodation in old cats functions almost as effectively as it does in young ones. The average man of 60 years has an eye accommodation less than one-tenth that of his youth; the very old cat's accommodation remains 75% efficient at the very least. Mellen claimed that the cat's pupil changes with age, beginning as a pointed oval in the kitten and becoming gradually rounded with age. She also stated that sickness pales the color of the iris. I have found no references in other literature to verify either of these facts.

NICTITATING MEMBRANE. To protect its eyes, the most essential sense organs with which it is equipped, the cat has a third eyelid called the nictitating membrane or haws. Not opaque like the standard eyelids, it allows the cat some vision when it is drawn over the eye. This the cat does in such cases as a fight or a prowl through dense undergrowth in order to keep the eye safe from abrasions and scratches. The membrane also cleanses the eye when closed over it.

In certain disorders and in worm infestations the membrane is kept continually drawn up over the lower portion of the eye. During the grasshopper season a cat who indulges too much in this feline delicacy will also have its eyes partially covered by the membrane. The reason for this phenomenon remains unexplained as does the fact that some cats, well or not, exhibit the haws at all times.

VISUAL EXPRESSION. A cat's face is as expressive of its feelings as is ours, and its eyes are the most expressive part of its face. Love, hate, fear, every emotion can be read in them; as with man they are a mirror of its soul.

> Stately, kindly, lordly friend,
> Condescend
> Here to sit by me, and turn
> Glorious eyes that smile and burn,
> Golden eyes, love's lustrous meed,
> On the golden page I read.
>
> ALGERNON CHARLES SWINBURNE

XII
Nose

"In the new moon gather the herb nepe, and dry it in the heat of the sun, when it is temperately hot: gather vervain in the hour of Mercury, and only expose it to the air while the Sun is under the earth. Hang these together in a net, in a convenient place, and when a cat has scented it, her cry will soon call those about her that are within hearing; and they will rant and run about, leaping and capering to get at the net, which must be hung or placed so that they cannot easily accomplish it, for they will nearly tear it to pieces. Near Bristol there is a field that goes by the appellation of the *'Field of Cats'*, from a large number of these animals being drawn together there by this contrivance."

THE CONJURORS' MAGAZINE 1791

FROM the quantity of literature about the cat's delight in inhaling scents you can almost believe that it uses its nose for no purpose other than pleasure. Consequently the odors that excite cats the most seems to be the logical beginning for a discussion of its nose.

SNIFFING FOR PLEASURE. 1. Catnip (*Nepeta cataria*). By analyzing the catnip plant chemists have isolated the substance that produces the so-called catnip response in cats and have called it nepetalactone. Nepetalactone is present in the volatile oil of catnip and concentrations as low as one part in 10^9–10^{11} are sufficient to excite cats. So far no attempt has been made to explain *how* it attracts them or affects their nervous system to produce the results that it does.

The catnip response is inherited as a dominant autosomal gene, but all young kittens tend to avoid catnip as if it were something disagreeable. Under six to eight weeks of age even those kittens who have inherited a taste for nipping do not react positively to the plant, and complete response is not fully developed until they are about three months old. In potential addicts the original avoidance gives place to curiosity while in cats who have not inherited a love for the plant the avoidance becomes indifference. Many Siamese show indifference or merely a mild attraction toward the plant while ordinary cats who aren't nippers appear to be rare. Studies on the inheritance of catnipping give no estimate of, nor breakdown in, the percentage of addicts versus the nonaddicts.

For simplicity, catnip response has been broken down into (1) sniffing, (2) licking and chewing with head shaking, (3) chin and cheek rubbing, and (4) head-over roll and body rubbing. Claw sharpening and washing are considered to be displacement activities as they are in other behavior patterns.

A cat's response to catnip is independent of sex or the presence of gonads. It does not result in an increase in killing, fighting or sexual mounting when experimental cats have been paired with live rats or a stuffed cat-size object, but the reacting cat does show an increased interest in the stuffed object with a decreased interest in rats. The type of interest in the object is comparable to that shown males by oestrous females. The rolling response is said to resemble closely that of oestrous females, and a possible connection between the two responses has been suggested.

My observations on cats' reactions to catnip add to those of the experimentalists. Dried catnip and catnip mice do not produce similar reactions. Response to the mice is generally restricted to the sort of mad play seen most often in kittens, with a minimum of the actions enumerated above. Also, the live plants don't appear to elicit as great a frenzy as the dried, and when they are available cats more or less scorn the dried. Throughout the growing season they avidly eat all parts of the plant.

During the winter months they respond to the dried leaves in similar fashion to the laboratory cats, and certain individuals eat them consistently. Purring while nipping is frequent, and there may be growling. Males, entire or castrated, act with more abandon and intensity than females. They become quarrelsome and start fights with other cats of either sex, and the grand finale to their orgy is urinating on what remains of the catnip. I have never observed a female do this. Those cats who eat the leaves do not roll, rub and carry on to the extent that the noneaters do.

Other members of the mint family stimulate cats the same way that catnip does. One of these is cat thyme, *Teucrium marum,* another the East Indian patchouli. The latter is prized by humans also, being used in a perfume or dried and made into sachets.

2. Valerian (*Valeriana officinalis*). "The root of the herbe *Valerian* (commonly called *Phu*) is very like to the eye of a cat, and whersouer it groweth, if cats come thervnto, they instantly dig it vp, for the loue thereof, as I myselfe haue seene, in mine owne Garden, and not once onely, but often, euen then when as I had caused it to bee hedged or compassed round about with thornes, for it smelleth marueilous like to a cat." Edward Topsell

Cats respond to valerian as vigorously as they do to catnip. It would be an interesting experiment to see which of the two plants would be preferred if they were presented together. Strange as it may sound, an analysis of valerian has indicated that it has tranquilizing qualities. Preparations of it used on cats with hypertensive disease produce the same results as standard regularly-used tranquilizers. It is difficult to reconcile the fact that something which excites an animal outwardly has the opposite effect systemically. Catnip is said to have a similar tranquilizing effect.

3. Silver Vine (*Actinidia polygama* and *A. kolomikta*) In 1708 Kaibara mentioned in volume 16 of *Yamato Hanza* how fond the cat was of matatabi (*A. polygama*). He said that the cat ate it and rubbed its body with the roots, stems and leaves "well knowing it is its superlative panacea."

The story is told that in China when cats got so numerous as to become a nuisance a smudge was made of these plants. Attracted from great distances the cats would congregate in large numbers around the smoking plants, and as the fumes stupefied them they were easily disposed of.

The passion that cats have silver vine, in particular the *polygama* species, is so great that gardeners must protect the entire plant from their depredation. They won't leave it alone until they have completely uprooted it. In 1906 David Faichild, the botanist-explorer, gave a good description of their actions.

"It has taken half a lifetime for Americans to discover the delicious qualities of the pomelo, but it has taken the cats of Boston only six months to appreciate a new cat delicacy.

"Professor Sargent, of the Arnold Arboretum, near Boston, imported from Central China a new vine, only a few plants of which were securable. As the species (*Actinidia polygama*) was a rare one and had never before been introduced into this country, the plants were put in the greenhouse and carefully watched, but before they had made much growth the propagator, Mr. Dawson, observed that some animal was eating their tender shoots. There were no rats, as a cat was kept constantly about and Mr. Dawson was puzzled to discover what new kind of pest he had in his greenhouse. The thought that the damage was done by cats never occurred to him, until, after the plants were severely injured, when he discovered some cat hairs on the half-eaten branches, and, watching more closely, he caught the hothouse cat eating not only the small tender shoots, but the large woody twigs as well.

"In the spring he set out over a hundred small vines in a cold frame but, to his surprise, after removing the protection which the sash afforded, the cats of the neighborhood destroyed the whole bed, eating the plants to the ground. They were not just nibbled, as are catnip and valerian, the only other plants known to be eaten by cats, they were completely destroyed—gobbled up—even to stalks as big as a lead pencil.

"No place in the arboretum is now concealed enough to be safe from ravage, and the few two year old vines in it are completely protected by wire nettings. Every leaf or twig on these caged vines which is near enough the wires to be within reach of claws is scratched and torn to bits. In a few months time this entirely new plant from the interior of China has become the most relished vegetable which our American cats have ever tasted.

"The plant has no odor that we can detect, neither has it any distinct taste. Did the cats scent it, or do cats, which are carnivorous animals, make a practice of tasting every new plant that comes within their ken? If they do, they certainly excel in investigative faculties the most civilized races of human beings. Then too, how did the news spread so that in a few months after its introduction all the cats of the neighborhood knew of it? Did the greenhouse cat communicate his discoveries to his friends, or did each cat make the test independently?

"The whole story throws an interesting sidelight on cat instinct and intelligence and starts a score of questions. It is difficult to see how there can be here an instinct inherited through long generations of ancestry, for the plant has been unknown in Europe and America until a few years ago. It seems to show an alertness of cat intellect which is most remarkable and which is in sharp contrast with the reluctance of the average human being to taste new things."

Tennent in his *Sketches of the Natural History of Ceylon* describes the plant and the cat's reactions to it still further.

"The matatabi (*Actinidia polygama*) is a climbing shrub of the order *Ternstroemiaceae,* which also comprises the tea plant and *Camellia japonica.* As its pentapetalous flowers bear a resemblance to the celebrated Japanese plum (*Prunus Mume*), its blooming branches, intentionally deprived of the leaves, are often used in flower arrangements and called summer mume. Its fruit resembles the jujube, but with acrid taste, and is salted and eaten by mountaineers. Besides, the plant produces a sort of gall flattish in form and tasting more acrid than the fruit. It is dried and sold by druggists under the name of Matatabi. The cat is so fond of it that a widespread proverb compares one's dotingness to the cat and Matatabi. When it is given the gall, it behaves as if suddenly possessed—caressing and rolling it about before its tasting, and drivelling and ejaculating during its eating. All its distempers, no matter how serious, are cured thereby. Moreover, the burning of the Matatabi is held to be the surest means of recalling a stray cat. It appears from the following quotation that a similar plant occurs in Ceylon. 'In connexion with cats, a Singalhese gentleman has described to me a plant in Ceylon, called Cuppa-may-niya by the natives; by which, he says, cats are so enchanted, that they play with it as they would with a captured mouse: throwing it into the air, watching it till it falls, and crouching to see if it will move. It would be worth inquiring into the truth of this; and the explanation of the attraction.' "

4. Snowball Tree or Guelder Rose (*Viburnum opulus*) A correspondent wrote to *Notes and Queries*: "Is the cat's liking for guelder rose-wood smell acknowledged? Several of my pets have delighted to roll in the sawdust where I had been cutting some logs. My present friend not only rubs against a piece kept indoors for over a year, but has found that by licking it well first, and then rubbing his chin to it, he gets a longer spell of the sweet savour."

5. Herbs in General. Cats enjoy lying among and sniffing most herbs, but it is a passive enjoyment and not wild as with catnip and

valerian. Rosetta Clarkson in her herb book *Magic Gardens* describes the quiet pleasure that cats get from the fragrance of herbs.

"My tiger cat, taught only by nature, is a great believer in the efficacy of fragrant breathing and nibbling. For long intervals Orphie will sit in his favorite spot surrounded by catnip, thyme, burnet, and rue, swaying and rocking gently back and forth singing to himself—his eyes slowly closing—his nose high, sniffing, sniffing—this side, now that side—the collected fragrances of the garden. Orphie knows the virtues of my herbs. Occasionally he picks his way delicately among the plots nipping off a leaf here and a flower there, then stretches out on his favorite flagstone, the fragrant thyme all about him, and goes to sleep feeling that all's right in his world, at any rate." [*and*]

"My twenty-pound cat, Orphie Whiffendorfer (just Orphie in hot weather), trails me about the garden all summer and assumes the responsibility of overseer of the harvest by practically living in the drying room, particularly watchful that his own pet herb, catnip, is being taken care of properly. While I am making sweet bags and pads, he sits up opposite to me and superintends that process. Just as grandmother made the last of the batter into a gingerbread man for me, so I fill the last pad with catnip. Orphie carries it to his master's desk and lays it over a grille covering the radiator. There he takes his afternoon naps and any attempt to move the pad only makes Master Whiffendorfer very unhappy."

It is curious that Mrs. Clarkson included rue in her list of herbs. The ancient Greeks and Romans claimed that cats detested its smell. One sure way to keep them away from hens, they claimed, was to tie a bit of rue under the hens' wings; a little cat gall mixed with the poultry feed made the safeguard still more effective. Dovecotes were protected by placing rue in their windows. Has the modern cat changed its tastes, or is our rue different from that of the ancients?

6. Other Plants. The fragrance of many flowers pleases cats. Those most often mentioned are: lily-of-the-valley, rose, violet, carnation, baby-blue-eyes (*Nemophila*), mimosa and Heliotrope. Fernand Méry claims that the preferred plants are those that originated in a warm climate thereby substantiating the theory that cats originated in Egypt or thereabouts. One thing is certain; cats avidly eat species of the genus *Cyperus* two of which are the papyrus and umbrella-plant.

7. Perfumes and Cosmetics. The Byzantine empress Zoë (980–

1054) liked to concoct her own perfumes, and the furnaces which she needed for doing this kept the room too hot for anyone's comfort except her cat's. In the fragrant heat, history tells us, it passed its days in indolent pleasure.

Although their sense of smell is acute, cats inhale with obvious delight perfumes and other overpowering odors that are far too intense for our less sensitive noses. If a particular smell appeals to them they can literally bury their noses in its source. Topsell misconstrued this pleasure, for he remarked that "they cannot abide the savor of ointments but fall mad thereby."

As with food, the taste for man-made smells varies from one cat to another. A cosmetic that attracts one often repels another, yet there is a general consistency. Camphor, of all things, appeals; at least it never repels.

Theophile Gautier, speaking of one of his cats says: "She delighted in perfumes, stuck her little nose into bouquets, and bit with little spasms of pleasure at handkerchiefs on which scent had been put; she walked upon the dressing-table among the scent bottles, smelling the stoppers, and if she had been allowed to do so would no doubt have used powder."

8. Miscellaneous. When cats and dogs are discussed the statement is often made that in its sense of smell the dog has low tastes compared to those of the cat, its idea of a smell thrill being putrefying matter while that of the cat is perfumes. In all fairness to the dog it should be noted that cats aren't above enjoying earthy odors. Their discovery of a smelly dried-up mouse, frog, worm, or other animal will set them off into an orgy of olfactory pleasure. The odor of excrement can entrance them and that of human perspiration can excite them to the point where they become as uncontrollable as when they indulge in catnip. As with cosmetics, each cat has its own preferences but all succumb to some form of what we like to term vulgar tastes. To a cat's discriminating nose, however, the musky smell of sun-dried lizards is probably more precious than the rarest scent concocted by man.

THE FUNCTIONAL NOSE. The external nose, extending down from between the eyes, ends in two nostrils which are surrounded by an area of thick hairless skin containing many glands. The Japanese have a saying that a cat's nose is always cold except on midsummer's day, and it is true that in a healthy and active cat this skin is usually cool and moist. If it is

"Mid-Victorian Vase" by Marguerite Zorach.

warm and dry, however, this does not necessarily indicate that the cat is sick. A sick cat's nose can be cool and moist and a healthy one's warm and dry depending on numerous factors such as its activity and atmospheric conditions.

The color of the nose skin ranges from unpigmented pale pink, found most frequently in predominantly white cats, through rose and brown to black. It can also be multicolored, especially in tortoiseshells. Age occasionally changes the original color.

Other than a protective covering for the cat's breathing and smelling apparatus, the external nose is an indicator of its owner's feelings. When its nose is wrinkled in rage, a cat's mood can't possibly be misinterpreted; nor when puckered in anxiety. Those acquainted with cats can often evaluate their emotional stresses by observation of the nose alone. Cats also show affection with the help of their noses. By touching them rather than their lips to the noses of those they care for they indicate their love.

The internal nose is lined completely with mucous membrane. Its anterior and ventral, or respiratory portion is lined with ciliated cells that clear the air of foreign particles before it passes into the lungs. Arrangement of the passageways also helps in the cleansing process. The tissues are highly vascular in order that the air may be warmed as well as cleansed in cold weather.

An especially thick and spongy mucous membrane covers the dorsocaudal, or olfactory part of the nose. Scattered through it are the spindle-shaped olfactory cells; each sends up tiny hairs which collect odors, and each sends down a process which connects it to the nervous system that will interpret the odors received.

The remote location of the olfactory center necessitates an actual act of sniffing to bring the air to it. Ordinary breathing alerts the cat to a smell by means of slow diffusion to the center, but it must go through the act of sniffing if the smell warrants investigation. Cutting off a cat's whiskers does not deprive it of its sense of smell. It does handicap it in spatial orientation, which can slow it down in locating something.

Uses of the Sense of Smell. Cats select and find their food through olfaction, and a kitten cannot initiate the sucking response on its mother if it is unable to smell, although it can learn to suck a bottle.

The hunting cat relies in large part on its sense of sight but apparently only the sense of smell is used in locating food. Everyone who has watched a cat searching for a piece of meat on the floor can verify this. The meat can be a few inches from the cat's nose, and it would have to be blind in order not to see it, but it continues the search by smell alone. Sight and smell seem to operate independently of each other. This is not so difficult to believe as the fact that an animal with a keen sense of smell is so inept in locating something at close range. Its long-range olfaction is remarkable, but its locating of the source of a smell at close range is poor.

When a cat does locate the source and begins to analyze it by sniffing it frequently opens its mouth in the process. This has been described as an attempt to clear the air passages of too intense an odor. Considering the interplay of the sense of taste with that of smell it is more logical to assume that the mouth is opened in an attempt to strengthen and interpret the odor. This assumption better helps to explain why the mouth is opened only at those times when an extensive examination of the smell is being made. Besides, as has already been mentioned, cats are not troubled by intense odors except for those that repel like the smell of citrus fruits.

The cat's use of olfaction for pleasure was described above. Sex is the third area utilizing this sense. Each cat has its own unique identification odor, which also classifies it sexually, and the oestrous cat announces her condition through still another odor. Lack of a sex odor in neutered cats confuses complete ones, and toms attack both male and female neuters as fiercely and indiscriminately as they do other toms. Even when they live in the same household entire cats seldom are friendly with neutered cats, and the dislike is mutual. The entire cat, however, is not always the dominant animal in such a situation. Once the antagonism is established, castration of the complete cat does not guarantee amity.

In ordinary day-to-day living a cat's coat picks up innumerable odors which narrate what it has been doing to those who can interpret them. Cats find these smells on each other irresistible and begin an immediate investigation. Seldom, however, is the cat under investigation tolerant of the affront to its privacy unless it, in turn, is interested in the smells on the investigator. In that case all is well and a mutual and prolonged smelling takes place. Swats and spits soon end the sniffing if it is one-sided.

Cats' noses forewarn them of danger, but though they may become more cautious after such a signal, they investigate it not by more thorough sniffing, but with their eyes and ears. All things considered, the organ of smell in cats (if you consider food and sex forms of pleasure, which both cats and humans seem to) is truly an organ of delectation.

XIII
Mouth

THE cat's rounded head delimits the size of its jaws, or, looking at it the other way around, a cat's shortened jaws give the head its rounded shape. In breeds with wedge-shaped heads, like the Siamese, the shortening is not so obvious. Leverage is diminished by it but the muscles for mastication acquire greater power. These muscles are highly developed in the cat, especially in the male, and contribute to the head's roundness by adding width. A study of feline dentition indicates that the short muzzle of today's cat evolved from a much longer ancestral one.

The lower jaw is incapable of any lateral movement, the lips possess no sphincter muscle, and the under-lip is shorter than the upper-lip, the last a characteristic shared by all animals that drink by lapping. Unable to pucker its lips in the form of a kiss, a cat shows its affection by dainty tongue licks instead.

Inside the mouth are the salivary glands, the teeth and tongue, and the palate or roof of the mouth, hard anteriorly and soft posteriorly. In light-colored cats the palate is pink; in black or partially black cats it can have varying amounts of pigmentation. Ridges, or rugae, run across it, their number varying from five to nine and averaging seven. The number of ridges is thought by some to distinguish a good from a poor mouser, but there appears to be no agreement on what the significant number is. Actually, if the ridges do have a function it has still to be discovered, and their inheritance has not been studied.

The Tongue

Cultivate your garden, said Goethe and Voltaire,
Every other task is wasted and dead-born;
Narrow all your efforts to a given sphere,
Seek your Heaven daily in a bit of ground.

So my cat behaves. Like a veteran,
He brushes well his coat before he sits to dine;
All his work is centered in his own domain,
Just to keep his spotless fur soft, and clean, and fine.

His tongue is sponge, and brush, and towel, and curry-comb,
Well he knows what work it can be made to do,
Poor little wash-rag, smaller than my thumb.

His nose touches his back, touches his hind paws too,
Every patch of fur is raked, and scraped, and smoothed;
What more has Goethe done, what more could Voltaire do?

"Practice" by HIPPOLYTE TAINE,
Agnes Repplier, translator

FUNCTION. Taine's "poor little wash-rag" does other things besides what he mentioned. Its principal duties number six.

1. *Drinking.* After the tongue's muscles have shaped it roughly into a spoon, it is used to lap up liquids, the number of laps before each swallow averaging 3, 4, or 5. A study of the so-called lick rate in cats was made by R. W. Schaeffer and R. Huff. After deprivation of liquids for 6, 12 and 24 hours, cats were measured for their lick rate when given milk and water. After 12 hours of deprivation they were also tested with 4%, 8%, 76% and 32% sucrose solutions. It was found that the mean lick rate was constant for all cats and independent of the length of deprivation and type of liquid offered, and age and sex of the animal.

2. *Thermoregulation.* Panting is initiated by a rise in temperature, overexertion, or excitement, and the rate averages 11.5 cycles per second. This frequency is too high to be very effective, and the cat supplements the panting by licking itself with saliva, a practice shared by many mammals. Under extreme heat conditions it is said to lick every part of its body that can be reached, to the point where it is dripping wet.

3. *Washing.* "Now she proceeds to clean herself all over, having a just sense of the demands of her elegant person,—beginning judiciously with her paws, and fetching amazing tongues at her hind-hips." (Leigh Hunt) The washing ability of cats is remarkable no matter what part of the body they cleanse. Their tongue can reach every portion except the back of the neck and between the shoulder blades, and as they seek out-of-the-way places it seems to grow in length to fulfill the need. Unable to reach the head except for chop-licking, they wash it by proxy through the paws which, when moistened, perform a good scrubbing. Washing becomes extremely exaggerated during parturition when the female licks almost constantly—herself, her young and the area around her.

As Taine pointed out in his poem, licking is not always employed for cleansing but can become a sponging and towelling to dry the cat should it get wet, and a smoothing down should it get rumpled. It is frequently performed as a sort of emotional release or displacement activity, as it is called.

A peculiar action of the tongue, a reflex, should perhaps be mentioned here. When cats scratch a certain area of their shoulder they will frequently open their mouth slightly and the tongue will glide in and out in rhythm with their scratching. The area roughly coincides with that which produces the well-known scratch reflex in animals. When he is artificially stimulated in that spot, the animal's hind paw will come up and begin rhythmical scratching movements. In the case of the tongue, it appears that an actual itch and subsequent scratching of the area produces a tongue-licking reflex.

4. *Display of Affection,* already mentioned above. Humans, cats and other animals can be the recipients of a cat's kisses. The licks are not the effusive slobberings of the dog, but are relatively dry and delicate. Occasionally they may progress into a vigorous washing of the recipient, and they can be accompanied by another form of caress, the nose contact.

5. *Eating.* Food is not only moved into the mouth by the tongue but

the tongue's rasp-like surface is used for removing meat from bones and for extracting-purposes of a similar nature.

6. *Taste.* Finally, it is primarily with the tongue that the cat is able to taste, although a few taste buds are also located on the soft palate and surrounding areas.

STRUCTURE. The tongue is long, flat and muscular and is coated with mucous membrane. Its underside is smooth and soft and not distinctive from the mouth lining. Its upper surface is covered with papillae of four kinds.

1. The circumvallate papillae are few in number and are located on the posterior part of the tongue. They are arranged in two rows which meet posteriorly to form a V-shape.

2. The fungiform papillae, more numerous than the circumvallate, are located anteriorly along the sides of the tongue.

3. The conical papillae, very numerous, are for the most part large and horny, resembling claws whose points are directed backwards. They are set closely together on the tongue's surface and give it its file-like looks and quality.

4. The flattened papillae, large and soft, are restricted to the root of the tongue in the area behind the circumvallate.

TASTE

Gustatory cells are scattered over the tongue in its less exposed spots, especially in the mucosa of the papillae. Through their pores they send filaments to the outside which collect and transmit tastes to the underlying nerves. The nerve fibers respond to thermal stimuli as well as to taste, and it has been found that taste sensitivity in the cat is greatest at 86° F., the temperature of the tongue itself. Prolonged cooling of the tongue with ice water was found to abolish all responses to gustatory stimuli.

The number and distribution of the taste buds have been investigated in the kitten at birth. The cells were found in both the tops and sides of the fungiform and circumvallate papillae but many of the former possessed none. Other than these, an average of 473 were found elsewhere: the very small percentage in the anterior third of the tongue, 50% in the mid-third, and almost as many in the posterior third. The taste center shifts to the posterior region but thins out again with next to no buds beyond the posterior circumvallate papillae. Apparently no mapping of the taste buds has been made in the adult cat, and it is questionable whether their numbers and locations would coincide more than roughly with those of the neonate kitten.

All taste sensations fall into the categories of salty, bitter, sour, and sweet, or their combinations. In the cat, the apex and anterior lateral margins of the tongue are sensitive to salt, the base and posterior lateral margins to bitter and the entire surface except the mid-dorsum to sour. Separate taste buds are said to respond to hypertonic saline, hypotonic saline and water.

Until quite recently it was believed that the taste for sweetness was unknown to the cat, and the location for the sensation has not been established. Frings, going on the premise that cats could distinguish sweetness if the conditions were right, worked with very hungry cats. He presented them with milk which was diluted four times and which did or did not contain sucrose. The dilution was necessary because a cat's fondness for milk will cause it to ignore adulterations. This did not hold in the extreme 4X dilution.

In all cases the hungry cats chose the milk which contained the sucrose. Their bodies, craving nourishment, recognized it in the sucrose milk. This indicates the presence of receptors for sweetness on the cat's tongue. Sweet stimulation may ordinarily be ignored because it is unessential to the cat's everyday existence much as is color perception.

Experiments by Pfaffman on taste stimulation in young kittens, done much earlier than Frings's work, bear out this fact. He found that a hungry kitten would not suck plain water but would suck a solution of sugar and water. Pfaffman further discovered that sensitivity to the four basic tastes develops early. Day old kittens responded differentially to a mixture of salt and milk; 10–20 day old kittens to salt and bitter. A sensitivity to sweet-sour was also indicated at about this age.

Sweet sensation in the adult cat is weak at best. Salt is a little stronger, then bitter, and sour produces the greatest stimulation.

TEETH

The milk teeth, or deciduous teeth, are 26 in number in the cat and begin to make their appearance when the kitten is between 2 and 3 weeks old. The incisors come first, next the canines, and then the molars, and by the end of the sixth week all 26 teeth have usually appeared. Their replacement with the permanent teeth begins around 6 months, seldom sooner, the true molars of the lower jaw making their appearance before the deciduous molars are lost.

Adult cats have 30 teeth, 12 less than the dog and 2 less than humans. The upper jaw has 6 incisors, 2 canines, 6 premolars and 2 molars; the lower jaw differs by having 4 instead of 6 premolars. The small transversely placed upper first molars have lost any function that they may have had and oftentimes are missing, like human wisdom teeth. When they are present they are highly variable, an indication that they are vestigial structures. In his study on the genetics of Singapore cats Searle found that 9% of the cats examined lacked upper first molars and 22% lacked one or both upper front premolars, an indication that the cat's jaw is possibly still undergoing transition to its shortened form.

The shape of the cat's teeth is that of the typical carnivore. None of them has grinding power. The tusk-like canines rip, tear, stab and hold, and are used for fighting and feeding. The sharp-pointed serrated molars play against each other, top with bottom, like scissor blades, to cut food into pieces small enough to be swallowed. The incisors are so small that the tongue oftentimes protrudes from the mouth between them, the cat apparently being completely unaware of it. This happens most frequently after a washing session.

Feline teeth are formidable weapons but little mention is made of this fact, emphasis usually being placed on the claws. Anyone who has seen an angry cat attack, however, will look with respect at his cat's teeth the next time it yawns.

XIV
Integument

For whoso woldé senge a cattés skyn,
Thenne wolde the cat wel dwellen in hir in;
And is the cattés skyn be slyk and gay,
She wol nat dwelle in house half a day.
But forth she wol, er any day be dawed,
To shewe hir skyn, and goon a-caterwawed.
GEOFFREY CHAUCER

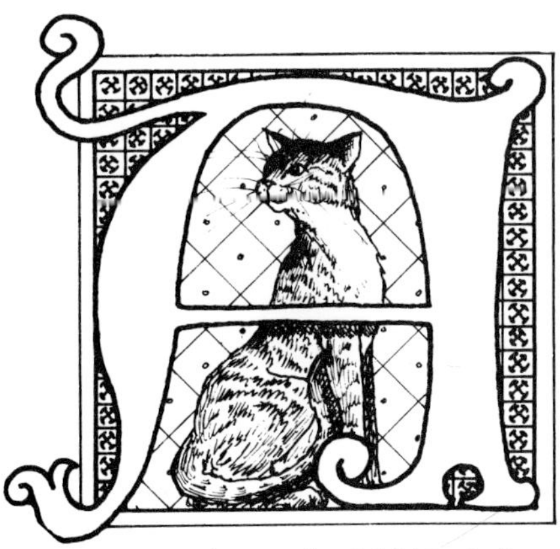

AND well may the cat be proud of her skin. It is a thing of beauty both in looks and function. The looks, that part to which Chaucer referred, is discussed in the section on genetics. Here the function and functioning of the skin are considered—everything covered by the term integument except the claws, these being best treated with paws in the section on appendages. Integument, in its total claws-fur-skin sense, accounts for approximately 13% of the adult cat's body weight; the new born kitten is 20% integument by weight.

SKIN. The principal function of the skin is to provide protection and the sense of touch to the cat it encloses. It is extremely loose and flexible as in other carnivores, possibly to help prevent wounds from penetrating beneath it even though it may be badly lacerated itself. If a fight goes against a cat, the slipperiness of his skin allows him to break away from his antagonist with minimum damage. The looseness is greatest in the vulnerable neck region, a favorite site of attack.

When it does get injured, cat skin heals rapidly, and this can be a distinct disadvantage in cases where the injury, such as a puncture wound, has penetrated deeply. The infection spreads beneath the regenerated skin creating an abscess which is difficult to heal. Such an occurrence is not uncommon because deep puncture wounds from tooth and claw are frequent despite the skin's flexibility.

Skin thickness varies. Thickest on the cat's head, especially in the neck region, and on the outer sides of the limbs, it gets progressively thinner from dorsal to ventral on the torso and from proximal to distal on the limbs. This evaluation does not include the specialized skin areas: the paw pads, the naked part of the nose and the lips. The epidermis of these is thicker than on any other part of the body and contains special nerve structures.

GLANDS OF THE SKIN. Sweat glands are distributed throughout the cat's body. However, it is only in the paw pads that they are of the type similar to ours; this may account for the general belief that the pads alone possess them. The similarity between human and cat sweat glands ceases in their ductile parts, and it is thought that this accounts for the fact that a cat's sweat is isotonic while ours is hypotonic.

Elimination of impurities is the main duty of cat sweat glands. They are not considered very effective in thermoregulation. Skin resistance and impedance activity appear to be controlled entirely by their activity, and toughening of the skin to protect it from mechanical injury is considered to be the result of so-called arousal sweating. Activity in the glands is continual even though it may be too low to produce obvious moisture.

Psychogenic drives activate paw-pad sweat glands in the cat in exactly the same way that they activate those in the palms of our hands. Some high-strung cats have damp foot pads frequently; other cats, the calmest individuals, retain dry pads even during a traumatic experience like a trip to the veterinarian.

Sebaceous glands are found in the vicinity of hair follicles and occasionally in the teats. They are largest in the dorsal tail region, the lips and beneath the chin. Their ducts empty into the hair follicles and the sebum which they secrete lubricates the hair. It is this protective covering that produces the sheen to the fur. Cat sebum, unlike that of most dogs, is odorless to humans.

FUR.
All your wondrous wealth of hair
  Darke and fair,
Silken-shaggy, soft and bright
As the clouds and beams of night,
Pays my reverent hand's caress
Back with friendlier gentleness.
ALGERNON CHARLES SWINBURNE

Whether short or long, black or white, striped or spotted, the fur of a cat is one of its best and most distinctive features. It is so species specific that it has been suggested that hair characteristics be used as a means of classifying the *Felidae*.

Each hair grows out of a follicle or sac which is imbedded in the skin and has its own blood supply and nerve. In the normal coat there are four different hair types.

1. *Guard Hairs*: long, straight, thick and evenly tapered.
2. *Awn Hairs:* bent distally, and markedly thickened before tapering abruptly. They are part of the overfur like the guard hairs.
3. *Awned Down-hairs:* proximally thin and crimped, distally thickened; intermediate between awn hairs and down-hairs.
4. *Down hairs:* evenly thin and crimped.

Of these four types only the guard hairs are entirely distinguishable; the others grade into each other. All are similar in length but awned down-hairs and down-hairs appear much shorter because of the crimping. The normal cat averages 4 guard hairs to 15 awn, 45 awned down, and 190 down.

Regardless of the above specifications, the fur of domestic shorthairs exceeds in looking different in each individual. There are the sleek stream-lined cats whose fur, coarse, fine, or inbetween, appears to be all guard hairs. There are the fluffy chocolate-box cats whose fur never lies flat and close to the body. And there are the woolly ones with so padded an undercoat, summer or winter, that the coat parts in places whenever they move. Some feel like velvet when you pet them. In others the fur is so coarse that it seems that you can feel each individual hair. Fur texture is as variable from cat to cat as its color and patterning.

Rex cats possess only down-hairs or a combination of awned down-

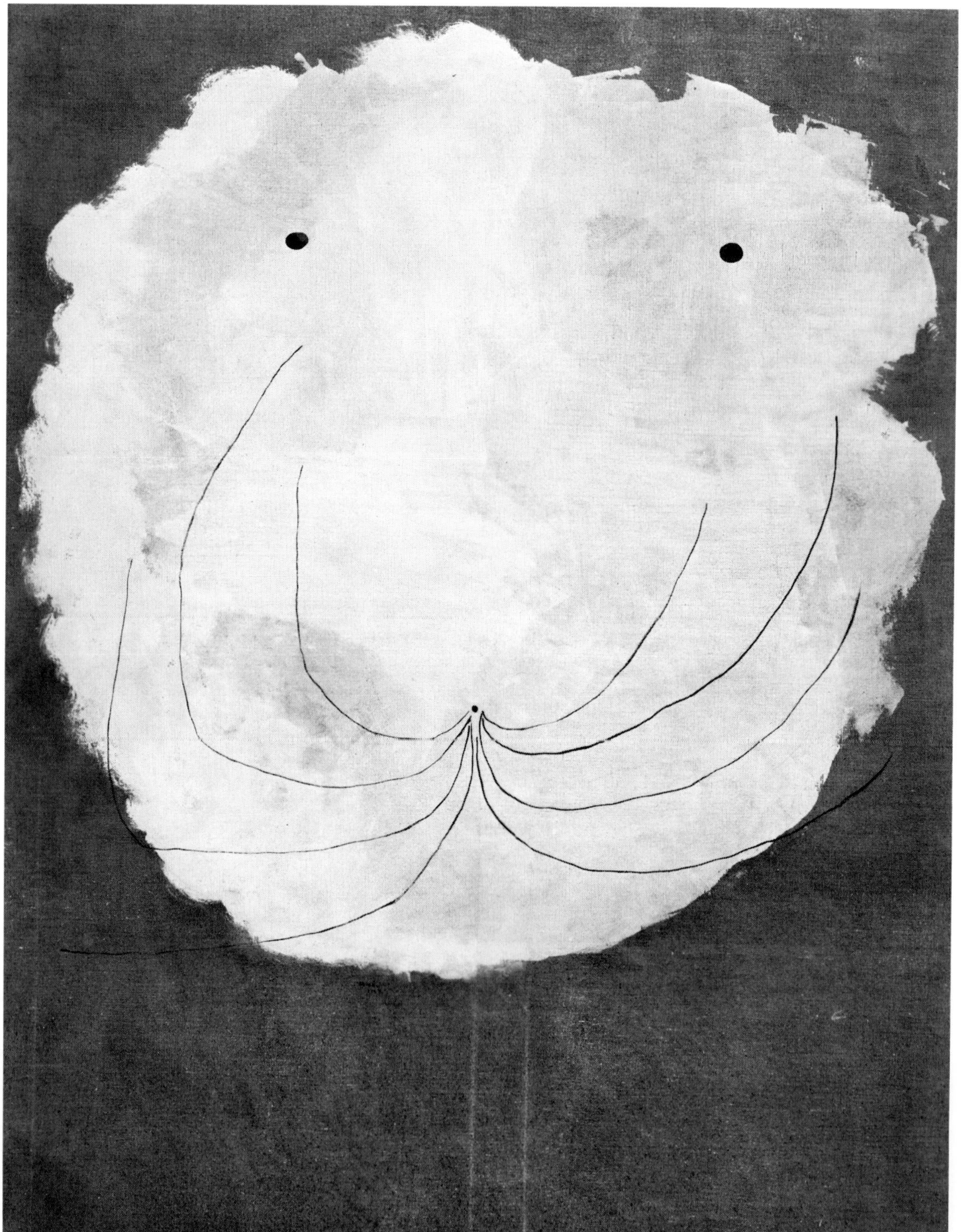

"The Cat's Whiskers" 1927 by Joan Miro. (From the collection of Mr. and Mrs. Burton Tremaine, Meriden, Conn.)

hairs and down-hairs in frequencies comparable to normal. The former are the English rex (now called Cornish rex to distinguish them from Devon rex), the latter the German rex. The wavy juvenile coat of the German rex becomes straight in the sub-adult, then once again becomes wavy. The length of the hairs in both types averages half that of normal cats and its thickness is about 60% of normal.

Fur length varies from one part of the cat's body to another. It is shortest on the face, ears and paws, longest on the abdomen and tail. Each hair is inserted obliquely into the skin, directed backwards toward the tail and more or less downwards on the limbs. The hairs can be made to stand erect by means of tiny erector muscles which connect the skin to the roots of the hairs. These muscles are most highly developed in the dorsal regions, especially in the tail, and are triggered by anger, fright, excitement and temperature. Other muscles in the form of an extensive sheet are closely connected with the skin and make possible its twitching and rippling movements at which the cat is so adept and which are activated by the slightest touch.

House cats shed their fur the year round but more in spring, summer and early fall in climates where there is a seasonal fluctuation of temperature. In late fall the coat becomes noticeably thicker and fluffy cats appear to be growing baggy breeches. Fluctuation in coat denseness with fluctuation in temperature is indicative of the fur's use as an insulator. By fluffing it in hot weather and holding it close to the body in cold, the cat can further regulate body temperature. Fat in the subcutaneous tissues also aids in regulating heat loss.

WHISKERS AND OTHER TACTILE HAIRS. Whiskers, eyebrows and the tactile hairs found on the cheeks and at the wrists of the forelegs—all these are modified hairs. There are no eyelashes as such but there is a noticeable overhang of fur on the upper eyelid.

The whiskers in particular are delicate sense organs, well supplied with blood vessels and nerves, to aid the cat in spatial orientation. However, only by a rough estimate at best can they tell it whether it can squeeze through a small hole or not. But Topsell's observation, that "if the long hairs growing about her mouth be cut away, she looseth hir corage," is correct. Lacking them, her space perception at night is so reduced that she must proceed with caution.

Whiskers supplement the cat's vision at all times and all but replace it in darkness. Normal cats evade objects skilfully at night; a cat deprived of its whiskers will frequently collide with objects or clumsily evade them if its head has made a slight contact. A dewhiskered cat is less precise in all its movements and under experimental conditions, at least, was found to be very slow in discovering exits to barriers impeding its progress. It was inept in navigation and did not find its food as readily as a normal cat. This suggests that contact sensitivity supplements olfaction which is poor in the cat at close range, and it no doubt accounts for the belief that a cat whose whiskers are cut off can't smell. More complex in structure and still more complex in function compared with ordinary hairs, whiskers nevertheless develop faster and appear in the embryo well before the fur.

Each cat usually has whiskers of only one color—white or black—but some cats, particularly tortoiseshells, can have them of both colors, and others, like the Siamese, can have them striped black and white. Arranged in 4 rows, the longest and strongest whiskers are found in rows 2 and 3. There is an average of 12 fully grown whiskers on each side of the face. They operate not only by contact but by detection of the ever present minute currents and pauses of air which signal the presence of solid objects. Their most effective contact stimulus is movement in particular directions, downward for the upper 2 rows and upward for the lower 2. Forward movement also causes a response while pulling and pushing seldom produce discharges that indicate stimulation. Spontaneous discharges that have been found to occur are thought to be triggered by abnormal irritability associated with stimuli above the threshold.

Whiskers are most sensitive to the initial stimulus they receive from contact with an object, and adaptation to a stimulus is slow. This is probably necessary to allow the cat to make the postural adjustment that the stimulus indicates are needed.

Excitement and other emotions cause a cat's whiskers to bristle, and under severe stress those from each side will almost meet in front of the face. When cats sniff noses with each other in greeting they may mingle whiskers. To judge by what follows, this ritual may help to convey their feelings to each other, friendly or hostile.

The tactile hairs at the wrists of the cat's forelegs, which have not yet been honored with a specific name, have been studied in the same fashion as the whiskers. Bending these hairs results in increased discharges indicating a response to stimulation similar to that of whiskers. When a bend is followed by a compensating bend in the opposite direction it often causes the stimulus discharge to cease. Other than this no directional sensitivity for these hairs has been found. As with whiskers they are slow in adapting.

HEAT AND COLD SENSITIVITY. A cat's face is only slightly less sensitive to changes in temperature than ours. But the animal as a whole is far less sensitive to thermal stimulation than we are, especially on the warm side. It is probably this tolerance that makes it capable of withstanding exposures to extreme heat to which a human would succumb.

Cats show no response to a mild warming of the skin but do react to a mild cooling. That they are sensitive to warming, regardless of this lack of obvious response, is shown by their delight in basking in the sun or other warm place until the heat becomes too intense. Their skin temperature must reach about 126° F before they show signs of painful discomfort; for us 112° F is sufficient to produce pain. They exhibit no response to temperatures between 60° and 112° F. Changes of temperature, however, do affect the responses of touch units to mechanical stimulation.

In experiments testing for temperature sensitivity in cats four areas were selected: the area around the nose, the footpads, the inner thigh, and the back. It was in the last three that response to mild cooling but not to mild warming was detected. Even so, the sensitivity shown was not significant when compared with humans. At an adapting temperature of 84° F a person can detect a temperature reduction of 2.7° while the cat requires a drop of 16° before it responds. Despite the skepticism one may feel about these figures it *is* true that the cat is a temperature-tolerant animal. It lies in ease on radiators almost too hot for us to touch. Then, of its own volition it will leave the heat to go and frolic in the snow in sub-zero cold with not even a shiver to indicate the extreme and quick change in temperature.

An experiment in cold acclimatization was carried on by Thomas Adams. One group of cats was acclimatized to a temperature of 77° F, another to 41° F. Each group was then tested at exposures of 73°, 50° and 32° F. It was found that although resting at 73°, the cold-acclimatized cats had lower rectal temperatures. They also were able to maintain higher internal body temperatures during exposures to cold than were the non-cold-acclimatized cats.

The cold acclimatizing mechanism in cats involves a redistribution of body heat. There is an increased heat flux at the expense of higher metabolism, a greater ability to increase heat production accompanied by more flexibility in the peripheral blood vessels for expansion and contraction plus an increase in functional tissue insulation.

Pigment formation in the Siamese is directly proportional to heat loss from the skin: the extremities where the heat loss is greatest have the most pigmentation. Temperatures between 37° and 60° F result in pigmentation of portions of the body as well as the extremities, principally in the shoulders and hips. Still lower temperatures can result in the entire body becoming dark brown.

This color change due to temperature explains the shift from dark to light fur during sickness, injury and other traumatic experiences, while tabby stripes that sometimes appear in the Siamese coat may be the result of the stripes having a lower thermal threshold. The thyroid gland can also contribute to color change in this breed; the less active the gland, the greater the pigmentation.

There appears to be no explanation for the white hairs that may suddenly appear and then disappear in pure black cats. A patch of white hairs frequently replaces the black at the site of an injury, perhaps as the result of temperature gradation as in the Siamese; but single white hairs and sometimes a whisker make their appearance from time to time on any part of a pure black cat for no obvious reason. These hairs may well have saved the life of many a black cat. Charms and folk remedies which so often included black cats in their specifications almost always required a *pure* black cat.

Touch. As was pointed out by Mivart and others, the sense of touch, though basically a feeling of contact, has many extensions. Through it the animal learns to distinguish the relative nature of objects in respect to density, hardness, texture, resistance, size, shape and distance. The kitten, ever busy with its paws, soon learns that tree trunks are rough, metal smooth and water wet. During its entire lifetime a cat explores new objects by touching them with its paws. The sense of touch for its forepaws is controlled by a relatively large portion of its brain, an indication of its importance.

The adaptation of the cat's toes to touch has been investigated through electrophysiological experimentation, and the time constant was found to be 0.04 seconds. This is 0.01 seconds more than that determined for humans through psychophysical methods. The question is, does a comparison of results from two different types of experimentation have significance? Observation alone indicates that the toes of cats are extremely sensitive.

Besides its paw pads, the skin of the cat's muzzle and its tongue are the most sensitive to tactile stimulation, but the entire animal is highly attuned to this sense. In the head and dorsal region the barest contact of one hair with an object can trigger a response.

The small raised tactile areas called touch spots or tylotrich pads scattered over the skin are responsible for this awareness. When a hair or hairs are moved these are depressed causing a discharge of impulses which convey both spatial and temporal information from the contact to the cat's nervous system. Each touch spot or tylotrich pad is the triggering portion of a tylotrich follicle, the unit of the sense of touch. A gnat grazing a hair in the cat's ear will, through one of these follicles, set off a series of ear twitches. One minute particle of water landing on its back will cause its skin to ripple from head to tail in protest.

The specific way in which whiskers and other specialized hairs respond has already been mentioned, as well as how the cat's sight is supplemented by that of touch. Touch also supplements its hearing. It has been demonstrated that deaf cats feel intense sounds through what has been called tremor perception, and the source of this perception has been traced to their fur.

Sensual animal that it is, the cat enjoys being stroked and petted but only if this is done properly and at the proper time. It enjoys having its whiskers rubbed so much that it frequently rubs them itself on any available object. It enjoys an all-round tickle or petting, particularly around the ears but never the toes, possibly because of their oversensitivity to contact.

The administrator of feline pleasures must know his cat in matters of petting as well as other idiosyncrasies, or, past a certain point, he may find his efforts rewarded by bites, scratches and kicks. All of his pet's inhibitions will have vanished because of over-stimulation.

Electricity. On a cold dry day, unless you like electric shocks, there is no pleasure in stroking a cat. Gilbert White wrote in 1784: "I must not omit to tell you that, during those two Siberian days, my parlour-cat was so electric, that had a person stroked her, and been properly insulated, the shock might have been given to a whole circle of people." After the first mutually felt shock the cat itself will seldom tolerate a petting. Not only the shock but the disarray of its fur from the electrical charge disturbs it. Nevertheless, unpredictable creatures that they are, some cats are said to purr from the sensation.

Cat fur generates electricity easily whether it is on the live animal or is a pelt, depending on atmospheric conditions. Vigorous petting may produce only sparks, or sparks and crackling, with no shocks. In the dark the sparking produces a miniature fireworks display.

Black cats do not generate more electricity than other cats. The color of the fur is no more related to electrical potential than is carrying or wearing a piece of cat skin a cure for rheumatism. Both have been and still are popular beliefs. In the latter, the electrical properties of the skin are somehow supposed to provide relief for the aches and pains accompanying rheumatism.

A fantastic reason for the electrical properties of cat fur was submitted in 1754 to *Scots Magazine*. "Natural electricity is common almost to all animals, especially those destined to catch their prey by night. Cats have this property in the greatest degree of any animal we are acquainted with. Their fur or hair is surprisingly electrical. If it be gently raised up, it avoids the touch till it be forced to it; and by stroking their backs in the dark, the emanations of electrical fire are extremely quick and vibrative from it, followed by a crackling noise, as from glass tubes when their electrical atmosphere is struck. It appears to me of singular use to animals destined to catch their prey in the dark. They give a sudden and quick erection of their fur, which raises the electrical fire, and this, by its quickness rushing along the long-pointed hairs over their eyes, and illuminating the pupilla, enables them to perceive and seize their prey. It would be worth while to inquire, whether all the wild sort that catch their prey with the paw, are not endowed with the same vibrations of electrical fire. The cat is the only domestic animal of that species, but such a discovery in the ferocious kind, would still be an additional demonstration of that infinite wisdom so easily discoverable in the minutest executions of all his works, and so perfectly adapted to a proper end."

XV
Appendages

And let me touch those curving claws of yellow ivory, and grasp the tail that like a monstrous asp coils round your heavy velvet paws.
OSCAR WILDE

PAWS.

WHAT can better describe the soft quiet padding of a cat's paws than Carl Sandburg's portrayal of fog as coming on little cat feet? The downy softness of feline paw pads admirably muffles their footsteps, and fur tufts between the pads make walking still more quiet. Composed of fibrous tissue and fat, the pads serve as shock absorbers and protect the bones which bear the cat's weight, besides guaranteeing the stealthy tread.

But a cat's movements aren't completely silent. All cats readily hear each other's approach, and under favorable circumstances so can a human. In cats that have access to the outdoors the paw pads soon lose their smooth satiny texture to become tough and leathery, but they don't lose their sensitivity.

There are 7 pads on each forefoot, one for each of the 5 toes (the fifth or thumb being rudimentary) plus the large tri-lobed central pad and the small wrist pad. Lacking the wrist pad the four-toed hindpaws have 5 pads each. Less flexible than the forepaws, the toes of the hindpaws are far more powerful, the better to perform their heavy duties in fighting, running, and jumping. In comparison to them the forepaws look dainty and delicate, especially when seen toying with a flower or insect, but they are amply strong to stun their prey.

Cats use their forepaws in almost every situation, and their importance and versatility cannot be overestimated. They help to cleanse as well as walk the cat; they examine and test strange objects; they ascertain texture, attract attention and show affection. They test for density and temperature and knead for pleasure. They retrieve food from inaccessible places and raise it to the mouth to be eaten or hold it on the ground to be chewed and gnawed. They pull down objects from a height and they swat and cuff in anger or play. They stun prey and play with and fondle objects that please.

J. Cole tested 60 cats for forepaw preference by having them reach into a glass tube for their food. Assuming that the use of the same paw for 75% of 100 reaches indicates a preference for this paw he arrived at the following figures. 38.3% of the cats were left-handed, 20% were right-handed and 41.7% were ambidextrous. His overall conclusions? Innate anatomical structure is probably of greater significance in determining the preference than are environmental psychological factors.

Two types of toe abnormality are inherited in cats: polydactylism, or extra toes, and ectrosyndactylism, or the absence of some toes with a fusion of those that remain. The former, first reported around 1880, is relatively common, the latter seldom encountered.

Polydactyls can have as many as ten extra digits on all four paws, but the usual number is six or eight, two more than normal on each hind foot and one or two more on each front foot. V. A. Chapman and F. N. Zeiner found eight different anatomical types of extra toes in their study of polydactylism, using one extra-toed male to sire all the cats examined.

A duplication present in all of them, including the sire, involved the skeleton, muscles and nerves of the second toe. One type of digit was integumental only, consisting merely of skin and a claw. Another was caused by the splitting of the lateral second metatarsal or metacarpal and still another was the duplication of the fourth toe. Some cats had one kind of duplication on the forepaws and another on the hindpaws;

others had a different type on each foot. Hind feet varied more than front feet.

Results show polydactylism to be genetically dominant, but simple dominance doesn't explain the many varieties of extra toes produced, nor does anything else so far proposed, especially when cats with different types of duplication on each paw have to be considered. Much more data are necessary before any conclusions about the puzzle can be made.

Claws. "Touch not a cat without a glove" is a proverb shared by many countries, and for good reason. More colorful if less succinct is Paul Verlaine's description of cat claws.

> The cat did hide, right treacherous,
> Beneath her gloves of jet-black sheen
> Her deadly, deadly agate points,
> As razor clear, as razor keen.

At birth the claws of a cat are not retractile, and the claws of some adult cats like the Siamese, although partially retractile, protrude enough to be seen and produce a clicking when the cats walk. In most mature cats, however, they are completely sheathed until needed, thereby guaranteeing quiet walking and stalking and protection from blunting and injury.

Cats use their claws when walking on slippery surfaces and steep inclines or declines, when climbing trees, seizing and clutching, tearing, eating and fighting. The hind claws are also used for disembowelling. As with the paws, they are much more strongly constructed than are the front claws and they are not as curved or wickedly pointed. Neither are they as versatile. If a cat wishes, it can use only one foreclaw at a time to hook onto something. Hindclaws are not capable of such delicate manipulation principally because of the limitations of hind toe movement.

The so-called sharpening of claws is restricted to the forepaws. Its purpose is considered twofold. First, it removes the old worndown outer sheath of the claw to leave a new sharp one in its place. Discarded sheaths can be found imbedded in all frequently used scratching areas. In the case of the hindclaws, cats chew off the old and dulled outer coats.

Secondly, cats indulge in claw sharpening to exercise and keep fit the mechanism by which the claws are retracted and protruded. They obviously enjoy the act, and a physically fit cat will exuberantly attack almost anything outdoors or in, especially when it is happy. A disturbed or unwell cat never goes through the motions. As soon as a sick cat once more takes an interest in claw-sharpening you can be sure it is convalescent.

Thomas Huxley, in a letter to his daughter, wrote about the family cat's delight in this occupation. "I wish you would write seriously to M ——. She is not behaving well to Oliver. I have seen handsomer kittens, but few more lively and energetically destructive. Just now he scratched away at something that M —— says cost 13s. 6d. a yard, and reduced more or less of it to combings.

"M —— therefore excludes him from the dining-room, and from all those opportunities of higher education which he would naturally have in *my* house.

"I have argued that it is as immoral to place 13s. 6d. a yardnesses within reach of kittens as to hang bracelets and diamond rings in the front garden. But in vain. Oliver is banished, and the protector (not Oliver) is sat upon. In truth and justice aid your Pa."

Claw retraction and protrusion is a simple mechanical process. The small terminal bone that bears the claw is fastened to the preceding bone by a ligament which in its relaxed state raises the terminal bone, with its claw, over the preceding bone. The result is the claw retracted in its fold of skin. The protrusion of the claws is a little more complex. Tendons are fastened to the lower portion of the toes' terminal bones. Muscles to which the tendons are attached pull the tendons, which in their turn move the terminal bones, hinge-like, so they open like a book to form a straight line with the preceding bones which have been holding them closed by means of the retraction ligaments. The maneuver lowers the claws for action almost instantaneously.

Moncrif remarked about the great restraint that cats exhibit in keeping their claws sheathed during their contact with humans; yet at the slightest infraction of this, their own code, they are condemned. It is only during uncontrollable excitement, fear, or justifiable rage that their claws whip out. At all other times humans are treated to the velvet paw.

Legs and Locomotion. Since the cat walks on its toes (that is, is digitigrade) its wrists and ankles form what appears to be the lower portions of its legs, while its elbows and knees are situated close to the trunk.

Only when it sits up in a begging position does the animal rest on its complete hind foot, plantigrade fashion, like humans.

The limbs of the cat move very freely, backward, forward, and in a rotary direction. Their angular joints, combined with the tough, wiry, but extremely flexible muscles and ligaments, give them great power and the ability to move uncommonly fast. Those enormous jumps that a cat can execute are the result of the great muscular power plus the closed angles of the leg joints. But the requisites for these abilities curtail other movements. The cat's stride is limited and it cannot attain great speed. The mighty acceleration from a standing start, for which they are famous, only partially compensates for this. For short distances a cat can outdistance an enemy but it must seek safety in height or some sort of shelter or eventually be caught.

The standing jump is utilized not only as a means of escape but also as a means of catching prey, particularly birds and insects. Mice are more often stalked closely and pounced on. Cats have been credited with 10 foot jumps, but the distance covered is not so marvellous as the ability to change direction during the leap. This can happen when the cat is being overtaken during escape or is attempting to catch a flying object. Under such conditions it can, during the jump, twist its body 180°, 90°, or whatever angle it has predetermined so that it will face its enemy for attack or bring down its prey. The maneuver is best observed when the cat leaps for butterflies. Its midair twist follows the insect's flight and can be credited for the successful capture.

Vertical jumps can be equally spectacular. If the cat is attempting a leap to a particularly high place for the first time, it will sit and gaze upward at it calculating the exact impetus needed to execute the act. To overleap could be as disastrous as to underleap because that could land it on something dangerous that it cannot see from below. The higher the objective, the longer the pause and preparation. Tail straight out behind, the cat crouches, bracing its hind legs for their surge of power. The rear end quivers from one side to the other as the legs adjust to their task. Suddenly, in a seemingly effortless move, the cat soars to its desired goal, balances itself delicately on the edge of it and begins to wash.

If there is an urgency to the leap, if for instance, the cat is hard pressed by an enemy, it will make the leap with only split-second calculations. Under these conditions it may overleap but the jump is seldom unsuccessful.

Giraffes and camels are the only other animals that walk like cats. The common quadruped walk is the alternate movement of a left front leg with a right hind leg and a right front leg with a left hind leg. Giraffe, camel and cat alternately move the front and back legs, first on one side and then the other. Cat footprints form a straight line as if the animal were always walking a fence top. Animal trainers can easily teach a cat to walk a tightrope because of this natural habit.

A. Brazier Howell in *Speed in Animals* says of cat locomotion: "The cat, though certainly not built for speed can easily out-distance most dogs of equal size in short sprints. That they are so gifted in this respect in spite of what one expects from the length of their limbs is due to a combination of factors. They are notoriously limber animals and have a high percentage of white muscle fibers which permit high twitch action of the muscles. Also, their vertebral column is extremely mobile allowing their powerful back muscles to arch and straighten the back and thereby aid the limbs. To utilize this to the fullest extent, the hind legs act in unison when the cat wishes to travel at top speed . . .

"Felidae progress by a walk, trot or gallop. In the cat the gallop is modified into the half-bound. The true gallop is asymmetrical, the half-bound symmetrical. The cat springs from both hind feet at once, lands on one front foot, and immediately shifts its weight to the other front foot which has stepped ahead as in the true gallop. Other small mammals which like the cat are good leapers and have fairly short legs, like squirrels, weasels and rabbits, employ this same sort of gait. It is advantageous to them in that during the long leap the animal has more opportunity to get its rear end in position for another thrust than it would have at the regular gallop."

Walking, running, leaping, jumping, crawling, climbing, squeezing into tiny openings—all the cat's actions are done with ease and precision. No one can deny this after watching a cat pick its way daintily on a shelf filled with bric-a-brac without disturbing a single piece. Its entire body cooperates to make each movement one of harmonious beauty no matter how inelegant the purpose.

"Anon she scratches her neck with a foot of rapid delight, leaning her head toward it, and shutting her eyes, half to accommodate the action of the skin, and half to enjoy the luxury." (Leigh Hunt)

Tail. Watch a cat's tail and you will know how it feels and what its thoughts are.

"Puss in Perplexity" by Theophile Steinlen.

She sits like any gossip at the casement,
Her agile tail reporting what she sees.
KATHERINE VAN DER VEER

There are broad generalizations that can be made for an interpretation of the cat's tail movements despite the usual pronounced individuality of any cat action. A wide-awake contented cat waves its tail slowly and gently to and fro to indicate pleasure. A sleepy contented cat will languorously move only its tail tip. A walking cat shows its contentment and happiness by carrying its tail erect, a flag announcing that everything is fine. Cats with very flexible tails carry them flat on the back like a squirrel to denote extreme well-being.

An angry cat's tail lashes violently from side to side. The intensity of the lashing is indicative of the intensity of the feeling—from slight annoyance to battle attack. The tail tip of an excited cat quivers. When preparing to leap on its prey, real or imagined, the entire cat is poised and motionless except for the tail tip which twitches in anticipation, the only manifestation of the animal's extreme tenseness. During threat of attack, stealth, and fear the tail streams straight behind its owner, while extreme terror swings it between the legs.

Cats flick their tails in situations where humans would thumb their noses, and you can't mistake the gesture before they disdainfully stalk off. This response comes most often when they are asked to do something that is beneath their dignity like coming when called. If the demands are repeated the tail will jerk in indignation.

Cat tails come in many styles—long and short, fat and thin, tapered and sausage-like, straight and kinked, knobbed, twisted, curled and bobbed, sometimes double like the fierce nekomatas of Japanese folklore. But no matter what their appearance they can adequately express their owner's feelings.

The number of vertebrae in a cat's tail determines its length. Not taking into consideration abnormalites like kinky and bobbed tails there are usually 18 to 23 but there can be as many as 28. The average length is 10 inches, with a range of from 8 to 12, giving the tail between 2 and 3 bones per inch, the reason for its flexibility.

What function the tail has, if any, is questionable, because cats with abbreviated or twisted tails or no tail at all don't appear to be handicapped by the abnormality. For those who do possess them they are an emotional outlet and a toy with which to amuse themselves. The mother cat uses hers not only to amuse but to instruct her kittens, and even a dignified elderly cat can't resist chasing its tail on occasion. In cold weather tails give protection to the noses of sleeping cats, a common use of this appendage in mammals.

Opinions to the contrary, a tail does help to balance a cat. In trees, along narrow fence tops and in other delicate maneuvers a false step sets a cat's tail spinning round like a propeller until the animal can regain its balance. A cat accustomed to owning a tail is clumsy after losing it until it adapts to a tailless existence. Finally, tails add the finishing touch to a cat's elegance and all cats seem aware of this fact as they wrap theirs round their body and paws.

Many tales have been told about how Eastern cats, in particular the Siamese, got their kinked tails, and how the Manx cats lost theirs. The favorite story explaining the origin of kinky-tailed cats (of which there are numerous versions) relates how, long ago, a cat had to guard a chalice or goblet over a long period of time. Unable to remain awake continually it wrapped its tail round the base of the vessel to keep it safe from theft. When the faithful animal was finally relieved of its trust its tail, having remained in the same position for so long, was found to be permanently kinked. And all its offspring have continued to inherit such a tail.

Another story tells of a princess who, wishing to go bathing, placed her rings on her cat's tail and knotted it to keep them secure. The knot remained and was perpetuated through all the following cat generations.

Loss of the Manx cat's tail is usually placed at the time of the Flood. The cat in that faraway time, like the cat of today, was slow in obeying. Noah's command that it board the Ark irritated it. When it finally decided to do as told, Noah was so exasperated that he impatiently closed the Ark's door too soon and accidentally cut off the cat's tail.

A dog and not Noah is blamed for the lost tail in another Ark narrative. After the Ark had grounded, the dog, as was his wont, ran after the cat. The cat was quick enough to escape him but not quick enough to save her tail which was snapped off. To this day her offspring show, by the lack of tails, how narrow was her escape.

XVI
Voice

They no instrument use ever,
  Each is his own flute and viol;
All their noses trumpets are,
  Bellies, drums, and no denial.

They in chorus raise their voices,
  In one general intermezzo,
Playing fugues, as if by Bach,
  Or by Guido of Arezzo.

Wild the symphonies they're singing,
  Like capriccios of Beethoven
Or by Berlioz, who's excelled
  By their strains so interwoven.

HEINRICH HEINE
[*E. A. Bowring*, trans.]

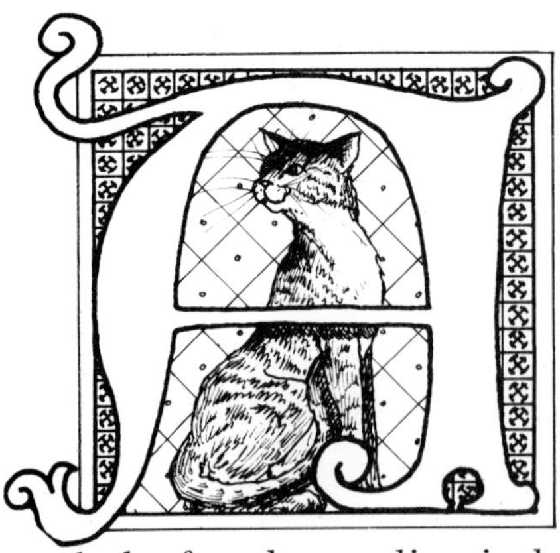

ANYONE who owns a cat may well wonder at the old expression, "liquor that would make a cat speak," because most cats are capable of a great deal of speech without any outside help. Human inadequacy alone keeps us from understanding the variety of sounds with which our pets bombard us. Through voice and action they attempt to converse with us, and their annoyance at not being understood is as amusing as our lack of understanding is deflating. Most cat owners never progress far beyond an understanding of *out, food, hello, take care* and a few other simple concepts. Cats understand human speech and action far better than the human understands that of cats.

The newly born kitten is capable only of purring and distress vocalization. Those investigators who claim that only 16 or so sound patterns are distinguishable in the adult cat say that a 3 month old kitten is capable of only 9 of these. Even to the untrained ear it is obvious that a kitten's speech is limited compared to that of the adult cat.

To express itself vocally the cat uses a great range of sounds. Its meow, purr and caterwaul are unique in the animal kingdom, and human words to describe its repertoire are many if inadequate. Those most commonly heard are spit, hiss, huff and puff, swear, whirl, sing, hum, whine, chatter, yowl, growl, scream, screech. Variant spellings for the word "meow" are also many, an indication of the range obtainable by that familiar sound. It is said that there is no ancient Greek or Latin word for "purr," a fact favoring the assumption that early Greeks and Romans were unfamiliar with the domestic feline or at least did not keep them as house pets.

Because the cat's language is so uniquely expressive and extensive in comparison to that of other animals it has received much study. Dupont de Nemour's and Marvin R. Clark's findings are the best known to people interested in cats, and Ida Mellen gives a résumé of the subject in *The Science and the Mystery of the Cat.* Mildred Moelk's study of cat vocalization published in 1944 (a summary of which appears at the end of this section) is the most recent and generally accepted scientific contribution to the subject. Comprehensive as it is, it does not cover all aspects of the cat's voice, for example the chatter, or machine-gunning, resulting from a cat's excitement and irritation at seeing birds or other prey that are unobtainable.

Vocalization of cats among themselves reaches its peak during the mating season. As discussed in the section on reproduction there are the growls, snarls, spits and yowls which accompany the quarrels and fights of the males. There are the urgent cries of the oestrous female to announce her condition, the cries of the males in reply and the wheedling, coaxing croons of both sexes to indicate their desires. Finally there is the copulatory cry of the female and later her angry rebuffs of the male. Just as the mating behavior follows a certain pattern yet is varied depending on the individuals, so the voice patterns during mating are similar and yet different due to the individual voices.

The mother cat talks to her kittens in distinctive murmurs and chirps. Soft crooning serves to reassure and quiet them much as lullabies soothe the human infant. Every time she approaches her nest after being away from it she murmurs gentle greetings to which the kittens will reply as they grow older. The chirps by which she instructs them and directs their activities are never used at any other time. This is a pity since they are a delight to hear.

Those particular sounds which denote danger and warn the kittens to hide or follow closely are always heeded, but boisterous kittens seldom heed reprimands even though these may turn into growls and other sounds of anger. Only actual chastisement will make them stop chewing on their mother's tail or roughhousing in general. Rather than go to this extreme, however, many females prefer to leave the place of action to get the peace and quiet they desire.

It has been asserted that as in humans, the voice of a male cat can be distinguished from that of a female. That well may be, but there are mighty few of us with ears comparable to those of a cat who no doubt readily distinguishes the difference. And what, if anything, happens to a neutered cat's voice? There are many male cats with high squeaky voices and females with deep melodious meows so that the difference can't be one of pitch. Caterwauling cats, male, female or neuter, range from high to low with such ease, depending on the mood of the moment, that it would be a rare feat to be able to tell one's sex by voice alone. E. S. Russell in *The Behaviour of Animals*, comments on the fact that both sexes of the cat caterwaul: "An increasing severance of the links between voice and hearing on the one hand and love-life on the other is observable among the higher vertebrates. Even the horrible caterwauling of love-sick cats can't be construed as a lovesong designed to attract the female, because both sexes join in the song."

Whether during the mating season or at other times, caterwauling variations are endless. According to a correspondent quoted in R. K. James's *The Angora Cat* there can be regional differences. "He who has only heard caterwauling on English roofs can have no idea of a cat-serenade in Malta. In England it has often a close and painful resemblance to the distressful cries of young children; but in Malta it is identical with the wide range of screams uttered by imps while they are dragging each other into hotter and still hotter pools of brimstone and fire. It is the discord of torment and of rage and of hate, of paroxysms of revenge, and every note grumbles away into despair."

A number of musical compositions give credit to the cat's voice for their inspiration, and no doubt others have inadvertently materialized

Story illustration by Everett Shinn.

from both the pleasant and unpleasant sounds a cat can utter. Addison wrote in *The Spectator*: "A Fellow of the Royal Society who is my good friend, and a great proficient in the mathematical part of music, observes very well that musical instruments took their first rise from the notes of birds and other melodious animals; and what, says he, was more natural than for the first ages of mankind to imitate the voice of a cat that lived under the same roof with them? He added that the cat had contributed more to harmony than any other animal, as we are not only beholden to her for this wind instrument (the cat-call), but for our string music in general."

Although no one has attempted to render caterwauls into a musical score (which should be relatively easy in our electronic age), the simple purr has often been interpreted. Young cats are said to purr in monotone; older cats are credited with two to three notes. S. P. Cheney in *Wood Notes Wild* gave his version and that of Dr. F. Weber of the cat's purr.

"Made close observations this morning on Tim's purring. I find that he varies the intervals. Have now heard him in a perfect fifth. He ranges, then, from one to five of the scale.

"The rhythm also is varied; there is a crescendo and *retardando* as well, and the dynamics are good. So far the higher tone is always given with the inhaling."

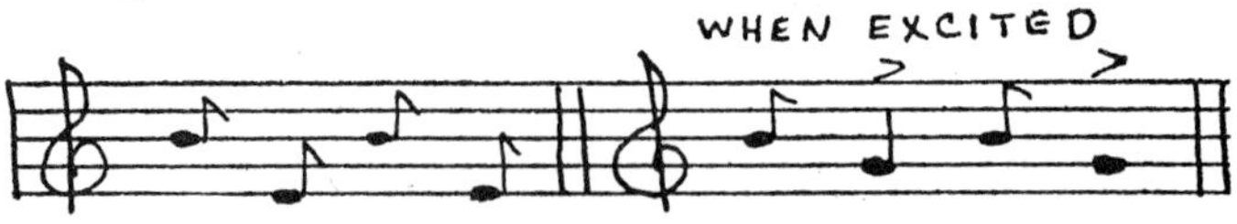

How cats accomplish their purr is still unknown. Since they possess both true and false vocal cords it is thought that the true are used for vocalization and the false for purring, which really doesn't settle anything, but is the most plausible explanation proposed thus far. What *is* known is that the phenomenon originates in the infundibular region of the brain; electrical stimulation of the purring center causes the cat to begin purring immediately.

All cats purr but in some it is inaudible and can be detected only by feeling the vibration that the purr produces. This, too, can be undetectable at times except by special methods. Other cats purr so loudly that the entire room which they are in seems to hum from their song. The intensity is never constant and may fluctuate from one extreme to the other, the degree depending on the height of the cat's feelings.

Purring may continue into the sleep of a cat or begin during sleep, no doubt being initiated through a dream. Although some cats purr when in deep distress or pain the sound usually seems to signify contentment, and extreme happiness in many cats is demonstrated by a deep purr accompanied by drooling. Parturition is usually accompanied by a great deal of purring, and a mother cat nursing her young never seems to stop her dynamo. A cat's contentment is easily transferred to humans through its purr, and many a human problem has been solved as people listen to their pets' avowal that life is fair.

> Whene'er I felt my towering fancy fail,
> I stroked her head, her ears, her tail,
> And, as I stroked, improved my dying song
> From the sweet notes of her melodious tongue.
> Her purrs and mews so evenly kept time,
> She purred in metre and she mewed in rhyme.
>
> JOSEPH GREEN 1733

The Bretons have a folk tale about why cats purr. A king and queen who for years had longed for a daughter finally had one born to them. They were the happiest people on earth except for one thing. A year before the princess was born her birth had been predicted along with a warning by a sorceress. It was the warning that weighed heavily on the hearts of the two monarchs.

"Your daughter will fall dead if she ever gives her hand in marriage to a prince," they had been told. "Heed this advice. Find three pure white cats and let them grow up with your child. Give them balls of two types to play with—balls of gold and balls of linen thread. If they ignore the gold and play with the linen, all will be well, but should they ignore the linen and choose the gold, beware!"

The three cats were duly found and became good friends. Better yet they learned to love their young mistress and she them, and as the months passed and became years the linen balls continued to be the only toys the cats chose to play with. The gold balls would have gathered cobwebs had they not been dusted regularly, and everyone began to forget their original purpose.

When the princess grew old enough to learn how to spin the cats were as happy as she was. They leaped at the wheel as it turned and at the thread as the princess made it. She begged them to leave things alone but they paid no attention to her and continued to play gaily. The queen, happy as she was in their continued neglect of the gold balls, laughed and indulged their frolicking.

The princess was now 16 years old and very beautiful. People came from far and near to see her beauty, and princes continued to ask for her hand in marriage, but she remained indifferent to all. She seemed perfectly content to continue living as she was with her three beloved cats.

One day, however, a prince arrived who was so good and wise and handsome in her eyes that she knew she would marry him at once if he asked. But although he visited the palace often and brought many gifts he never mentioned the subject of marriage. As he was leaving from one of his extended visits she finally could bear it no longer and confessed her love for him, and he, in delighted surprise, expressed his for her.

The cats were in the tower room playing with the linen balls but no sooner had the prince and princess professed their love for each other, than they seemed to see the gold balls for the first time in their lives and gave chase to them. The news spread throughout the palace but it wasn't the princess who was affected by the switch in balls. The prince became gravely ill and nothing the physicians tried helped to cure the strange malady which had struck him down.

In desperation the princess sought the sorceress who had made the prophecy about the cats and balls. What she learned from her was almost as bad as knowing nothing. There was only one almost impossible way to save the prince. Only 27 days remained before Christmas but in that time she would have to spin 10,000 skeins of pure white linen thread if her lover, whose thread of life had reached the breaking point, would live. No hand but hers could spin the 10,000 skeins and the prince would die at midnight of Christmas night if they weren't finished by then.

The sadly frightened girl rushed home to her spinning wheel and worked steadily until dawn. More discouraged than tired she gazed at the little she had accomplished and burst into tears. Through her sobs she seemed to hear her cats call to her.

Ready to believe anything she gazed lovingly at them. "If you only knew what was wrong I know you'd help me if you could," she told them.

"We know what's needed and can and will help you," they replied. "After all, we don't have hands but paws so we can do the spinning for you and no one will be able to object. Now please let us get to work. Even for us the time left is very short."

And so it was that the three cats began to spin, each at a wheel provided for it. And spin they did—rapidly and beautifully. All day the three wheels hummed and when they were silent as evening came the princess looked into the room to find her beloved cats sound asleep next to 300 skeins of thread.

As the days passed and the skeins grew in number the prince's health began to mend and the princess's spirits soared. On Christmas day the 10,000 skeins were ready for the sorceress and the prince was almost well.

The sorceress was more than pleased with the cats' work and told the princess to be sure and show her gratitude to the cats for saving the life of her lover. Such a reminder was unnecessary. The girl had always loved them as much as she thought possible but her gratitude had increased even this great love. She gave them all her jewels which she found they had always greatly admired, and at the wedding feast, decked in these jewels, they sat in a place of honor on magnificent cushions.

As the feast continued the cats curled up contentedly on their cushions and suddenly from all three came a pleasant hum. It was the wonderful, happy sound of purring, the reward, the cats explained to the princess, they had received for their help to her. Strangely enough the sound was very much like the whir and hum of a spinning wheel. And from that day to this cats have continued to purr whenever they feel contented.

"Vocalizing in the house-cat; a phonetic and functional study" by Mildred Moelk is well worth reading in its entirety. The author generalizes in the introduction that "The house-cat, unlike man, has enforced upon it no model of traditional language and no standard of correct pronunciation to which it must conform. Variety of phonetic form in the vocalizing of these animals is due to an unstudied modification of a voiced column of air during inhalation or exhalation, by means of tensional changes in the mouth and throat, by speed and energy of the column of air, and by the extent, time, and rate of the opening of the mouth. Thus vocalization basically derives its form from the constitution and the physiology of the cat. Association with man plays a large part in conditioning the vocalizing situation, but it does not affect the phonetic form, except in so far as such conditioning affects the strength and temper of the vocalizing effort. In other words, this conditioning affects utterance indirectly by way of the cat's somatic condition, not directly through a choice among vocal patterns. The fact that vocalizing is not artificially stylized in cats into conventional patterns or words means that an indefinitely wide variation of sound and of patterning is possible."

Moelk places vocal sounds of the cat into three classes depending on their intensity.

1. Murmurs, or sounds produced with the mouth shut. These include
   a. The purr, produced by continuous vibration, its rhythm derived from the breathing rhythm, each inhalation or exhalation consisting of a number of readily distinguishable vibrations.
   b. The purr-like sound used in greeting or request and differing from the purr in being a continuous sound rather than separately discernible vibrations.
   c. The call, varying from the soft appeal to the loud demand.
   d. The acknowledgement or confirmation, a short single murmur, coming when the cat gets, or is about to get, something that it wants, such as its meal.

In the kitten (up to three months) murmurs are limited to the purr, the greeting and the grunt.

2. Vowel patterns, or sounds produced with the mouth first opened and then gradually closed. These are divided into
   a. The demand which may develop from the coaxing murmur or begin as a loud clamor. Both can step up in intensity.
   b. The begging demand.
   c. Bewilderment, when the cat discovers that things aren't turning out as expected.
   d. Complaint, which can build up from bewilderment and in turn become a scolding cry.
   e. The milder forms of the mating cry.
   f. The anger wail (see "The Growl" below)

It is chiefly through the vowel sounds that cats' voices differ from each other and become distinctive. Here, too, kitten sounds are more limited. They are limited to the demand-wail and the sounds for distress and bafflement.

3. Strained intensity patterns, or sounds produced while the mouth is held tensely open in one position. This results in
   a. The growl. "When two cats are lined up nose to nose, growling away, ready to fight, each waiting for the other to make the first move, the next step vocally is the wail . . . produced by gradually opening the mouth wider during growling and closing it again to the growl position. This preliminary wailing is long drawn out, the mouth opened and closed slowly and steadily . . . Wailing, with modification, is continued throughout the fight . . . Slighter wailing, which may be termed angry protest, also occurs occasionally in connection with the growl in highly annoying situations which do not lead to fighting."
   b. The snarl.
   c. The mating cry, a much modified form of demand.
   d. Pain.
   e. Refusal.
   f. Spitting.

Strained intensity sounds in the kitten are the growl, the spit and the sound denoting anger.

In an attempt to reach a certain goal the cat follows a definite pattern. In the human household it vocalizes chiefly for two reasons—food and asking to have a door opened. Intensity, quality and quantity of vocalization depend, of course, on the strength and type of need. Often, too, the voice response comes automatically, the result of an oft-repeated stimulus such as a can being opened. The kitten will wail to attain its goal, the adult cat coax or demand unless the need becomes so strong that, like the kitten, it breaks into the begging wail.

Body position may take the place of vocalization in the adult—for example sitting in front of a door that it wishes to be opened. If the mute appeal brings no results the cat will usually give voice to its desires, first a murmur, then on to a loud demand. Success in the demand may elicit purring; failure will bring on the meow of bewilderment, then complaint.

In a turnabout of the above situation, the cat may be offered something which it usually finds desirable but to which circumstances have made it indifferent. If its feelings are sufficiently aroused from an affront of this sort it will give voice to them with the refusal pattern.

A petted cat will generally begin to purr regardless of who is doing the petting. Naturally it won't let any stranger be so familiar with it, but those it allows to approach and stroke it will be rewarded with a purr almost every time. A loved person (usually but not always one who supplies it with creature comforts) tends to be greeted with a happy murmur which becomes a purr when the welcome is returned.

A cat uncomfortable in either mind or body needs little encouragement to voice its discomfort, especially if the listener is sympathetic. And how true Moelk's observation is, that "nearly any unoccupied cat who is not in the state of maximal comfort, as represented by drowsing upon a full stomach in a warm, soft, safe spot with friendly hominids at hand, is in a sufficiently uncomfortable and disturbed state to find ready release through the noises of complaint."

The author enlarges greatly on all the above vocalizations which can more or less be considered stylized responses to given situations, including also some cat to cat talk. What she does not touch on are what might be called "conversations" between cat and human and cat and cat. Cats frequently carry on lengthy discussions with people who talk to them and whom they like, and in the many-cat household talk occurs among the cats themselves. The topics discussed, to judge from sound and action, range from mere chatting, both pleasant to unpleasant, to a buildup of belligerence. It could be said that the conversations parallel human conversations except for their relative brevity. In both cat-human and cat-cat talk, the sounds from the cat are tremendously varied, and one can well believe those who credit it with a large vocabulary. Moelk credits it with the following sounds: letters as in father, hat, let, comma, machine, yet, note; as in the French oeuf, and eux; food; as in the French vu or the German über; fun, go, halt, men, men, rung, rat, rat, we. These are varied by prolongation, nasalization, stressing, inflection, and wavering or discontinuity.

XVII
Genetics and Geography

SOME years ago I had extensive correspondence with a Japanese gentleman who was writing a cat book. I knew no Japanese and his English was limited but we managed to learn new facts about cats from each other. He sent me an old print by Yeisen of a young woman holding a cat in her arms—a piebald, short-tailed cat like those depicted so often in Japanese prints. Now, I thought, I'll find out the truth about these cats, and I wrote asking about them.

Mr. Kimura answered: "Such Japanese domestic cat as you have mentioned is not so specific species but very popular in Japan. According to the Japanese classical literature such domestic cat was introduced into ancient Japan from ancient China more than 1000 years ago.

"The tail length varies very much. There are cats white with black and light brown spots besides those white with black spots. My pet cat is tiger-striped Tom Cat.

"Most Japanese cat fanciers pay very little attention to the ordinary Japanese cat, unfortunately. And so I am sorry . . ."

I was sorry, too, that he could supply no more information than that. The people whose names he gave me could give no further detail. But the thing that had bothered me the most was settled. Some Japanese cats' tails are naturally short and are not docked as you so often read that they are. The short-tailed cat in Japanese prints is undoubtedly a form of the geneticists' kinky-tailed cat described below.

An understanding of the variation in cats throughout the world is being gained from a not too intensive investigation by geneticists of cat populations in chosen locations. Such investigations are difficult to perform and evaluate but the results justify the work involved and we can hope that the program will continue and become more thorough. General conclusions from the studies to date are incorporated in the summary of cat genetics that follows, and the accompanying chart compares the results on selected characteristics. Descriptions of and inheritance in specific varieties are not included; they are outside the scope of this book.

Cats must agree with the human evaluation of them—that structurally they are well-nigh perfect for the sort of life they are intended to lead—because they have changed little in the centuries that we have known them. The mutations that have occurred have been, for the most part, minor as well as temporary, and human attempts to alter the basic cat structure have accomplished little, while attempts to perpetuate variations that do occur are not always successful.

Natural selection continues to be an important factor in the evolution of the cat, unlike other domestic animals. Arbitrary choice of a mate continues despite increasing environmental difficulties. Through controlled matings geneticists in the laboratory and breeders in the cattery have discovered many whys and wherefores concerning natural selection but these facts are few compared to what remains unsolved.

GLOSSARY

In a discussion of genetics, no matter how elementary, some technical words are unavoidable. For those completely unfamiliar with the subject, the words used in what follows, with their definitions are:

1. *Allele.* One of two or more contrasting characters transmitted by alternative genes.

2. *Autosome.* Any ordinary paired chromosome as distinguished from a sex chromosome.

3. *Chromosome.* Small, dark-staining, more or less rod-shaped bodies in the nucleus of a cell. They contain the genes or hereditary factors, and are constant in a number for each species.

4. *Epistatic.* Superimposed; said of a Mendelian character which is superimposed upon another, hiding the appearance of the latter.

5. *Gene.* The biologic unit of heredity, self-reproducing and located in a definite position on a particular chromosome.

6. *Genotype.* The fundamental hereditary constitution of an individual.

7. *Heterozygous.* Possessing different alleles in regard to a given characteristic.

8. *Homozygous.* Possessing an identical pair of alleles in regard to a given characteristic.

9. *Phenotype.* The outwardly visible expression of the hereditary constitution of an organism.

CHROMOSOMES. Not much investigation has been done on the chromosomes of felines. The domestic cat has 19 pairs, 38 chromosomes in all, the same number as the lion and Chinese leopard, and the characteristics of these are similar in all three animals. As in man, there is a female X-chromosome and a male Y-chromosome, the former being of medium size, the latter very small, approximately half the length of the X. Also, as in man, faulty division in the chromosomes can occur to produce abnormal individuals. Some male tortoise-shell cats, those freaks of the cat world, have been found to possess abnormal sex-chromosome combinations, an explanation in part as to how and why these cats occur.

Old descriptions of cats tell of the rarity of these toms in the Western World. They also tell of regional variations in cats: the tri-colored from Spain, the Chartreuse from France, the long-haired from the Near East, the tabbies common everywhere—all interesting but, like today's varieties, beyond the scope of this book.

THE CAT'S COAT

Coat color and pattern were and are the most diversified part of the cat, the easiest to study genetically and to change through selective breeding. Cat colors vary in intensity but basically are red (also called ginger, marmalade, orange or yellow), cream, black, gray (also called maltese or blue), white, ticked (also called agouti) silver, brown. Cats can be one solid (self) color or have more than one color arranged in a pattern or random spotting as in tabbies and tortoiseshells respectively.

TABBY. Today, tabbies, or tiger cats as they are sometimes called, continue to be the most common type of cat throughout the world. This fact, as has been mentioned elsewhere, is one of the principal reasons supporting the accepted theory that the domestic cat's ancestors were two tabby-marked wild cats, *Felis lybica* and *F. silvestris.*

A tabby cat is one whose fur is a combination of solid striping and ticking. Generally speaking, the designation of tabby means the melanistic cat whose striping is black, but the red-striped cat is as much a tabby as the black-striped.

You may have noticed that the fur on the foreheads of cats forms a pattern of its own due to differences in length. The distinctness of the pattern varies from cat to cat becoming particularly obvious in a dirty light colored cat where the ridges formed by the longer hairs are well defined from the dirt. The color pattern in tabbies follows this fur-length pattern, the tabby stripes coinciding with the shorter hairs or furrows.

Tabbies fall into three main groups according to their patterning: the striped or mackerel tabby, the blotched tabby and the lined tabby. Each of these is not distinct but grades into the others.

Striped tabby is the ancestral form of the tabby pattern. The ground color varies from grey to brown, with a yellow tinge, and is ticked. The black stripes are not always continuous but may form broken lines. On head, body, limbs and tail they are relatively constant from one individual to another. Their resemblance to the pattern in wild cats is very marked.

Blotched tabby color and markings on the face, lower legs and tail agree with that of the striped tabby, but the stripes on the body have become whorls and spirals. This difference in pattern is considered to be a mutation from the striped tabby and an extremely successful one. It apparently originated in Europe and was already common there by the middle of the 18th century. It is this form of the domestic cat that Linnaeus describes and gives the name *Felis catus* in his *Systema Naturae* (see chapter on general natural histories). So successful is the blotched tabby mutation that striped tabbies are becoming uncommon in parts of Europe, by comparison, and, if the trend continues, will soon be extinct.

Blotched tabbies reached India by the middle of the 19th century and have not yet begun to exceed the striped type there. The striped and uniform Abyssinian tabbies are still the commonest throughout the entire East. Patterning of the Eastern blotched tabby is still unstable and varies considerably, being readily distinguishable from that of its English counterpart which has become more or less standardized.

The extremely high frequency of blotched tabbies in London in no way implies that the same proportion is found throughout England. Studies of cat populations in other parts of England point to the probability that London cats are not consistent with the rest of the country.

There is nothing to indicate why natural selection favors blotched tabby over other tabby types. Human preference for it, which would increase its numbers through artificial selection, is not indicated. In Queensland feral blotched tabbies have been reported as holding their own. This, in addition to the data showing the great increase of blotched types elsewhere, reveals that the mutation is successful in all types of environment, and is here to stay. No possible wild ancestors for the cat exhibit this pattern.

Lined, or Abyssinian tabbies, differ from the ancestral striped tabby by having narrower striping. The Abyssinian cat is considered an extreme lined tabby where the stripes have almost disappeared except on the face. Stripes on other parts of the body as well are not uncommon in these cats.

The large percentage of Abyssinian tabbies in South and Southeast Asia suggests the possibility of hybridization between the domestic cat and the wild cat *Felis chaus*, found in the area. According to experts, however, this is highly improbable. *F. chaus* is a large wild cat, and Eastern domestic cats average much smaller than those in Europe and the United States, making matings between the two unlikely. Still more significant is the fact that the pattern of *F. chaus*, although it resembles that of the lined tabby, is only superficially similar.

Tabby variants other than the above three are infrequently encountered. One type is the spotted tabby where the stripes have degenerated from broken lines into spots. Another looks as unlike a tabby as the unlined Abyssinian. Its entire body is solid grey, but face, legs and tail show some striping.

Striping in tabbies shows a wide variation and it has been found that the modifications are not due to a common cause but to independent genes. A limited number of matings made by P. W. Whiting in 1918 gave the following results. (I have found no other attempt made at unravelling tabby inheritance.)

Lined X Lined → 2 Lined; 2 Blotched
Lined X Striped → 17 Lined; 2 Striped
Lined X Blotched → 12 Lined; 4 Blotched
Striped X Blotched → 19 Striped; 8 Blotched
Blotched X Blotched → 4 Blotched

Red and Tortoiseshell. Rufinism is produced in the cat's coat by a gene which modifies melanistic development in the tabby. Red rather than black stripes are the result, and the ticking that is present in melanistic tabbies is almost eliminated.

No possible ancestral form of the cat shows the color red. It is incompletely recessive to black, and tortoiseshell is the heterozygote. Tortoiseshells are red and black or red and tabby with intergrades between the two. The two colors can be distributed in splotches or be broken down into smaller and smaller spots resulting in the salt-and-pepper effect of roan horses. The color in larger patches is considered the true tortoiseshell.

The gene for red is sex-linked although recently red has been found to be autosomal and recessive in the Abyssinian breed. Its sex-linked character is demonstrated through the following matings.

Male		*Female*		*Male*	*Female*
red	X	red	→	red	red
red	X	black	→	black	tortoiseshell
red	X	tortoiseshell	→	red	red
			→	black	tortoiseshell
black	X	tortoiseshell	→	black	black
			→	red	tortoiseshell
black	X	red	→	red	tortoiseshell
black	X	black	→	black	black

Black females and tortoiseshell males occur in some of these matings, and no satisfactory explanation for their appearance has yet been found. Why the tortoiseshell male is almost always sterile also remains a mystery. Extensive breeding experiments have been in progress for over 50 years in an effort to discover the reason for this cat's occurrence and its sterility, and various explanations have been proposed. The variety of these explanations has led to the opinion that these cats are not the result of one type of situation but of many different types. Literature on the subject is too extensive, technical and inconclusive to be reviewed here. Anyone wishing to acquaint himself with it should consult genetics periodicals.

In the world cat populations studied to date the incidence for red in New England is found to lie between that of London and Singapore. The frequency for red increases gradually from Western Europe to Eastern Asia, just as the frequency for blotched tabby decreases. In Asia, the gene for red is between three and four times more frequent than in London. As yet, there is no indication where, and whether, the intermediate frequency in the United States enters into the scheme. Human preference for the shift cannot be ruled out completely. However, the method employed in taking the cat censuses revealed preferences for some cat types but none either for or against red anywhere. Preponderance of red in the East results in a good percentage of male tortoiseshells, and much of the research on this cat is consequently being carried on in Japan.

THE ALBINO ALLELES: FULL COLOR THROUGH SILVER, BURMESE AND SIAMESE TO ALBINO. The genetics of this series is only partially known. Here, red coloring is reduced very quickly, black more slowly, modifying to brown and increasing in thermosensitivity.

1. Silver is recessive to Full Color.
2. Silver crossed with Black gives Smoke.
3. Burmese is completely dominant to Siamese and is considered a mutation from the Siamese.
4. Siamese is an imperfect albinism and is recessive. (See section on Integument for a discussion of the effects of temperature on fur color.) The Siamese factor is becoming common in urban cat populations both in the United States and Europe.
5. In the Silver, Burmese, and Siamese the extremities, i.e. ears, nose, feet and tail, are darker than the body. This is emphasized when the genes are combined with black.
6. In the gradation from Full Color to Albinism the eye color as well as the fur color becomes modified.

MALTESE (OR BLUE) DILUTION. The presence of this character dilutes the color of the fur. Through it Black becomes Slate Grey (Blue) and Red becomes Cream. It appears to be recessive.

NON-AGOUTI. Self Black is the alternative to agouti, or ticking, and is generally epistatic to tabby striping. Tabby stripes can be seen as a ghost pattern in the black kitten the same way that spots can be detected in the black leopard. In strong light the pattern can be seen in some adults. A shift from black to stripes can also take place. In such cases the kittens are born black with no indication of a pattern; their noses are brown like those of tabbies. As they mature tabby markings begin to appear, the black stripes being very broad, and the ticking silver: a casual glance at one of these cats will give the impression of a full black.

Melanism is frequently encountered in wild animal populations, so a relatively even occurrence of black cats throughout the world can be expected and does actually occur. Black cats are more frequent in London and Japan than elsewhere, but the numbers are not significantly higher. The British have always considered it lucky to own a black cat and the large percentage of these in London reflects this human preference. An explanation for the greater number in Japan is not known; the tortoiseshell rather than the black cat brings luck in that country.

DOMINANT BLACK. Considered to be an extension of melanism by a dominant gene, the inheritance of dominant black has not yet been completely worked out.

DOMINANT WHITE. The result of a dominant gene, the pure white cat is, nevertheless, uncommon throughout the world. Selective disadvantages have been proposed as an explanation for this, the two principal ones being that the color is too conspicuous and is associated with deafness. Pure white cats can have blue or yellow eyes or one eye blue and the other yellow. It is the blue-eyed white that tends to be deaf, and records of this fact date back to 1828. Deaf white cats with other eye colors have also been reported. In early literature highly bred Persians were reported to be deaf frequently, a fact which no longer seems to be the case.

Dominant white and polydactyly, often linked together, have been found to assort independently and to have a minimum recombination value of 25%.

Brown or Chocolate. Brown is recessive and is of relatively recent origin. It is thought to have originated through Siamese, and its genetics is not yet completely understood.

White Spotting (Piebald) The degree of white spotting ranges from a few white hairs on the throat to a completely white cat. The placement of the spots in the progression to all-white is not random but follows a loose order.

1. A bit of white on the throat or chest
2. Spots on the feet; in the armpits or groins; on the belly
3. Spreading of the spots over the legs and sides of the body and around the neck
4. The white encroaching on the color and breaking it into patches on head, back and tail
5. The white covering most of the body and the color reduced to a few small random spots

There is evidence of an independent inheritance of restricted white spotting and dominant white spotting, but the genetics of spotting in general is not known. Like the color red it is incompletely recessive.

Not only is white spotting commoner in the East than elsewhere but the spotting is also more extensive. Compared with those in London almost three times as many Singapore cats have over two-thirds of their coat white. Calcutta cats are also heavily white. This high percentage of white with a correspondingly low percentage of black could be the result of an equatorial climate. The intensity of solar radiation close to the equator may result in natural selection for white over black.

POLYDACTYLY

The gene for super-scratchers as they have been called is dominant but not lethal as it was once thought to be.

Polydactyls in the New England states have their epicenter in Boston where they are greatly favored over cats having a normal number of toes. Elsewhere around the world they are relatively rare, being found

"Longhair" by Henriette Ronner.

"Cat and Snake" by Katherine Schmidt.
(The Metropolitan Museum of Art)

sporadically in isolated sections. Where they do exist there tends to be a high concentration of them. With fanciers now breeding for extra-toed cats they are bound to become more common.

EYES

At birth all cats' eyes are blue. The color in adult domestic short hairs ranges from grey-green through yellow, the yellow extending into orange and copper in the purebred. Some coat-color genes affect eye color, but eye color is not determined by one gene alone.

Grey-blue eyes are found with a silver coat, topaz-blue with Burmese, and opalescent-blue with Siamese. The squint or crossed eyes in Siamese is also an inherited character.

FUR TYPE

Long fur is recessive to short fur. Castration in male cats can produce longer fur and confuse the genetic picture.

In the survey of Singapore cats, none was found with long hair. As with the color black, long hair may be at a selective disadvantage in an equatorial climate.

Rex type fur is due to a single recessive gene; it masks the dilute tabby pattern. Hairlessness is also recessive. It seldom appears and when it does has not been successful. Breeders, however, have come to the rescue, and hairless cats are now obtainable for a price. A pair of Siamese in France consistently produced some hairless offspring which, mated with each other, were found to breed true. This mutation appeared most recently in Canada and apparently has been successfully preserved by breeders who claim it as a new breed and have given it the name "Sphynx." Hairlessness does not mean that the cats are completely bald; their body is covered with a very fine downy fuzz.

KINKY TAILS

Kinky-tailed cats are exclusively Eastern. The only time they make their appearance in the Western world is through the Siamese or other cats whose origin was Eastern. Kinky tails should not be confused with short tails, which 1.3% of the cats in the London census were found to have. These abbreviated tails are manifestations of the Manx factor in British cats which is in no way connected with the so-called kinky tails.

Kinks in individual tails vary. There may be only one slight distal bend or a tight spiral which reduces the tail to approximately one-third of its normal length. The extreme is a tail which looks like a rosette or pom-pom. The degree of distortion depends on the number of caudal vertebrae affected by the anomaly. These not only are individually distorted but fuse with each other making it impossible to untwist the kinks.

Hong Kong had the smallest number of kinky tails found in East and Southeast Asia—about one-third of the cat population. Four northern Malay states averaged two-thirds kinky tails, and Singapore topped that with 69%. Such a preponderance of distorted tails points to their superiority over straight tails for a tropical climate, but what they can offer a cat in a hot climate that straight tails can't is anyone's guess. Human selection is definitely ruled out, so we have a problem similar to the blotched tabby in Europe.

MANX

Of interest to both geneticist and anatomist, the Manx cat has a good share of scientific literature devoted to it, probably second only to the tortoiseshell tom so far as cat types go.

The Manx phenotype is due to an autosomal lethal factor. Variation in the tail length—from the dimple of the genuine Manx to a respectable tail—has been traced to an apparently incomplete penetration of the tailless gene. The presence of a tail of any length from this lack of penetrance assures the cat of a normal life providing it is not destroyed at birth by the breeder. The true Manx will suffer from its abnormalities as long as it lives. A malfunctioning of the anal sphincter muscles is one of its more annoying afflictions and can become a problem.

The entire vertebral column and not just the tail is affected by the Manx factor although most of the reduction in the length and number of vertebrae is concentrated posteriorly. Vertebrae can be missing in the lumbar and sacral regions as well as in the caudal. The greater these deletions, the greater are the associated malformations. And the greater the malformations the greater becomes the infant mortality rate. Cats pay a high price for the loss of their tails.

SOME CONCLUSIONS FROM THE CAT CENSUSES

1. Random mating is indicated in all areas, no significant difference being found between the adult cat and kitten populations. There is very little evidence of human selection except for a slight tendency toward uncommon types.

2. In the East female cats surpass the males in number probably because they are considered better mousers. In the West males are preferred because the nuisance of getting rid of kittens is not wanted. In the East next to no males are castrated; in the West a large proportion are.

3. Cities seem to provide a peculiar environment for cat inheritance. Both Paris and London cat populations are significantly inconsistent with the rural areas surrounding them. For example, there is an extremely low frequency for red in Paris whereas the country surrounding it has higher frequencies than those in London. The same applies to the high ratio of blotched tabbies in London in comparison to outlying areas, as already mentioned.

4. The cat population of the northeastern United States probably came from the same gene pool as London cats, and Paris and London cat populations would appear to have a common origin.

5. Cats in the northeastern United States appear to belong to a single, stable, and distinct gene pool.

6. The frequency for blue dilution in London has declined rapidly during the last 150 years. This is brought out by the fact that this mutant in the northeastern United States (the cat population of which was established from England by the mid-17th century) and in eastern Australia (whose population was also established from England but not earlier than the beginning of the 19th century) are very similar to each other but very different from that of London. The same holds true for the blotched tabby.

7. Shifts in gene frequencies have been taking place in western Europe for over three centuries.

8. London, Paris and rural France show a general homogeneity in cat populations as does the northeastern United States.

9. Paris cats are more similar to London cats than to rural France cats.

10. On the average, the alleles for darker coats have higher fre-

quencies in urban areas than in rural ones, a characteristic shared by other animals.

HYBRIDS AND BREEDS

The weird, unhappy product of tabby's indiscretion,
Who sacrificed the spotless name that was her proud possession,
Now roams in hybrid misery among the loveless hills,
The hapless child of selfish sins, the fruit of thoughtless thrills,
"My father was a rabbit and my mother was a cat,"
He wails in shame and loneliness—"Now who can equal that?
I'm just a mixture and a mess; I'm neither cat nor rabbit.
If you insist on naming me, just label me 'catabbit.'
My curse on fragile tabby cats with tendencies to swoon
For Casanova bunnies in the fullness of the moon!"

JACK BURROUGHS

Many people still believe that rabbit-cats, cabbits, catabbits, or whatever you want to call them, are an actuality, especially after they see a Manx-type cat for the first time. The short tail and hopping gait resulting from long hind and short front legs certainly belong more to a rabbit than a cat. In extreme cases the front quarters of such an animal look and move like a cat while the hind quarters appear all rabbit.

Logical as the conclusion is—that these cats have to be the result of a cat-rabbit mating—it is as impossible as this tall-tale published in 1858 in *Yankee Notions:*

"A cat belonging to a widow lady in Ohio, lately sat upon a dozen of duck's eggs and continued her attention until the eggs were hatched, and there is now a fine brood of six young ones, half duck and half cat, having duck heads and cat tails; but what is more wonderful, they mew and quack alternately."

The only authentic cat hybrids are those resulting from the mating of a cat with a bobcat or other small wildcat, and this doesn't happen as frequently as stories would have you believe because of limitations such as chance meeting and size discrepancy. The American coon cat has no raccoon ancestors. It is a large and powerful breed of cat with fur approximating a coon's in length, so that one with a blotched-tabby type of coat does resemble a raccoon superficially.

The American Cat Association, the first and oldest cat association in

VARIATION IN CAT POPULATIONS
GENE FREQUENCY

	Tabby Striped	*Tabby Lined*	*Tabby Blotched*	*Non-Agouti*	*Red*	*Silver*	*Siamese*	*Long Hair*	*Blue Dilution*	*Dominant White*	* *White Spotting*
New York City	?	.004	.473	.752	.145	.130	.069	.130	.443	.013	?
Rochester, N.Y.	?	.044	.444	.643	.196	?	?	?	.421	.007	?
Boston	.557	—	.443	.642	.193	?	?	.302	.426	.022	.440
Philadelphia	?	—	.48	.68	.262	—	—	.23	.47	.01	?
N. Carolina (W.)	?	—	.20	.58	.067	?	—	?	.40	—	?
Atlanta, Ga.	?	?	.481	.703	.224	—	—	.250	.415	.031	.526
Columbus, Ohio	?	—	.312	.637	.289	—	—	.394	.501	.01	?
Chicago	?	—	ca .34	.714	.225	.44	?	.37	.455	.02	.476
London	.185	.002	.814	.762	.107	.202	?	.09	.142	.004	.607
Paris	.215	.001	.76	.74	.066	.19	.10	.27	.33	.015	.640
Rural France	.386	—	.614	.640	.148	.227	—	.167	.286	.006	?
Mayenne	?	—	.58	.66	.140	.26	?	.18	.26	.005	?
Chamonix	.24	—	.76	.70	.12	.25	—	.29	.31	.01	?
Marseille	.31	—	.69	.70	.07	.15	—	.28	.30	.002	?
Venice	?	—	.483	.579	.058	.60	—	?	.348	.007	?
The Hague	.34	.004	.66	.66	.21	.32	.04	.18	.26	.013	?
Reunion	.63	.05	.32	.76	.25	—	.24	—	.33	—	.05
Bloemfontein	.52	—	.48	.78	.08	.38	—	.13	.49	.02	—
Brisbane	.315	—	.685	.815	.14	?	?	.17	.455	.022	.650
Melbourne	.393	—	.607	.849	.14	?	?	?	.468	.039	.375
San Francisco	?	—	.50	.70	.32	?	?	?	.13	.02	?
Caracas	?	?	?	.77	.149	?	—	.264	.310	.001	?
New Zealand	?	—	?	.81	?	?	—	.47	.33	.036	?
Bangkok	?	.11	—	.76	?	?	.29	—	?	.02	?
Singapore	.651	.24	.113	.604	.315	.31	.13	—	.128	.012	.754
Mishima +, Japan	Common	?	?	.79	.39	?	?	?	?	.02	?

*Phenotype Frequency

this country, recognizes the coon cat as a specific breed. It also recognizes the breeds which are listed here in order to show how basically stable the cat is genetically. Body conformation in all the cats is limited to the stocky body with round head of the Persian type and the slender body with triangular head of the Siamese type, with intergrades or combinations of the two.

Persian. White with blue, copper-blue, copper or odd-eye eyes; cream, black, blue, red, smoke (black or blue) with copper eyes; silver and shaded silver with blue-green eyes; cream, blue, brown, red, mackerel and blotched tabbies with copper eyes and silver tabbies with blue-green eyes; tortoiseshells either blue-cream, calico, tortoiseshell and tortoiseshell and white with copper eyes; cameos either shell, shaded, smoke or tabby depending on the distribution of the red and creamy-white colors, also with copper eyes.

Peke-face Persians. In red or red tabby only with copper eyes.

Balinese. Essentially a long-haired Siamese (lilac, blue, chocolate or seal points with blue eyes).

Himalayan. Essentially a Persian with Siamese coloring lilac, blue, chocolate, seal, red, or tortie points with blue eyes).

Sacred Cat of Burma. Also called Burman. Essentially a Himalayan with white paws. Lilac, blue, chocolate and seal points with blue eyes.

Maine Coon Cat. Emphasis on body conformation; all else incidental.

Domestic Shorthair. Coloring as in the Persian except that the eyes are gold rather than copper.

Colorpoint Shorthair. Points red, tortie and lynx, the last having either lilac, blue, chocolate or seal points; all with blue eyes.

Albino Foreign Shorthair. Essentially a Siamese with a solid white coat and pink eyes.

Lavender Foreign Shorthair. Solid mauve or lavender with deep green eyes.

British Blue. Emphasis on compact body conformation. Blue with orange, yellow or copper eyes.

Russian Blue. Emphasis on plushy coat. Silver-tipped blue with lighter lavender color preferred; vivid green eyes.

Burmese. Intergrade type body; sable brown or beige (champagne) with yellow to golden eyes.

Havana Brown. Intergrade type body; solid, warm mahogany brown with chartreuse green eyes.

KORAT. Intergrade type body; solid blue tipped with silver; brilliant green or amber-green eyes.

ABYSSINIAN. Emphasis on ticking and color which can be either red or ruddy; eyes gold, green or hazel.

SIAMESE. Lilac, blue, chocolate or seal points with blue eyes.

A few other cat types are not yet recognized as breeds in the Fancy. One is the "hairless," already referred to. Another, which appears to be new to *Felis catus,* is wire-haired with a coat similar to that of the Wire-hair terrier.

As yet, thank goodness—recognized or not—all cats still look and act like cats, and let's hope they always will. Let's hope, too, that breeders will finally cease distorting the innate beauty and intelligence of basic cat as they persist in doing, particularly in the Siamese.

XVIII
Disease

THE first report of disease in cats would appear to be in 1348 when the Black Plague was rampant in Europe. At Rome and elsewhere it was noted that cats, dogs, fowls and other animals, besides humans, were taking sick and dying. Later, many other instances of cat epidemics were recorded, a few in detail. Noteworthy ones were as follows.

1414. Germany. A severe form of dysentery affecting horses, cattle, dogs and cats as well as man ravaged the country.

1513. England. An epidemic among cats only occurred, but no details were given.

1578. Paris. An unspecified disease of both cats and poultry raged throughout the city.

1613. Constantinople. The plague in man still persisted. Because cats, too, were still suffering from some sort of epidemic they were transported to Scutari under the supposition that they were the cause of the plague in humans.

1630. Padua. A contagious disease among cats was reported.

1671–72. Westphalia, Germany. A disease, almost always fatal to the cat who contracted it, spread throughout the province. It was described thus: "The head was covered with scabies, and at first the ears were inwardly crusted with scaly matter. The eyes seemed as if they were covered with a film, although the animals could see until suppuration took place; after this period they died. Sleep continually oppressed them; and so drowsy were they, that they appeared as if they had heard that celebrated speech on the joys of sleep after dinner. The skin disease did not proceed further than the head and neck. There was scarcely a house in which some were not infected; and unless common rumour be false, it seemed that it could be communicated from one to another, as well as generated spontaneously. As a proof of this, it attacked some which were closely shut up, so that they might be free from all contagion from the diseased. Some are supposed to have been cured by the fat of a whale; in the case of most, however, medicine was of no avail, and few survived."

1679. Vienna. Great epidemic during which cats and birds died.

1713. Hungary. In Kaskov, an epizooty raged among cats during the spring, and so deadly was it, that in many villages not one survived. As a consequence mice increased by leaps and bounds, and they did great damage.

1724. Silesia. In April mice died in huge numbers from some sort of disease and lay in heaps in granaries and elsewhere. Cats and pigs refused to eat them so they had to be collected and buried.

1762. Lyons. An "eruption of itch," apparently often fatal, attacked cats.

1763. France. In Gatinais cats were attacked by a malady that resembled a disease then rampant among dogs.

1764. Moravia. Milk from cows infected with a form of fever transmitted the disease to cats, dogs and people who drank it.

1765. France. "The disease amongst dogs and cats has continued throughout the year, though not so extensively as in the last year, but with the same accidents. Some cats have been attacked by itch, which has made them blind." Mem. Ac. Royale des Sciences, 1764–65.

1774. France. Cats, dogs and pigs were blamed by some for a plague that broke out among the cattle, the symptoms of the disease being analogous in all these animals.

1782–84. France. Around Chartres an epizooty prevailed among both cats and dogs. Symptoms were the same in both animals. Farmers in the area, who usually had at least 20 cats each, lost all of them during the winters of 1782, '83 and '84. The disease was apparently distemper.

1791. England. "An epidemic distemper prevails at this time among those domestic animals the cats, which ends in madness. Valerian root boiled in milk is a specific; but if they refuse to lap it, they should be directly killed, to prevent the most fatal consequences to families." Dr. Darwin of Darby wrote of this disease: "The *parotitis suppurans,* or mumps with irritated fever, is at times epidemic among cats, and may be called *parotitis felina*; as I have reason to believe, from the swellings under the jaws, which frequently suppurate, and are very fatal to those animals. In the village of Haywood, in Staffordshire, I remember a whole breed of Persian cats, with long white hair, was destroyed by this malady, along with almost all the cats in the neighbourhood; and as the parotitis or mumps had not long before prevailed amongst human beings in that part of the country, I recollect being inclined to believe that the cats received the infection from mankind, though in all other contagious diseases, except the rabies canina can be so called, no different genera of animals naturally communicate infection to each other..."

1796. Holland. The epidemic skin disease that attacked cats here approximates that in Westphalia in 1671. Both were described as resembling scabies. The Holland cats "had also an acrid, stinking discharge from the eyes, which at last blinded them. It was observed that in the previous months, from February to April, they were excessively lascivious and their night cries were particularly loud."

1797–99. Europe and America. A particularly virulent disease raged among cats at the same time that yellow fever was plaguing humans. The symptoms and spread of the disease were extremely well documented and found their way into scientific and lay periodicals alike. The succession and nature of the symptoms varied greatly from one animal to another and also geographically. Generally speaking there was great drowsiness, trembling, vomiting, discharge from the nose, jaundice, great debilitation, and finally torpor and death at about the sixth day, the animal eating and drinking little during this time.

Post 1800. Major epidemics after this date occurred in 1803 in Europe, later reaching America; in 1809 in Switzerland; from 1919–1921 in Europe, attributed to infectious enteritis; and from 1933–1938 in different parts of the United States, also attributed to enteritis.

So much for the historical aspects of cat disease. Lady Cust's booklet

"The Cat, Its History and Diseases," published in 1856, is credited with being the first English book on cat care. Since then cat care books have been published in almost too much profusion, and most are of inferior quality. No attempt will be made here to duplicate their contents, but a brief resumé of the diseases and parasites that torment cats must be given to complete their natural history.

Cats suffer from many of the same things that plague man: colds, asthma, eczema, rheumatism, anemia, tetanus, rabies, tuberculosis, leukemia, pneumonia, epilepsy, diabetes, brucellosis, and cancer to name the more common ones. They also suffer from diseases which are, or would appear to be, specific to them alone. The foremost of these is feline distemper, the name by which most people know it; but it also has many other names, principally infectious enteritis and panleukopenia.

Cats play host to fleas, ticks, mites, lice and worms, both flat and round, and anyone who allows his pet outdoors freedom might as well forget trying to keep it free from worms. No cat that eats prey can avoid worm infestation because the prey itself is almost always infested. Continual deworming is far more debilitating to a cat than the actual worms: a healthy animal doesn't suffer from them because a balance between it and its parasites is normally maintained.

A cat's response to drugs and chemicals oftentimes differs from that in other animals, the classic example being its reaction to morphine which is one of excitation rather than sedation. Easily poisoned by drugs and chemicals that don't affect other species, as well as by "natural causes," cats are used extensively in experiments about food poisoning and similar experiments.

Fortunately, their natural environment and mode of life offer only a few toxic hazards such as mushroom poisoning. Although most cats are overly-anxious for new taste thrills it is the completely indoor cat that usually gets into trouble. In quest of greens to eat it will nibble house plants and bouquets and frequently gets poisoned.

In spite of the many health hazards that a cat must face, however, especially in man's world, it continues to be, as it always has been, a hardy animal; proof that it does, in fact, have nine lives.

XIX
Sleep

THEOCRITUS stated it around 270 B.C. and it has been said a good many times and in a good many ways since—cats like to sleep soft. Not only that, but they prefer their beds to be cozily warm. Peter, an ingenious cat, found both requirements in a most unlikely spot. J. A. Russell, whose cat he was, wrote:

"My mother used to make her own bread. Every week she set a sponge in a large iron-ware pan, placed on a small table behind the kitchen stove. On Friday evening she set the sponge as usual, threw a clean remnant of freshly laundered Turkey-red tablecloth over the bread bowl, and retired for the night.

"The next morning as we entered the kitchen, Mother glanced in the direction of the rising bread dough. Strangely enough, the tablecloth was not to be seen although the bowl still remained in its usual place and position. Then I discovered that Peter, the house cat, becoming chilly during the night, had jumped upon the bowl. His weight had gradually carried the cloth downward into the dough while the sponge had risen high around him, making a warm and springy mattress.

"As ours was a thrifty Yankee family, Mother shooed Peter off the tablecloth, removed the covering, decided that no harm had been done, and baked the bread as usual."

Cats always give preference to high, secluded places in choosing a bed, other things being equal. Once an acceptable spot has been found it will be occupied consistently for days and even weeks only to be abandoned for a new location and sometimes never used again. Many favorite places, however, to which a cat will return again and again, and for which there may be competition if there is more than one cat, appear to have nothing in their favor. They fulfill none of the requisites for sleeping that cats are known to crave, in particular the isolation, warmth and softness already mentioned, and cleanliness. But the cat has always been unfathomable to humans so we can't expect to understand completely its selection of a bed.

Because he knew cats and could describe their idiosyncrasies so well, William Cowper's cat poems are quoted in almost every cat book. This one is no exception, because "The Retired Cat" so adequately describes the subject of sleep and the cat.

A poet's cat, sedate and grave,
As poet well could wish to have,
Was much addicted to inquire
For nooks to which she might retire,
And where, secure as mouse in chink,
She might repose, or sit and think.
I know not where she caught the trick—
Nature perhaps herself had cast her
In such a mould *philosophique,*
Or else she learned it of her master.
Sometimes ascending, debonair,
An apple-tree or lofty pear,
Lodg'd with convenience in the fork,
She watched the gard'ner at his work;
Sometimes her ease and solace sought
In an old empty wat'ring pot,
There wanting nothing, save a fan,
To seem some nymph in her sedan,

Apparell'd in exactest sort,
And ready to be borne to court.
  But love of change it seems has place
Not only in our wiser race;
Cats also feel as well as we
That Passion's force, and so did she.
Her climbing, she began to find,
Expos'd her too much to the wind,
And the old utensil of tin
Was cold and comfortless within:
She therefore wish'd instead of those,
Some place of more serene repose,
Where neither cold might come, nor air
Too rudely wanton with her hair,
And sought it in the likeliest mode
Within her master's snug abode.
  A draw'r—it chanc'd, at bottom lin'd
With linen of the softest kind,
With such as merchant introduce
From India, for the ladies' use—
A draw'r impending o'er the rest,
Half open in the topmost chest,
Of depth enough, and none to spare,
Invited her to slumber there.
Puss, with delight beyond expression,
Survey'd the scene, and took possession.
Recumbent at her ease ere long,
And lulled by her own humdrum song,
She left the cares of life behind,
And slept as she would sleep her last,
When in came, housewifely inclin'd,
The chambermaid, and shut it fast,
By no malignity impell'd,
But all unconscious whom it held.
  Awaken'd by the shock (cried puss)
Was ever cat attended thus!
The open draw'r was left, I see,
Merely to prove a nest for me,
For soon as I was well compos'd,

Then came the maid, and it was closed:
How smooth these 'kerchiefs, and how sweet.
O what a delicate retreat!
I will resign myself to rest
Till Sol, declining in the west,
Shall call to supper; when, no doubt,
Susan will come and let me out.
   The evening came, the sun descended,
And puss remain'd still unattended.
The night roll'd tardily away
(With her indeed 'twas never day),
The sprightly morn her course renew'd,
The evening grey again ensued,
And puss came into mind no more
Than if entomb'd the day before.
With hunger pinch'd, and pinch'd for room,
She now presag'd approaching doom,
Nor slept a single wink, or purr'd,
Conscious of jeopardy incurr'd.
   That night, by chance the poet, watching,
Heard an inexplicable scratching,
His noble heart went pit-a-pat,
And to himself he said—what's that?
He drew the curtain at his side,
And forth he peep'd, but nothing spied.
Yet, by his ear directed, guess'd
Something imprison'd in the chest,
And doubtful what, with prudent care,
Resolv'd it should continue there.
At length a voice, which well he knew,
A long and melancholy mew,
Saluting his poetic ears,
Consol'd him, and dispell'd his fears;
He left his bed, he trod the floor,
He 'gan in haste the draw'rs explore,
The lowest first, and without stop,
The rest in order to the top.
For 'tis a truth well known to most,
That whatsoever thing is lost,

We seek it, ere it come to light,
In ev'ry cranny but the right.
Forth skipp'd the cat; not now replete
As erst with airy self-conceit,
Nor in her own fond apprehension,
A theme for all the world's attention,
But modest, sober, cur'd of all
Her notions hyperbolical,
And wishing for a place of rest
Anything rather than a chest:
Then stept the poet into bed,
With this reflexion in his head:

MORAL

Beware of too sublime a sense
Of your own worth and consequence!
The man who dreams himself so great
And his importance of such weight,
That all around, in all that's done,
Must move and act for him alone,
Will learn, in school of tribulation,
The folly of his expectation.

Not only does the cat select odd places to sleep but it sleeps in odd positions. The cat photographs being published in such profusion nowadays illustrate both facts. Choice of place and position are almost infinite but show consistency in regard to weather. Cold weather finds the cat in a snugger hideout and more compactly arranged when it sleeps, frequently balled into a sphere with its nose buried beneath its tail or under its paws. Hot weather finds it in a more exposed place with body attenuated, the extreme of this elongation being an on-back pose with tail and legs sticking straight out from the body. All the graceful and not-so-graceful contortions between the sphere and the straight line which a sleeping cat can assume are best observed in the cat itself.

Everyone knows what a cat-nap is whether he owns a cat or not. Sleep in cats is preponderantly on the light side. The only time I have observed profound sleep in them has been at night when they were sleeping on the bed with me. Buffon's correspondent (see p. 84) had the same experience, and like him, the first time I observed it I thought the cat had died.

Tayi had the habit of creeping under the blankets when I was asleep and nothing I did could keep her from doing it. When I awoke, there she'd be at my feet moving grumpily out of my way when I changed positions. On this terrible night I must have stretched in my sleep, and my feet contacted solid resistance. Instantly I was awake, my brain having registered what I always feared—that Tayi had suffocated under the heavy comforter. I dragged her from under it as usual, but this time there were no loud complaints about such treatment. There she lay, completely limp, and there I sat in a panic. I moved her front legs out and in, thinking to pump air into her lungs; I shook her, I screamed at her, I don't know what else I did. Nothing helped and time passed, how long I don't know.

Suddenly the limp bundle rose languidly, blinked and yawned, and began to burrow under the blanket for the second time that night. I couldn't believe the resurrection and I still can't in spite of having seen it repeated by Tayi and a few other cats. Abo, Tayi's son, was the only one who went into his comas during the day when the weather was very hot, and these never lasted as long as the nocturnal ones.

The Rev. W. Bingley said that this form of sleep happens most frequently in winter, particularly when snowy weather is on the way. Actually, it seems to depend on the individual cat. Little notice has been taken of the phenomenon so it can be assumed that it is not very common.

In the chapter on the ear it was noted that a sleeping cat's ears sort the sounds impinging on them, and as soon as one signals danger the cat is alerted. This does not hold true for the type of sleep just described. If cats fell into this form of deep sleep often, they would soon become extinct.

In ordinary deep sleep the cat is completely relaxed but easily awakened by sound or touch. It can dream and the dreams are often vivid. Whiskers twitch, tail lashes, fur stands on end, and there are growls, purrs and meows and the motions of eating and chop licking and fighting. If the cat is a male it may become sexually aroused.

When I was young we had a large black tomcat at home whose interests, like those of most toms, were limited to brawls and sex. In the lulls between these pursuits he enjoyed spending his evenings at home.

One night the peace and quiet of the last few days must have proved too tame for him. He was dreaming in my lap when suddenly he let out a shriek and attacked my thighs as he would a hostile dog. The dream was so vivid that it carried through momentarily into his waking state, a very short time altogether, but long enough to make my thighs a bloody mess. It was the most violent dreaming that I have ever seen or felt in a cat, and Kit never duplicated it.

Cats go to sleep so easily that insomniacs must hate them. If a blizzard is raging outdoors they sleep and sleep, perfectly content to wait it out whether it lasts for hours or days. They don't rant and rave futilely about anything. They sleep. But the second that circumstances are favorable they are up and away. They turn their sleep off and on as easily as we flick light switches.

Their time sense gives them specific sleeping habits and many house cats demand that their bedtime be yours or, at least that you maintain regular hours. Every cat owner knows the embarrassment of having his cat approach visitors who are keeping it up past its bedtime. Few people can tolerate its stoney stares and condemning meows for long, and the host whose cat goes no farther than this to show its displeasure is lucky.

The more cats you have, the greater the bedtime problem becomes. Happily, some cats are not cranks in this direction. I had one stray that never attempted to make the family conform to his sleeping habits. Every night at nine o'clock, no matter what was going on, Bum marched into his basket and slept there until morning. More wonderful still, he never showed any interest in sleeping on beds. What could his past life have been?

In one respect the cat's time sense is a godsend: its owner's sleep won't be disturbed too often. Cat owners like to think that their cat respects slumber, but if that were the case they wouldn't find it tramping back and forth on their chest and complaining on those mornings other than the weekend when they sleep longer. Most cats demand regularity, which makes them good alarm clocks and calendars.

Physiological Aspects of Sleep. Sleep has always puzzled man, and research on it today is extensive, with the cat, as usual, being one of the most satisfactory subjects. Cat sleep closely parallels human sleep and can be separated into three phases: (1) exploratory and preparatory, (2) light and (3) deep sleep.

Light sleep is characterized by moderate muscular tonus and basal

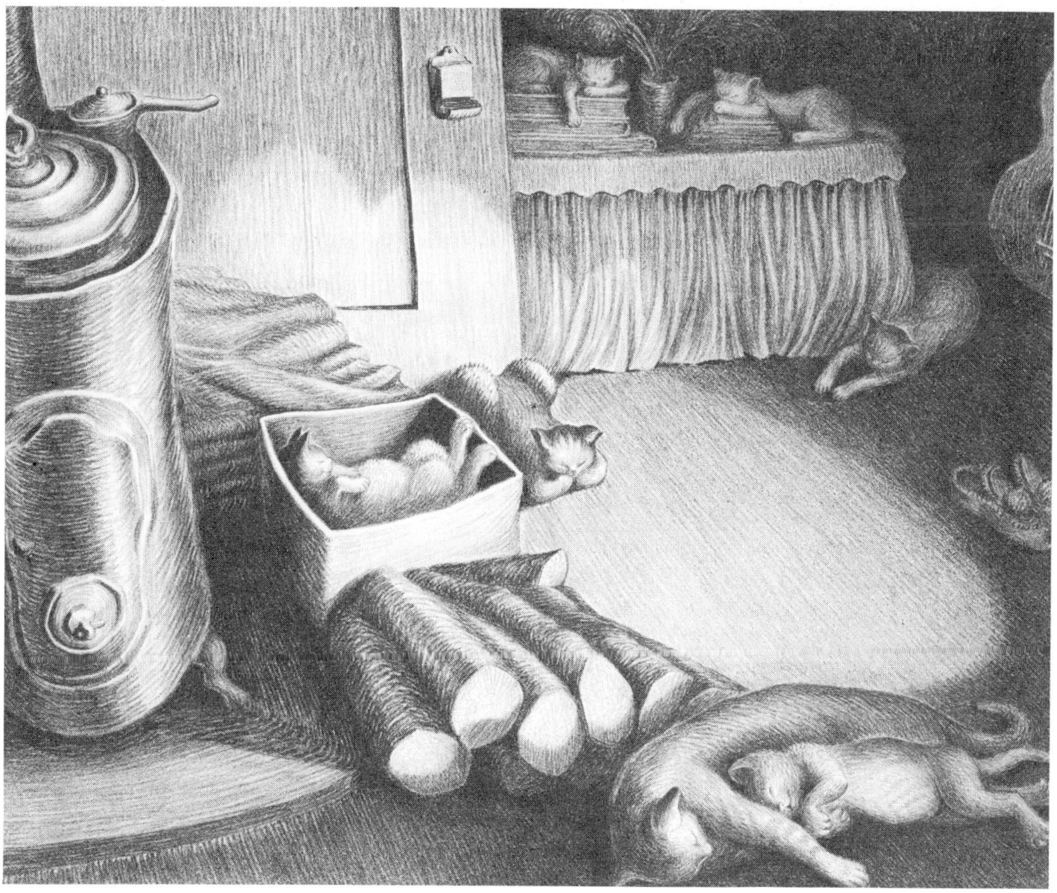

"Siesta" by Wanda Gäg.

blood pressure level with a decrease in temperature. Because of its electroencephalograph (EEG) pattern it is often referred to as slow wave sleep and sometimes as high voltage sleep. As the cat passes into this second stage from stage one, its ability to discriminate between tones of different frequencies is found to improve as has already been mentioned in the section on hearing. This could be of value to the animal in that it becomes more alerted to sound variation at a time when it is more vulnerable to harm.

Deep sleep produces complete muscular relaxation, a marked decrease in blood pressure and a slow rise in temperature. In the EEG it is characterized by low voltage and high frequency waves, and is comparable to the rapid eye movement (REM) sleep in humans. In the cat and other animals that exhibit it, it is referred to as paradoxical sleep, researchers being unwilling to think that animals and humans can experience similar phenomena. REM or paradoxical sleep, because of its implications, receives a great deal of attention. It is in this phase of sleep that cat and human alike dream.

Eye movements indicate when dreaming has begun and precede muscular relaxation, twitching and other external manifestations. The movement is usually grouped into bursts of twelve and may not be synchronized in the two eyes. The speed is slower than it is in the waking state, suggesting that different mechanisms are at work. During paradoxical sleep the cat's eyelids are partially open, and the pupil is wider and the nictitating membrane more retracted than in slow wave sleep.

Ear as well as eye muscles are highly active during paradoxical sleep whereas both are inactive during slow wave or light sleep. The activity level of the brain is also high, probably as high as when the cat is awake.

Deep sleep normally accounts for a third of the cat's total sleep time. When a cat is recovering from experimental deprivation of it, it accounts for 53%. The longer the cat is deprived of this sleep phase the greater must be the number of awakenings to prevent it from occurring. Humans follow a similar pattern, but whether the cat's behavior deteriorates from lack of REM sleep as does that of humans has not yet been satisfactorily determined. One thing is certain: deep sleep is essential to the well-being of both cat and human.

When a period of normal paradoxical sleep is over the cat usually awakens momentarily following a major body movement. It lifts its head, opens its eyes, shifts positions, possibly yawns and stretches a little, and then lies down again to re-begin the three-phase cycle. Mary B. Miller describes a cat's complete awakening.

The black cat yawns,
Opens her jaws,
Stretches her legs,
And shows her claws.

Then she gets up
And stands on four
Long stiff legs
And yawns some more.

She shows her sharp teeth,
She stretches her lip,
Her slice of a tongue
Turns up at the tip.

Lifting herself
On her delicate toes,
She arches her back
As high as it goes.

She lets herself down
With particular care,
And pads away
With her tail in the air.

XX
Reproduction

LECHEROUS, lascivious, libidinous, lustful—cats have always been considered the epitome of sexuality and labelled with every term connoting sexual excess. Why they gained this reputation is difficult to understand. Ungulates, for example, engage in far fiercer battles during the rutting season than do cats, and cat copulation is rapid and unspectacular in comparison to that of other animals, like dogs, where male and female are often tied for long periods. As for vocalization, it is definitely no gauge for passion, and caterwauling is not limited to courtship.

Since it usually occurs at night and in places inconvenient for observation if not audition, it is doubtful whether anyone has actually seen the uninterrupted and *natural* courtship of cats. As soon as toms hear and smell a female in heat they congregate in her vicinity, but seldom do the participants stay in one place to perform for our benefit the prolonged and varied repertoire which precedes coitus. And it is this fascinating display and vocalization that makes the reproduction in cats distinctive from that of other mammals. In the wild state it is improbable if not impossible that one female will attract so many males as she does in our cities and towns; but it is indisputable that she actively participates in the courtship instead of remaining impassive like a good percentage of female mammals. This behavior is no doubt a major reason for calling prostitutes cats.

Many a female cat ringed in by her admirers chooses her mate long before they do battle for her. Winner or loser, she will accept him and no one else, and Charles Duff claimed in his book *Ordinary Cats* that she may even do battle for him when the odds are against him. Other females will accept more than one male, more than one of whom can become father to her kittens. Mating orgies can last for several days with little or no breaks for either food or sleep, and impregnation may occur over the entire span. It could be these prolonged preliminaries to actual mating and the fact that a tomcat's life is one round of them after another that has earned cats their high rank in the realm of sex. But battle more than sex seems to be the byword of toms. It doesn't require the presence of an oestrous female for him to fight any cat in sight, and many maverick males indiscriminately attack males, females, neuters and kittens of every age. Their depravity is so far advanced that all that can be done is to destroy them before they themselves destroy. Normal tomcats are interesting creatures and some make good fathers, in particular the Siamese; many, however, will destroy young kittens if they find them, and this is said to be the usual case in the wild state. Most toms are good household companions when they choose to stay at home, but this is seldom. Some become far from pleasant: scarred in mind and body from the life they lead, they are reproducing machines and little else.

Tomcats of long ago were apparently no better than those of today (and actually no worse than other male animals). Herodotus, writing in the 5th century B.C., said of the Egyptian cats: "The number of domestic animals in Egypt is very great, and would be greater were it not for what befalls the cats. As the females, when they have kittened, no longer seek the company of the males, these last, to obtain once more their companionship, practice a curious artifice. They seize the kittens, carry them off, and kill them; but do not eat them afterwards. Upon this, the females, being deprived of their young, and longing to supply their place, seek the males once more, since they are particularly fond of their offspring."

THE SEXES. The male cat generally reaches sexual maturity when he is a year old, but precocious males can mate successfully at eight months (occasionally six) while others take 15 months or longer to mature. Unlike females, males are capable of mating the year round.

Before male kittens are four months old sex hormones are being secreted and the horny papillae of the penis have developed. Around this time they begin to exhibit sex play—neck grasping, mounting, etc. Sex play in female kittens is the same as that in males, there being no adult female behavior in kittens of either sex before puberty. The explanation given for this, which is now considered untenable, is that male hormones are present in both male and female kittens, while female hormones are never present until puberty.

The female cat usually becomes sexually mature when she is from five to eight months old. Although her heat periods can occur at any season of the year they are generally limited to twice a year in northern latitudes; in the south they can occur four times a year. Oestrous peaks in the north are reached from late January to early March and again in May and June, in the south from mid-December through January and from mid-July to the end of August. From late September to early January most cats are anoestrous.

Where I now live, in the vicinity of Chicago, I have never known a feral cat to have young at any other time than spring, and this restriction also applies to some females who live a completely outdoor life like the farm cats. In laboratories, regulation of illumination can produce breeding at any time of the year.

The oestrous phase lasts from three days to two weeks or longer and recurs as often as every two weeks if the female has not mated. Receptiveness to the male begins toward the end of the pro-oestrous phase and reaches its maximum about the third day of the oestrous period. If mated, receptivity can last up to six days, if unmated from six to ten days. Ovulation, except in rare cases, occurs only if coitus has taken place during the oestrous phase, and it takes place about 30 hours after the stimulation produced by the mating.

No one can mistake female in heat after the first time he has seen and heard one. She becomes very affectionate and seeks attention and caresses from her humans. She purrs and rubs herself against anything available—legs, furniture, trees. She rolls excessively much as cats do when they are happy and joyous, then jumps up hurriedly to rub once again. Particularly when petted, she goes through the positions and actions that precede copulation. And throughout the entire exhibition, which goes on and on, she will vocalize from a soft almost inaudible croon to loud calls. In the Siamese these can be raucous and become unbearable as they continue hour after hour and day after day.

All these actions are the usual pattern performed by all females. Individual temperaments produce various idiosyncrasies to make each performer and performance more or less unique. Some females in the oestrous phase can become fretful and irritable instead of mellow and loving, but regardless of how they behave most lead the tomcats, who come at their call, a merry chase.

Only cats in oestrous mate, and only cats in oestrous are approached by the male; rape, as practiced in other mammalian species, is unknown in the domestic cat. Neurohormonal processes augmented by sexual experience are responsible for and control the onset, maintenance and persistence of sexual behavior. The sex act, however, is not completely stereotyped, the female reacting differently to each male depending on his individual idiosyncrasies.

MATING. Courtship can be a whirlwind affair or prolonged, depending entirely on the individuals and their sexual experience. The male is completely oriented to the female, pursuing her wherever she goes, circling her, sniffing her genitalia and vocalizing in what has been termed the mating call. When she isn't avoiding him the female crouches, rolls, rubs her whiskers and treads while also vocalizing. If the male comes too close to suit her she may swat at him and spit and growl.

Gradually she becomes more submissive, and only then will the experienced tom attempt copulation. As she crouches with her rear end elevated he will seize the loose skin on the back of her neck in his teeth and mount her from the rear, first with his forelegs and then the hind ones. Rubbing her with his forepaws, his hind legs begin to tread as do hers. Back arched, he makes pelvic thrusts forward, the female swinging her tail to one side and bending her rear end in the direction of the stimulus. At this point nervous irritation may cause her to break away from the male's grip so that the procedure must be repeated, often more than once.

When a pelvic lunge results in intromission, ejaculation and withdrawal of the penis lasts only a few seconds. With a loud cry the female pulls forward and turns on the male spitting and clawing. It is believed that the barbs on the penis injure her vagina during withdrawal thus causing the hostile attitude and cry of what is considered pain. This stimulus is thought to be requisite to ovulation.

The cries of the female cat during copulation have been explained in many different ways through the centuries. One explanation, greatly favored, was that cat semen is so hot that it burns the female's internal organs causing her to cry out. Another explanation was that the male, in the extremes of his passion, scratched and bit her brutally. Still another, and the best of all, tells of one female cat whose love-making was interrupted by the appearance of a mouse, her gallant tom leaving her in an instant to pursue it. Chagrined, she swore that that would never happen again. To prevent it she screamed at intervals during future amours thereby scaring the mice and keeping them at a distance. This expedient proved so successful that all female cats have continued to do it to this very day.

After dodging the female's angry attack after coitus the male sits down near her and begins to wash his penis and paws. The female also washes her paws and genitalia, rubs her whiskers and begins to roll once more, meanwhile watching the male. Sometimes she will approach him and pat him with her paws. Some females, in order to arouse reluctant males to sexual activity, are said to mount them. As already stated they may mate several times, often over a period of days with the same or different males.

All normal cats have a tendency toward homosexuality, but it is much more common in males, as is hypersexuality. In laboratory colonies of cats, auto-erotic behavior in the male has also been observed, and penile erection and other acts associated with copulation are occasionally seen in sleeping pets.

PREGNANCY. In the cat, pregnancy follows the general mammalian pattern: appetite and weight increase as activity and agility decrease. In its later stages there is swelling of the vulva and distension of the mammae. Licking of the genital and abdominal areas become exaggerated due to increased cutaneous sensitivity of these parts. This facilitates place-fixation and other reactions attendant on the birth of the kittens.

In her search for a proper nesting site the female looks for a secluded, dry, dark, wind-protected location that has cover and a soft substrate. In the free-living cat this can be a hole in the ground, a hollow tree or a cave as it is with the larger cats, and she will hunt from such a site within a one or two mile radius. The domestic cat favors

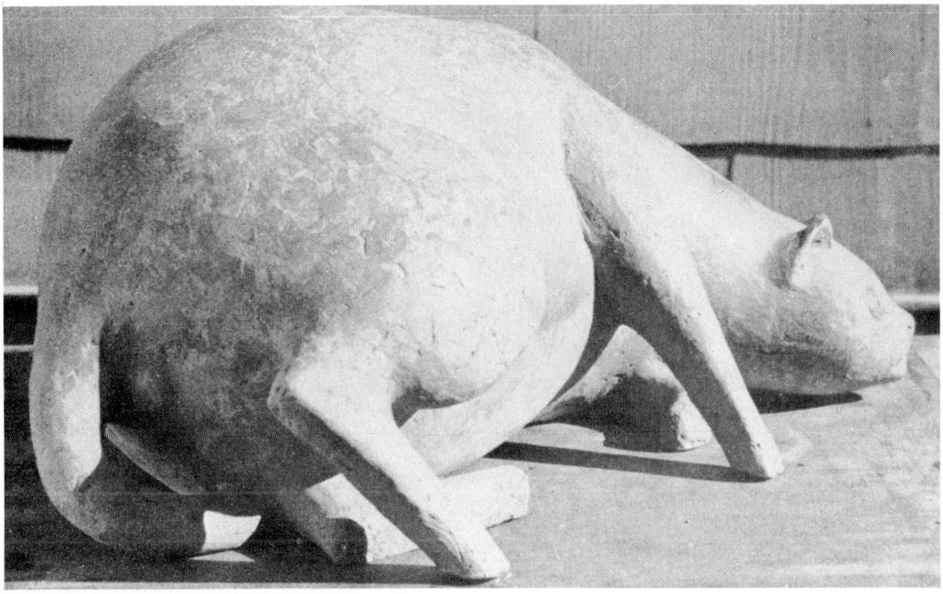

"Pregnant Cat" by Paul Frazier (From the collection of Mr. and Mrs. William C. Palmer)

"Mother Cat and Kittens" by Heinz Warneke. (From the collection of Mrs. J. B. Helms)

closets and cupboards, but her choice is unlimited as she is not opposed to an exposed situation like the outdoor cat who always goes into hiding. Beds are highly favored for the accouchement. Once selected, the place is usually slept in and otherwise frequented so that it becomes saturated with odors that will later serve to guide the kittens to their home site.

The young are carried, on the average, 60–65 days but gestation periods from 56 to 70 days are not abnormal. The gestation period of the indoor cat whose activity is curtailed tends to be in the far upper range, that of the active, outdoor cat in the lower. The number of young is from 1–7, but there can be 8 or more, especially in certain breeds like the Siamese. Plutarch had this to say about the number of young born to a cat: "For it is said that she brings forth at first one kitten, afterwards two, and the third time, 3; and that the number increaseth thus until the seventh and last birth, so that she bears in all 28 young, or as many as the moon hath revolutions." This is one of the reasons why cats were considered an emblem of the moon. He also remarked that the Egyptians gave to each female cat a suitable mate, that is, one that was compatible with her personality.

The young of cats are altricial, their strength and coordination developing slowly and their eyes opening around the ninth day. The Jews explained this phenomenon by saying that ritually unclean animals which see at night are always blind until they are nine days old.

The mean birth weight of kittens born in the average litter of five is greater than that of those born in smaller or larger litters, and the birth weight of kittens born to small mothers is greater than that of kittens born to large mothers. The average weight is 3.5 ounces and this is doubled within a week. As could be expected the growth rate is faster in those below average weight at birth. There appears to be no postnatal weight decrease as in humans. Female kittens average heavier than males at birth and continue to be heavier during the first five weeks, but after eight weeks males grow much more rapidly than females. The growth curve for all kittens is almost linear up to the eighth week.

PARTURITION. The imminence of parturition is heralded by increased vulvar distension sometimes accompanied by a mucous discharge; colostrum in the mammae; calling; and a general restlessness with scratching (similar to that used in covering excreta) alternating with squatting.

Parturition, like pregnancy, follows the typical mammalian pattern: contractions, emergence of foetus, delivery of foetus and delivery of placenta. Contractions and delivery intervals can take less than a minute or last over an hour. Most cats give birth to a kitten every half hour, their highly excited state at this time aiding the entire procedure, especially the expulsion of the foetus.

There is no stereotyped pattern followed in delivery: variations arise from the interaction of internal and external stimuli that occur at this time, principally the newborn, the placenta and accompanying fluids, the uterine contractions and the passage of the foetus. Much of the female's behavior, particularly licking, produces a bond between herself and her young, and this in turn forms the basis for the long period of maternal care which she will have to give them.

About 30% of her time during parturition is devoted to licking, some females devoting over 50% of their time to this activity. The foetal membranes must be licked off the neonate who is then licked dry. The umbilical cord is licked before being chewed to sever it from the newborn, and the placenta is licked before being eaten along with the cord. Previously born kittens are relicked for good measure, and the birth area is tidied up by still more licking. Finally, the mother cat attends to her own body with a general washing but still with concentration on the genital and abdominal regions. Other actions besides licking and those that accompany giving birth (squatting, crouching, straining, etc.) are rolling, rubbing, circling and scratching the floor.

In many ways the mother cat—even an experienced one—acts irresponsibly toward her young while in the process of giving birth. She will bump one along the floor as it hangs from her vulva; she will sit, lie and walk on previously born kittens; she will paw them and pick them up in her mouth far from gently. She is completely unresponsive to their cries over such rough treatment or when they accidentally become separated from her. Even after parturition she seems oblivious of their screams until these reach a certain intensity, and usually she responds to them only when they come from a kitten who has somehow become separated from her. Retrievals of stranded kittens are almost always accomplished by sound rather than sight.

Kittens begin to nurse within one half to two hours after birth. Firstborns may nurse before the entire litter is delivered but often there is no suckling by any kitten until parturition is completed. In his attempt to locate mother and nipple the neonate moves forward with pushing movements of his hind legs while moving his forelegs in paddle fashion. Simultaneously he moves his head continuously from side to side, his nose close to the floor, as he senses out the area. On making contact with his mother he responds to the thermal, tactile and olfactory stimulations he receives by nuzzling her and thereby eventually locating a nipple. The female lies with her young almost continuously for 12 hours after parturition, resting and allowing them to feed. Maternal behavior has taken over.

Kittens are able to distinguish their own mother from other nursing females shortly after birth. In their first few days of life they won't respond to a strange female's teats, but at the time when constancy on their mother's teats begins to wane they will accept a foster mother. Females often take advantage of this by pooling their young. Some indifferent mothers will leave their entire brood to a conscientious one to rear completely but usually it is a reciprocal affair, each female taking her turn in feeding and training.

Cooperation of a sort also exists during parturition. Matron cats will frequently act as midwives to females having their first litter or to those experiencing a difficult birth. As the kittens arrive they will take over completely to the obvious relief of the female in labor. Female cats are notorious in being able to defer the arrival of their kittens until the time is propitious. Most pet cats insist on having their loved owner in attendance and can hold off for days if necessary. Labor will commence as soon as that loved one arrives.

MATERNAL BEHAVIOR. Basic maternal behavior in the cat consists of the mother encircling her kittens in a horseshoe formation prior to feeding them; retrieving and returning them to the nest when they wander off; assiduously licking them and herself almost continuously when she is awake and never going any great distance from them when she has to leave them. In females with only one kitten the bond of motherhood is much weaker than it is with those having the average litter of four or five, and typical behavior may be greatly modified or completely lacking.

For two days after birth the mother barely leaves her young for any reason. From then on a daily routine of coming and going becomes established. At first she stays away for short periods only, one hour at the very most, and the kittens huddle together in a tight mound until she returns. In order to awaken them for nursing when she does come back she begins to wash them vigorously and encircle them. The encircling serves to limit their movements and simplify their finding nipples for feeding. It also produces a quieting effect on the kittens, along with her odor and those of the nest area. Familiar odors are essential to the well-being of the neonates. If their nest area is well cleaned the kittens become greatly disturbed and are unable to locate it again should they stray away, relying as they do on olfaction alone during the first few days of their lives. At three weeks of age, with their eyes and ears functioning, nest orientation presents no difficulties to them.

During their first two weeks kittens are unable to urinate or defecate independently, and if it weren't for the licking stimulation of their mother they would soon die. As soon as they are able to navigate sufficiently well—during the fourth to fifth week—she toilet-trains them, and many are the cuffs a youngster receives if he doesn't learn promptly.

Nursing diminishes a great deal during the kittens' first two weeks. Apparently it is governed by the number of kittens in the litter: females with the average number spend far more time nursing than do those with only one or two kittens. On the average, the young feed about one-third of the time before weaning begins. However, a female can spend as much as 70% of her time nursing since the kittens often suckle individually and in succession. After the fifth week feeding time is reduced to about 20%.

The oral drive in a kitten is very strong. It was found that kittens who were fed by stomach-loading would suck a nonlactating cat as much as if they were deriving their nourishment from the act. As with kittens feeding normally from a lactating cat, they didn't begin to suck less until after the usual five week period.

During the first three weeks or so of the kitten's life, the mother initiates the feeding, principally by washing, encircling, and presenting her nipples, and continual contact with her is essential for the kitten to develop the proper response. Usually by the second day after birth suckling habits have begun to be formed. Many kittens will have appropriated one, or sometimes two, specific nipples which they will claim as theirs. Others will select a specific location rather than nipple from which to nurse, and a good many others will suckle at any available place where they happen to get hungry.

By their fourth week when they have begun to totter around rather than crawl, the feeding is initiated by them as well as by their mother. They seek her out for nursing purposes but are incapable of initiating the actual suckling unless she is quiescent. At their approach she usually obliges them by lying down, encircling and presenting. She will also approach them herself of her own accord to feed them.

Beginning around the fifth week she almost ceases to approach them for feeding purposes, and the kittens must trail after her and pester her if they are hungry. Instead of giving in to their demands she will often rebuff them and escape to some location where they can't follow. Soon she begins to wean them by avoiding most of their approaches, and if she has access to the outdoors she starts to supply them with prey to eat. By the end of two months, three at the most, most kittens are completely weaned and are beginning to hunt for themselves.

There are many exceptions to this. Cats having only one kitten may continue to nurse it indefinitely, and cats who have a favorite child may refuse milk to all but him after the weaning period is over. An extreme case of preferential feeding was exhibited by a farm cat. She continued to nurse her entire first litter even after giving birth to subsequent litters which she ignored. Her first kittens, adults themselves, continued to take advantage of their good luck.

Interesting suckling behavior was reported by P. Courbon in 1928. Grandmother, mother and daughter cats—each had kittens of her own. Daughter sucked both mother and grandmother indiscriminately. Mother sucked only grandmother, her actual mother. Grandmother sucked no one and no one sucked daughter.

As could be predicted, more than at any other time in their lives, the three demonstrated their ability to unite when potential enemies such as dogs were present. Mr. Courbon concluded from his observations that cats have not only a maternal instinct but a family instinct, and that their intelligence is heightened during the period of childbirth and rearing of young.

The females were said to show an increase in sociability and to behave more maternally toward the young of their own species as the time of delivery approached. However, they mistreated the young of other species, in this case, rabbits. This is an interesting observation considering that female cats are notorious for adopting other animal species after they have kittens. (see chapter on friends and foes)

After kittens begin individual activity, family ties begin to weaken. There no longer is much eating or sleeping together as a unit, the aggregate action being replaced by play activity some time after the third week. After the fourth week, when nursing is reduced, this becomes greatly intensified. The increased activity tends to annoy most females and for this reason as well as weaning purposes she avoids her boisterous youngsters. When they play with her tail, pounce on her, and roughhouse in general she is just as apt to swat them, spit and leave as participate in the games. Nevertheless, she remains highly concerned about their welfare and in order to protect them is willing to sacrifice her life.

As everyone knows, a female cat generally moves her kittens to a new location as soon as danger threatens. Innumerable stories have recorded her almost impossible feats during some of these moves and the camera has recorded many more. Her tendency to shift locations is strongest at that critical fourth week period when so many changes are taking place in the cat family. Once more she becomes highly aware of the environment beyond her nest, the awareness of which was subliminal at the birth of her kittens and for many days afterward.

For moving purposes she generally grasps a kitten in her teeth by the nape of the neck, sometimes by the shoulders. The kitten responds by curling itself up as tightly as it can. Despite this precaution on the kitten's part and the fact that the female lifts her head high as she walks, it will often have a rough journey, being bumped and dragged to its new home. Size of mother and kitten determine how hazardous the trip will be, and if the mother is a nervous individual the kitten will have to endure many uncomfortable journeys before it is deemed capable of following instead of being carried

Mother cats are always one step ahead of danger so far as their young are concerned whether in the nest area or elsewhere. No matter what threatens their kittens—fire, water, predators, man, catastrophes of every sort—they meet it boldly, and anecdotes abound to attest to this fact. Their caution and bravery cannot be questioned and anyone who has owned a female cat with kittens, even a cat who is completely housebound, must have seen some demonstration of these. One of my cats exhibited the extreme nervousness that some human mothers show in regard to the safety of their offspring. During the years that we were apartment dwellers she hid her kittens at the approach of any unfamiliar footstep. She was so good at it that we often couldn't find the kittens, and more than once one was almost killed by her stuffing it into an impossibly tight spot. Never were they herded into one hiding place. Each was deposited in its own niche as if she reasoned "never put all your kittens in one basket."

"Cat Playing With Her Kitten," Egyptian.
(Musée du Louvre, Paris)

Another cat mother, a stray, had kittens on our farm when we were plagued by roving dogs, and both of us were always chasing them off the property. But her zeal often went too far. The retreating dogs frequently outran both of us and, not having one to leap on and attack, in her excitement she would attack me instead. Luckily a scream from me would bring her to her senses after her first onslaught. Otherwise her overzealousness could have been disastrous.

One of the most famous examples of a cat's protective behavior toward her young is that of Faith during the Battle of Britain. Her display of courage, although not in excess of other females, gained notoriety because of the circumstances. A stray, Faith was befriended by a rector and spent a good deal of time in the church where her behavior was exemplary. When the rectory came under attack during the air raids in the fall of 1940 she shielded her kitten from harm instead of seeking safety for herself.

"Roofs and masonry fell asunder, and the whole house blazed. Four floors fell through in front of Faith; fire and water and ruin were all around her. Yet she stayed calm and steadfast and waited for help. We rescued her in the early morning while the place was still burning and by the mercy of God she and her kitten were not only saved but unhurt."

The story is made more interesting by the fact that a day or two before the blitz Faith began hunting for a new nesting place for her kitten and finally settled on the secluded niche against a stone wall where she was found after the blitz. This could well be an act of prescience on the cat's part much as mother cats are said to be forewarned of coming floods and move their kittens to higher ground.

Cat Mother

Her gaze is tranquil and almost profound,
And seems to hold both mother love and pride;
She cups her paw protecting-wise around
The furry offspring nestled by her side.

She sings a song so very soft and low—
A song that soon each kitten can repeat;
It is the age-old song all felines know,
But mother love has made it doubly sweet.

MARGARET E. BRUNER

"Development of Behavior in the Fetal Cat" by J. D. Coronios is a 104 page study of the bodily functions of the cat from the time of fertilization to birth. Following is a brief portion of this very interesting investigation.

"The picture of the newborn kitten presents, essentially, an organism which is able to walk (although still in somewhat of a crawl), to feed, to maintain an upright posture, to find warmth and the source of food, and to breathe. It has developed a certain degree of sensitivity, although the auditory and the visual functions have yet to appear. The newborn kitten is somewhat of a "helpless" creature in coping with its postnatal environment, yet it has the necessary equipment for a certain type of biological adaptation. And we have seen that this equipment, such as it is, is the product of a long, continuous, and progressive course of prenatal development.

"On the basis of the results of the present investigation it is not maintained that the separate reactions which have been described appear on a definite, specified day in the course of development in all normal cat embryos and fetuses. Rather the emphasis is to be placed upon the developmental relations which exist among the various items. In some cases, as it has been previously stated, in the present experiment the intervals of the gestation age between observations were two or more days. This would preclude any possibility of definitely asserting that a certain item of behavior appears on a given day of the gestation period . . . With these qualifications, it is, perhaps, justifiable to make the following tentative conclusions.

"1. Before birth there is a rapid, progressive, and continuous development of behavior in the fetus of the cat.

"2. The development of behavior progresses from a diffuse, massive, variable, relatively unorganized state to a condition where many of the reactions are more regular in their appearance, less variable, better organized, and relatively individualized.

"3. In the early stages of prenatal development the behavior appears to be progressing along a cephalocaudal course.

"4. The development of the sensitivity of the reflexogenous zones passes through a continuous and transitional development from a time when rather vigorous stimulation of any 'spot' of the body within a large area serves to elicit variable, diffuse, uncoordinated patterns of behavior to a later time when a weak stimulus becomes adequate, within a much more circumscribed area, for precise, well-coordinated, uniform, and less variable patterns of behavior. The direction of such development is cephalocaudal.

"5. The 'primitive' reactions of breathing, righting, locomotion, and feeding are the products of a long and continuously progressive course of prenatal development.

"6. Behavior development appears first in the gross musculature, and in the fine musculature later.

"7. Behavior develops in each of the limbs from a proximal to a distal point, that is, the entire limb is first involved in the response and then gradually the more distal joints become, as it were, independent of the total movement."

•

XXI
Predation

Grimalkin, to Domestick Vermin sworn
An everlasting Foe, with watchful Eye
Lies nightly brooding o'er a chinky Gap,
Protending her fell Claws, to thoughtless Mice
Sure ruin.

JOHN PHILIPS, 1703

THE cat is a carnivore, a machine exquisitely constructed for killing. It is sensitive to minute movements. It localizes and reacts quickly to the slightest sound. It readily detects and traces odors. Its spatial orientation is highly developed and it can move quietly and quickly through cover, leap lightly, agilely, and far in any direction, and climb effortlessly. It can remain oriented to its prey for long periods, quiet and motionless. Its forelimbs are dextrous and work in close coordination with its mouth to seize and grasp, and its claws and teeth are efficient weapons. It is intelligent and learns quickly, easily outwitting its victims. Both mind and body are geared for efficient hunting; the method employed is inborn and not deliberate bloodlust and cruelty.

Long may you love your pensioner Mouse,
Though one of a tribe that torment the house;
Nor dislike for her cruel sport the Cat,

That deadly foe of both mouse and rat.
Remember she follows the law of her kind,
And Instinct is neither wayward nor blind.
Then think of her beautiful gliding form,
Her tread that would not crush a worm,
And her soothing song by the winter fire,
Soft as the dying throbs of the lyre.

WILLIAM WORDSWORTH

HUNTING. 1. *Birds and Mammals as Food.* After reading a book or two on cat care you get the impression that cats require a variety of foods and taste thrills daily to keep them fit and in appetite. Still, when they live on their natural food, mice, they relish each one despite the monotony of the diet and are adequately nourished by them.

Let take a cat, and foster hire with milke
And tendre flesh, and make hire couche of silke,
And let hire see a mous go by the wall,
Anon she weiveth milke and flesh, and all,
And every deintee that is in that hous,
Swiche appetit hath she to ete the mous.

GEOFFREY CHAUCER

Food habit studies to determine how destructive a cat is to song and game birds bear out the fact that rodents are the cat's principal food. These studies have been carried on in many states, major ones in Oklahoma, Wisconsin, Michigan and California. Results from these prove that outdoor cats are strictly rodent-oriented. All stomach content analyses reveal that their staple diet (including that of feral cats whose lives depend on their hunting prowess) is rodents.

Briefly, McMurry and Sperry in their Oklahoma census found the food of cats to consist of insects 12.5%, garbage 26.5%, reptiles 2.0%, birds 4.0% and mammals (chiefly rodents) 55.0%. Hubb's California count showed birds averaging 25.2% of the total bulk consumed and mammals (again chiefly rodents) 64.1%. There is an obvious local and seasonal variation in any investigation of this type.

In Baltimore, Maryland an urban-cat food census was attempted by means of fecal examinations to determine how effective cats were in rat control. They were found to be chiefly scavengers. It was estimated that only 10% of their entire food consumption consisted of rats. This small amount was considered to be only about 20% of the annual post-weaning mortality necessary to keep the rat population stationary in the area studied.

So much for an extensive literature on whether the cat in its role of predator is man's friend or foe. The fact remains that cats *do* keep down the rodent population and birds *do* breed successfully in their midst. Shooting, poisoning and trapping have eliminated most of the natural predators, and many of the birds in the rural area where I live; and if it weren't for cats, rodents would soon take over both land and buildings as those who live here soon find out. A farm that had no cats and was plagued by rats and mice befriended a stray. She was soon at work ratting in the barns and a few months and a few cats later the farm's rat problem was solved.

Ecologist Charles Elton studied the cat-rat problem on English farms. He found that farms on which cats were installed remained almost completely free from rats after they had been initially freed of a heavy infestation by other means. Farms that had no cats suffered recurrent infestations. The cats kept an area of approximately 50 yards free from incoming rats; beyond that range they were not too effective, and at distances over 120 yards their effectiveness was negligible.

Cats can prevent a territory from being overrun by rodents but cannot eliminate them completely according to Mr. Elton. That may be, but farms with well-fed cats very seldom have rodents in their buildings although they may have them on their land. It could be that other cats are like the puss in that well-known anecdote who, on finding that he had disposed of all the mice in his home went farther afield and carried his catches home alive to release them there for future hunting.

Cats kill all species of rats and mice but they refuse to eat some or, if they do eat them, they are soon regurgitated. House mice and meadow mice (voles), the year-round mainstay of hunter cats, are eaten and stay eaten, but deer mice are left untouched or are regurgitated shortly after they reach the stomach. Gilbert White in *The Natural History of Selborne* remarked that his neighbor noticed that the dogs ate all the red mice they could catch and rejected the common mice. The cats, on the other hand, ate the common mice and refused the red. There must be more examples like these in different geographical areas which remain unreported.

Rabbits, hares, squirrels, flying squirrels, thirteen-lined ground squirrels, chipmunks, moles, shrews, and bats are the other mammals

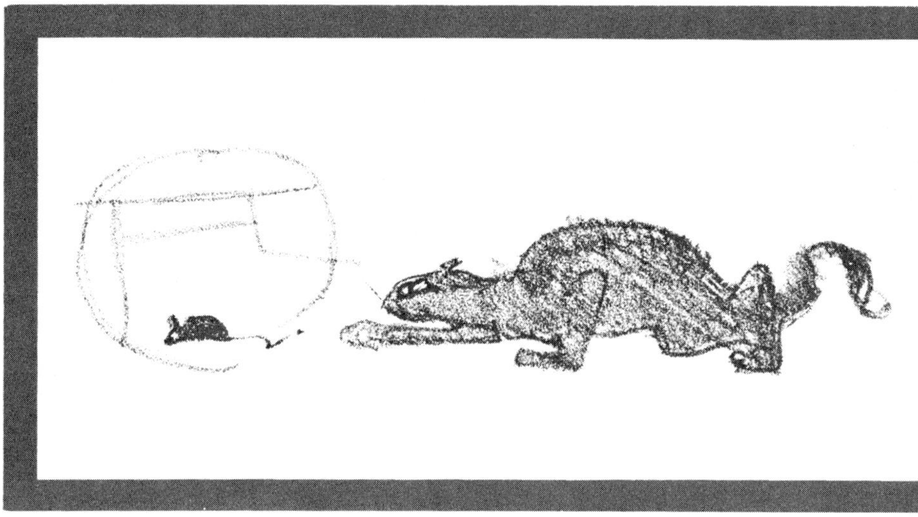

"Cat Stalking Mouse" by Henri de Toulouse-Lautrec.

most commonly preyed upon by cats. Shrews are killed in abundance but like the deer mice are seldom consumed. An exception to the rule was found during one food habit study. A cat was found with the remains of eight short-tailed shrews in its stomach. This was not due to starvation rations because other game was available where the cat was found. It must have been a definite food preference and one no stranger than that of many cats.

The evidence says no, but man has persisted from the earliest times in labelling the cat a great destroyer of birds. Even the fabulist Pilpay wrote on the subject (see folktale chapter). Actually only a small percentage of cats specializes in catching birds, and these become very successful at it. The majority find that birds are more trouble to catch than they are worth. Success in bird-catching by these non-specialists is the result of luck or the finding of a crippled or sick bird.

It is late April as I write this and birds have begun to nest. In a 100 foot radius around my home there already are nests of robins, grackles, mourning doves and jays. If it is like other years there will be still more—quail, brown thrashers, song sparrows, buntings and others—this in spite of the fact that 12 cats regularly police the grounds in full sight of the nest builders. And the birds will successfully rear their young unless a coon or some other misfortune comes their way. Seldom will the misfortune be a cat.

This is not to say that cats won't kill whatever song and game birds they can manage, or eat their eggs. Domestic birds, in particular the young, will also be attacked; but most cats can be trained not to attack them, while only a rare cat can be trained to leave wild birds alone. There appears to be a definite taste preference in both birds and their eggs, as there is with mice. A study of such preference indicates that the conspicuous birds are less palatable than the cryptic species.

2. *Insects as Food.* The outdoor cat relishes many other living things besides birds and mammals as it can find and catch them. It is so fond of grasshoppers that it frequently gets sick from overindulging in them. Crickets, flies, beetles, moths and butterflies are other favored insects, and to the housebound city cat, flies and cockroaches, when available, are a great delicacy. When larger insects are caught the objectionable parts like legs and wings are removed before the insect is eaten or are discarded during the eating process. Hugh B. Cott in *Adaptive Coloration of Animals* gives an interesting account of cats and their insect prey.

"Not only do members of the *Felidae* move up from the assault with wonderful skill, they also show considerable judgment according to circumstances. For example, my cat 'Queenie,' who is fond of insects, hunts for them with untiring zeal when in the mood for sport: but he uses a different technique for different types of prey. If the immediate attraction is a 'crane-fly' (*Tipulidae*), he knows by experience that he can easily overtake it by speed alone; the insect is pursued, struck down with a paw, and swallowed. But when a 'blue-bottle' (*Muscidae*) has to be captured, the difference in his mode of attack is nicely adjusted to the activity of his victim: employing all the stealth at his command, he will work up actively behind cover, then approach deliberately, slowly, until within a foot or so; then there follows the sudden rush, and the lightning stroke of a paw, and the disabled insect is transferred to the mouth. . . .

"From the time that the first grasshoppers appear in June to the time that the last one finally succumbs to a severe freeze, country cats enjoy the sport of catching them and making a meal of them. Young kittens soon learn the technique and continue it for the rest of their lives. An African species of grasshopper, however, emits an unpalatable secretion, and Dr. W. A. Lamborn describes its effects on his kitten. 'My kitten seized one in its mouth, but dropped it instantly, and commenced to salivate. Strings of thick mucous an inch long appeared at the corner of its mouth with much frothy saliva, and the animal retched but did not exactly vomit. It kept on rubbing its mouth against a tree in an endeavour to get rid of the cause, and was not its usual self for two or three hours. The Acridian had hopped off, apparently little the worse for its experience.' A cat's reactions after mouthing a toad parallel this description exactly."

3. *Reptiles and Amphibians as Food.* Frogs, newts, salamanders, snakes and lizards comprise the country cat's herpetological menu. Some reports also mention toads but this is hard to believe. As Dr. Cott pointed out in his discussion of cats and grasshoppers, a cat who mouths a toad will be unhappy for a long time and it is never stupid enough to try the same thing a second time. *Hortus Sanitatis* (15th century) says that the cat fights against toads "and though it be beaten off by their venomed darts, yet it is not killed." It further states that the cat is an unclean and poisonous animal itself. In the Middle Ages cats born in May also gained a poor reputation. They were said to be melancholy creatures who caught toads and reptiles in preference to anything else and were therefore poor mousers.

Snakes fascinate cats as much as they fascinate people. Cats will contemplate and play with them dead or alive for longer periods than with other animals, yet I have never seen one eaten, even by a hungry cat. They may well be on the list of highly individual taste preferences like shrews.

A sick feral cat arrived at our door one day with her three young kittens. She was no longer capable of hunting. Some intestinal disorder had left her weak and emaciated and she knew she needed help if she and her kittens were to survive. They were too young to be weaned so we concentrated on stuffing her.

The urge to provide for herself caused her to continue hunting, however unsuccessfully. Shortly after she arrived she came walking up the driveway very very slowly, dragging a large snake. All her energy had been expended in its killing and she had to stop frequently to gather the strength needed for the haul. By the time she reached the house she was so exhausted that she dropped down with her heavy burden and didn't even move when we approached her.

In spite of all the labor expended in procuring the snake she didn't eat it and the kittens showed no interest in it. Perhaps they were too young but kittens the same age grow extremely ferocious over mice brought to them. In her condition Calicat seemed incapable of catching anything except snakes, none of which was ever eaten. Later, when she grew better, her catches never included snakes.

Diodorus of Sicily (1st century B.C.) mentions the use of cats to kill snakes, but he makes no comment about whether they were eaten or not. "The cat is likewise useful against asps with their deadly bite and other reptiles that sting . . ." And many is the tale to this day, both fact and fiction, of how a cat, by attacking a poisonous snake, saves a person's life.

4. *Hunting Technique.* Seldom pure instinct, predation is learned by the kitten through play and the behavior of its mother. Play activity which teaches the proper hunting procedure begins around the fifth week and by the eighth the kitten is already well cordinated and agile; it responds to all types of stimuli and situations automatically and precisely.

In play or earnest the hunting cat or kitten follows a definite pattern. It stalks and approaches its prey stealthily, running swiftly in a crouching position, its belly close to the ground. As it closes the gap between itself and its prey it conceals itself as well as conditions allow. At close range it proceeds slowly and pauses often. When near enough to pounce it does so quickly with outstretched forepaws.Both claws and teeth grasp the prey in perfect coordination, the claws pinning it to the ground as the jaws seize it at the back of the neck. Often the cat will sit in some elevated position to watch for its victim. In such cases the stalking ritual is unnecessary, the cat pouncing on its victim from above as soon as the latter gets within range. It will also follow its prey up trees and into dens and burrows, but not being equipped for effective digging it prefers to lie in wait outside of them for the animal's reemergence.

A hungry cat will eat completely the animal that it catches except for the larger birds and mammals. A cat that isn't hungry will leave its catch or eat only the brain or a few entrails. Prey like full-grown rabbits that can't be finished in one meal, no matter what the appetite, are first eviscerated, the muscle meat being partaken of at the next meal. The long hair, feet, and tail of mammals will usually be left uneaten, as will the large feathers, wings and legs of birds.

Cats are neat eaters, as they are in all their habits. They seldom leave a trace of their bloody meals and they themselves remain clean. A washing isn't necessary after their meals but they always give themselves one anyway.

5. *On Some Hunting Cats.* "Latterly we saw at my house a cat lying in wait for a bird in a tree, and fixing each other with their eyes for some time, the bird allowing himself to fall as though dead between the paws of the cat, whether made drunk by his own imagination, or drawn by some attractive force of the cat."

MONTAIGNE

"Edmund is quite well, and Tommy Puss the same. A night or two ago, Tommy was lying at my feet and suddenly got up and stretched himself. 'What now, Tommy?' said I. He said there was no standing the want of a bit of meat; he didn't like this bread and tea work; and off he started. In half an hour, he came in at the window with a fine half-grown rabbit, and laid it at my feet."

CHARLES WATERTON in *Essay on Natural History*

"It is a well-known habit of some hunting, or poaching, cats to bring their captives to their master or mistress. I have met with scores—I might say with hundreds—of such cases. I remember an old gaucho, a neighbour of mine in South America, who used to boast that he usually had a spotted tinamou—the partridge of the pampas—for his dinner every day, brought in by his cat. Even in England, where partridges are not so abundant or easily taken, there are clever partridge-hunting cats. I remember one, a very fine white cat, owned by a woodman I once lodged with in Savernake Forest, who was in the habit of bringing in a partridge and would place it on the kitchen floor and keep guard over it until the woodman's wife came to take it up and put it away for the Sunday's dinner. A lady friend told me of a cat at a farm-house where she was staying during the summer months, which became attached to her and was constantly bringing her young rabbits. They were never injured but held firmly by the skin of the neck. The lady would take the rabbit gently into her hands and deposit it on her lap, and cover it over with a handkerchief or a cloth, and pussy, seeing it safe in her power would then go away. The lady would then walk away to a distance from the house to liberate the little trembler, devoutly wishing that this too affectionate cat would get over the delusion that such gifts were acceptable to her. One day pussy came trotting into the drawing-room with a stoat in his mouth, and depositing it on the carpet by the side of her chair immediately turned round and hastily left the room. The stoat was dead, not being a creature that could easily be carried about alive, and pussy, having other matters to attend to, did not think it necessary to wait to see her present taken up and carefully deposited in her mistress's lap.

"Cases of this kind are exceedingly common, and the simple explanation is, that the cat is not quite so unsocial a creature as some naturalists would have us believe. We may say that in this respect he compares badly with elephants, whales, pigs, seals, cattle, apes, wolves, dogs, and other large-brained social mammals; but he does not live wholly for himself. He is able to take thought for other cats and for his human companion—master hardly seems the right word in the case of such an animal—who is doubtless to him only a very big cat that walks erect on his hind-legs. I must, however, relate one more instance of a cat who hunted for others, told to me by a very aged friend of mine, a native of Fonthill Bishop, . . .

"When she was a young motherless girl and they were very poor indeed, her father being incapacitated, they had a cat that was a great help to them; a large black and white animal who spent a greater part of his time hunting in Fonthill Abbey woods, and who was always bringing in something for the pot. The cat was attached to her, and whatever was brought in was for her exclusively, and I imagine it is so in all cases in which a cat has the custom of bringing anything it catches into the house. The cat mind cannot understand a division of food. It does not and cannot share a mouse or bird with another cat, and when it gives it gives the whole animal, and to one person alone. When the cat brought a rabbit home he would not come into the kitchen with it if he saw her little brother or any other person there, lest they should take it into their hands; he would steal off and conceal it among the weeds at the back of the cottage, then come back to make little mewing sounds understood by his young mistress, and she would thereupon follow him out to where the rabbit was hidden and take it up, and the cat would then be satisfied.

"The cat brought her rabbits and di-dappers, as she called the moorhen, caught in the sedges by the lake in the park . . . Moorhens were not the only birds it captured: on two or three occasions it brought in a partridge and on one occasion a fish. Whether it was a trout or not she could not say; she only knew that she cooked and ate it and that it was very good.

"One day, looking out, she spied her cat coming home with something very big, something it had caught larger than itself; and it was holding its head very high, dragging its burden along with great labour. It was a hare, and she ran out to receive it, and when she got to the cat and stooped down to take it from him he released it too soon, for it was uninjured, and away it bounded and vanished into the woods, leaving them both very much astonished and disgusted."

W. H. Hudson from *A Shepherd's Life*

An old cat was sitting up mewing with half-closed eyes when two mice happened to see her. Astonished that their old enemy should be taking things so easily they said to each other, "Puss is evidently reformed; she is saying her prayers. We need have no fear." So they began playing about without noticing her. No sooner had they got within reach, however, than the cat sprang upon one and devoured it. Its companion rushed home and remarked, "Who would have thought that a cat who shut her eyes and said her prayers would act like that?"

Chinese Folktale

Fishing. "Catus amat piscem, sed non vult tangere flumen." Taken from a manuscript written in 1225 this is one of the earliest references to our proverb that a cat likes fish but doesn't like to wet its feet. The first part of the statement is true for most cats, but not the second. And since a discussion of the cat's liking for fish necessitates a consideration of its reaction to water it seems best to cover that matter first.

As the elephant is said to abhor slight tickling sensations like those produced by a scampering mouse, most cats despise an accidental sprinkling from a few drops of water or, at the other extreme, a downright drenching. Very few mind a mild wetting and most enjoy being out in misty weather or drizzling rain if there is no strong wind. In summer they drowse on the damp earth and in winter romp in the snow. They *do* dislike accidentally wetting a paw but when engrossed in fishing, getting a paw wet is deliberate and distaste over it is farthest from their thoughts. Even the indoor cat often braves exposure to water in order to fish in the household's fish bowl or aquarium.

The cats of the Egyptians, who are thought to share at least one ancestor with our modern cats, were often depicted hunting birds with their owners in the marshlands of the Nile. Wildcats are avid fishermen and good swimmers, taking to the water not only through necessity but desire. Housecats themselves swim instinctively and although most do not do so voluntarily there are many exceptions that do without any coaxing from humans.

It therefore remains a mystery why the misconception about their dislike for getting wet has persisted for over 700 years, and probably longer. Even scientists who should have known better repeated it as a fact. Topsell went a step further to say that cats die from a wetting. "A Cat is much delighted to play with hir image in a glasse, and if at any time she behold it in water, presently she leapeth down in the water which naturally she doth abhorre; but if she be not quickly pulled forth and dryed she dieth thereof, because she is impatient of all wet." Were cats of the 16th and 17th centuries actually so stupid?

The Negroes have a story about why cats don't fish. One day Brother Tom went fishing. He baited his hook and threw it into the water and almost immediately a big dogfish grabbed it and lit out with it. Tom was sitting on a log but he managed to land the fish. When, however, he went to pull it in, the dogfish grabbed his tail and gave it a good bite. Brother Tom was so surprised that he fell into the water and barely made it to shore. From then on he swore he'd only catch fish off a plate.

Literature abounds in anecdotes about fishing, boating and swimming cats, and there are reports on some who actually dived into the water to catch fish and water voles with their paws or mouths. Ordinarily the fishing cat frequents shallows or stream banks and deftly hooks its fish out of the water with its claws in the same fashion that the indoor cat hooks goldfish from an aquarium. Often it will wade into deeper water after its catch.

In his articles on feline fishermen E. W. Gudger tells about cats who used their eyes, tongue or tail as lures to attract fish to within reach of their claws. It could well be that these stories have some truth to them, far-fetched as they may sound. The cats may have used the "lures" accidentally at first and, noticing the excellent results, continued to use them from then on. Their mentality is sufficiently advanced for them to draw conclusions.

One of the earliest references to a fishing cat is Gray's oft-quoted poem "On the Death of a Favourite Cat Drowned in a Tub of Gold-Fishes" first published in 1748. According to Gudger the cat after whom the *Rue du Chat qui Peche* in Paris was named is the only earlier reference. When the floods of the Seine subsided around the middle of the 17th century they left many fish stranded in the cellars of buildings along its banks. The Parisian puss who frequented these because of the easy fishing they provided became a legend. Because of his activities a street's name was changed, thereby perpetuating him and his fishing proclivities.

Mother cats who are avid fishermen teach their young to fish as other mothers teach theirs to hunt, and adult cats have been known to teach other adults the art. A cat's liking for fish and fishing appears to be greater than that for mice and hunting, and it is always ready to accept a handout from fishermen. Clams, oysters and crabs are three more favorite feline aquatic foods. Cats search for crabs at low tide and when they find them they crack them open to get at the meat.

A CAT THAT CAUGHT TROUT

One of the shepherd's most interesting memories of his Doveton period was of a cat they possessed, which was greatly admired. He was a very large, handsome, finely marked tabby, with a thick coat, and always appeared very well nourished but never wanted to be fed. He was a nice-tempered, friendly animal, and whenever he came in he appeared pleased at seeing the inmates of the house, and would go from one to another, rubbing his sides against their legs and purring aloud with satisfaction. Then they would give him food, and he would take a morsel or two or lap up as much milk as would fill a teaspoon and leave the rest. He was not hungry, and it always appeared, they said, as if he smelt at or tasted the food they put down for him just to please them. Everybody in the village admired their cat for his great size, his beauty, and gentle, friendly disposition, but how he fed himself was a mystery to all, since no one had ever detected him trying to catch anything out of doors. In that part of the Wylye valley there were no woods for him to hunt in; they also noticed that when, out of doors, the small birds, anxious and angered at his presence, would flit, uttering their cries, close to him, he paid no attention. The only thing they discovered about his outdoor life by watching him was that he had the habit of going to the railway track, then recently constructed, from Westbury to Salisbury, which ran near their cottage, and would there seat himself on one of the rails and remain for a long time gazing fixedly before him as if he found it a pleasure to keep his eyes on the long, glittering metal line.

At the back of the cottage there was a piece of waste ground extending to the river, with a small, old, ruinous barn standing on it a few yards from the bank. Between the barn and the stream the ground was overgrown with rank weeds, and here one day Caleb came by chance upon his cat eating something among the weeds—a good-sized, fresh-caught trout! On examining the ground he found it littered with the heads, fins, and portions of backbones of the trout their cat had been feeding on every day since they had been in possession of him. They did not destroy their favourite, nor tell anyone of their discovery, but they watched him and found that it was his habit to bring a trout every day to that spot, but how he caught his fish was never known.

W. H. Hudson from *A Shepherd's Life*

Response to Prey. "Some years ago, at Mr. James Greenfield's in Maryland, was observed a most surprising sympathy between a cat and a rat. It was supposed to have happened thus. The cat had young kittens, and frequently carried them mice, and other animals, its prey, and among the rest a young rat. The kittens not being hungry, played with it; and when the cat came to give suck to the kittens, the rat likewise sucked her. This was observed by some of the servants, and they informed Mr. Greenfield of it. He had the kittens and rat brought downstairs and put together on the floor, and the cat was observed to carry away the young rat as tenderly as she did either of her young ones. This experiment was repeated as often as any company came to the house, till numbers were eye-witnesses of this preternatural sympathy. A rare instance of affection from lactation." *Scots Magazine*, 1752.

Occurrences like this are relatively common (see chapter on friends and foes) and the end result is that the adult cat often ceases to hunt rats, and her kittens never acquire the habit. Why cats may respond in friendly fashion to rodents and other animals that are their natural food has always bothered observers of this phenomenon. Experience, training and example are not needed to cause a good percentage of cats to kill their prey, but certain perquisites to bring out friendship usually are, such as nursing in the above cat. Circumstances make the cat-rat relationship vary from love to hate, killing to fearing.

In 1930 and 1938 Zing Yang Kuo published the results of his experiments aimed at explaining different types of cat-rat and cat-bird behavior, and they more or less settled a good part of the problem. They demonstrated the importance of the cat's early environmental experience to its future behavior. Mr. Kuo used three species of rodents for his tests—albino rats, ordinary wild mice and dancing mice—and he began his experiments by raising kittens in three separate environments.

1. 20 kittens were raised in complete isolation as soon as they were taken from their mother. They not only were kept from other animals including each other but were not allowed to see or hear anything outside their individual cages. When given rodents only nine of these kittens killed them and only three of the nine ate them. Mr. Kuo felt that this shows the concepts of habit and instinct are insufficient to describe an animal's behavior.

2. 21 kittens were raised in a rat-killing environment. They were kept with their mothers who were given rodents of one species only to kill, and these were removed as soon as they were killed. The kittens never saw one being eaten.

When offered rodents of their own 18 of these 21 kittens killed them. They always killed the species of rodent which they had seen their mother kill, and sometimes they killed other species as well. 9 out of the 18 ate their kill.

3. 18 kittens were raised in the same cage with rodents of one type only. Three of the 18 killed a rodent when given one but these were never of the same species with which they had been reared. Two of the three ate their kill.

The next step in the experiment was to see whether kittens could be trained to kill. Those kittens who had failed to kill mice—the 11 raised in isolation and the 15 raised with rodent companions—were allowed to see adult cats killing different kinds of rodents. Of the 11, nine became killers, but of the 15, only one did. This adequately demonstrates the difficulty of teaching a cat to kill something with which it has been reared. The one killer kitten and two of the other nine killers ate their kill.

It should be noted that in all the above situations some of the killer kittens ate their prey although they had never seen this being done. The action is independent of external stimulation and does not have to be learned.

In the three types of environmental conditions under which the kittens had been raised, half of each group had been fed a vegetarian diet while the other half received meat. Of all the kittens, totalling 59,

40 eventually killed rodents and 17 ate them. Of these 40, 20 or 50% had been raised as vegetarians, indicating that food habits do not govern the impulse to kill. However, only 4 of the 20 vegetarian killers, or 20%, ate their kill while 13, or 65%, of the meat eaters ate theirs. In a follow-up of this learned food preference it was found that the vegetarian kittens refused to eat meat in any form after they were 3–4 months old.

All the kittens were also divided into two groups according to hunger. Half were given their rodents immediately after they had eaten; the other half received theirs after a 12 hour fast. The well-fed kittens were found to kill and eat more rodents than the hungry ones, proving the contention that a well-fed cat is the best mouser.

Further findings from the experiments are equally interesting. The kittens raised in a rodent-killing environment began to kill much sooner than those raised in isolation. Cats learn readily through imitation. In this case the mother's behavior not only influenced her young to kill but to kill as soon as they were capable of it. The young kittens never attempted to attack the large albino rats, but began first with the small dancing mice. As they grew in size and dexterity they began to attack the larger wild mice, and finally graduated to the rats. No preference for killing certain species was shown other than this limitation caused by relative ability, except for the instances already noted, that is, the kittens' preference for killing species which they had seen their mothers kill and their refusal to kill species with which they had been raised. Once old enough and adept enough to kill rats they still continued to kill smaller rodents as well. There were, of course, a few individualistic kittens who killed only one type of rodent.

Summarizing his findings, Kuo classified the behavior of the kittens toward rodents into six categories: A) positive, B) negative, C) oriented, D) tolerant, E) playful, F) hostile.

1. F was closely related to A.
2. B and D were dominant in non-rodent-killing kittens.
3. Larger rodents called forth B and F more often than did smaller ones.
4. B, C, and E were found in kittens raised in isolation.
5. F was found in kittens raised in a rodent-killing environment.
6. B, D, and E were found in kittens reared with rodents. They also exhibited an attachment for and a protective attitude toward them.

This last held true, however, only when the rodent was the kitten's only companion. When a kitten was raised with its litter mates as well as rodents it formed no ties with the latter.

Each of four litters of kittens, shortly after birth and without their mothers, was raised with a pair of albino rats for a period of nine months. One month after they were separated from the rats they were again introduced to them, the test being repeated each month for four months.

During the nine month period all the kittens remained indifferent to and tolerant of the rats. Some attempted to play with them, but any sort of attachment was reserved for their siblings alone. None missed the rats if they were removed from the cage, and none showed any protective behavior toward them. When the pair of rats had young, 65% of the kittens killed and ate the newborn rats whenever they had the chance, but this did not change their relationship with the adults. (When the rats were in their nest they would attack the kittens who approached it. The kittens were afraid of them under these conditions and took the young only when the rats left their nest.)

In order to test whether their reaction to the adults was toward the individual rather than the species, rats of graded ages were introduced to the kittens. In each test two rats of the same age were used, one unshaved and the other shaved to make it resemble the naked young. The unshaved rat was given to the kitten first, the shaved after the unshaved was removed. All but one of the kittens that killed newborn rats killed and ate shaved rats regardless of age or size. Also, one kitten that had not killed the newborn rats did kill two young shaved rats. Unshaved rats were ignored.

The kittens' attitude remained unchanged toward their rodent cage mates which were reintroduced, as mentioned above. Even after they were allowed to watch other cats killing rats only 40% tried to attack them and only 20% persisted long enough to make a killing.

A similar experiment was performed using sparrows instead of rats. The birds were introduced to the kittens before their eyes were opened, and they were ignored until the kittens were two months old. They then began to follow the birds in their flight around the cage but lost interest in them as soon as flight ceased. If the birds panicked from being chased the kittens grew excited and intensified the chase. If one was accidentally caught it was played with but not harmed. After a number of catches, however, 20% of the kittens did kill and eat the birds.

When the kittens were allowed to live a free, normal life only this 20% showed any interest in small birds of any species, and they were seen to catch and eat not only these but frogs and mice as well. The other kittens showed no interest in birds.

A NOTABLE RAT-KILLER

Gip is the most inveterate rat-killer I have ever known. He is never seen hunting other creatures, not even mice, although it is probable that he does kill and devour them on the spot, but he has the habit of bringing in the rats he captures; and as a day seldom passes on which he is not seen with one, and as sometimes two or three are brought in during the night, he cannot destroy fewer than three hundred to four hundred rats in the year.

Let any one who knows the destructive powers of the rat consider what that means to an agricultural village, and what an advantage it is to the farmers to have their rick-yards and barns policed day and night by such an animal. For the whole village is his hunting ground. His owner says that he is 'worth his weight in gold.' I should say that he is worth much more; that the equivalent in cash of his weight in purest gold, though he is big and heavy, would not be more than the value of the grain and other foodstuffs he saves from destruction in a single year.

He invariably brings in his rats alive to release and play with them in an old, stone-paved yard, and after a little play he kills them, and if they are full-grown he leaves them; but when young he devours them or allows the other cats to have them.

W. H. Hudson from *A Shepherd's Life*

WHY CATS KILL RATS: A LIBERIAN FOLKTALE

Mrs. Rat owned a large farm that was difficult to manage. When her daughter was old enough to marry she decided that the best way to test the worth of each suitor was to see how well he could manage the farm.

As Miss Rat was very beautiful many sought her hand, but each lover, after attempting to run the farm, was soon found lacking by Mrs. Rat and sent away. After many months of losing prospective husbands because of her mother's whim Miss Rat began to wonder if she would ever marry. Suitors became scarcer and scarcer.

One day Mr. Cat presented himself at the farm and went to work immediately without any preliminaries. He worked so rapidly and so efficiently that the farm was soon in better shape than it had ever been before. Mrs. Rat was delighted and gladly gave her daughter to Mr. Cat. It was Mr. Cat's turn to be delighted, and he settled down joyfully with his new bride. He was soon to find, to his sorrow, that he had married beauty only: his young wife did nothing but complain.

A few weeks after the wedding she looked at him petulantly and told him that she would certainly love him far more if he had shorter teeth. Anxious to do anything that would please her, Mr. Cat filed them down at once and came back to her for her approval.

"Goodness," his wife exclaimed, "now you've made them much too short. This way I don't like you any more than I did before."

Mr. Cat, angered at being played for a fool, leaped on his wife and killed her. From that time on, cats have killed rats whether they are hungry or not.

XXII
Alimentation and Elimination

THE capriciousness of the cat is no better illustrated than in its eating habits. Presented with the food he ate with gusto the day before a cat may look at it and then you in shocked disbelief. How heartless can you be to offer him something unfit to eat? He turns again to the offending dish, goes through the motions of covering it up as he would his excrement, and turns his back to it. Not yet satisfied that he has rid himself completely of the noxious stuff, he shakes his hind feet, first one and then the other, as he does after an accidental wetting. Only then does he stalk off in a pique without a further glance at you or the cause of his displeasure.

It is for this sort of cat, the pampered, bored house pet, that the petfood companies prepare their great variety of cat foods. As pointed out in the section on predation cats never seem to tire of their natural food, and those lucky enough to live where they can hunt are not so great a problem to feed as the housebound pet. Still, they are difficult enough particularly when they smell human food that appeals to them more than their own fare. Cats being cats, exceptions to the rule are many, and I know of two cats who will eat only one type of dried cat food and nothing else, not even milk.

What do cats enjoy eating? Almost anything, depending on the cat and its mood of the moment. Carnivorous they may be but their tastes range far and wide from meat as the old nursery rhyme reminds us.

Pussy Cat ate the dumplings,
The dumplings, the dumplings.
Mama stood by and cried, "Oh, Fie!
Why did you eat the dumplings?"

Lafcadio Hearn listed the food eaten by one of his kittens as "beefsteak and cockroaches, caterpillars and fish, chicken and butterflies, mosquito hawks and roast mutton, hash and tumblebugs, beetles and pig's feet, crabs and spiders, moths and poached eggs, oysters and earthworms, ham and mice, rats and rice pudding"; a nice balance between civilized and wild viands.

In countries where the cocoanut palm grows, cats are fed cocoanut meat and are very fond of it. The Bagobo of the Philippines say that long ago the cocoanut used to be the head of the cat and that is why they like it so much.

With domestication the cat has learned to eat practically every sort of human food including most fruits and vegetables. As with us, it wants some foods in quantity, some only as an accent to the meal. Almost all cats enjoy corn, melons and asparagus, and of their liking for this last, Alphonse Toussenel, the French naturalist, had this to say. "A love of cats is a vice of inferior minds; a man of good taste, and with a keen sense of smell, has never had, nor could he have, sympathy with a beast passionately fond of asparagus." Needless to say, Toussenel despised cats as much as he doted on birds.

A cat's liking for grass (the coarser the better for most) appears to be strictly for utilitarian purposes. A small amount acts as an emetic, cleaning out the stomach. A large amount seems to act as a purge. It is not digested. According to a correspondent of *Notes and Queries* earthworms are also eaten for their therapeutic value. The author watched an adult cat dig them up in the garden to feed to a sick kitten. This she did daily until the kitten recovered. Earthworms were used in folk rem-

"An Oyster Supper" by H. H. Couldery. (City of Nottingham Museum & Art Gallery, in the Castle Museum)

"Caught in the Act" by Unknown Artist.

edies of the ancients, so there may be something in his observations and conclusion, unlikely as they seem.

Most cats like milk, and if not milk, cream, and they relish it in their daily diet. The Egyptians fed milk to their cats with bread crumbled in it, much as people nowadays do, besides giving them cut-up fish. People the world over are aware of the cat's love for milk. From the Hindus comes "The cat laps the moonbeams in the bowl of water, thinking them to be milk." Of the many proverbs on the subject there is "It's easy to teach the cat the way to the churn" from Scotland to "The cat has drunk the milk but you have given it to her" from Surinam.

The physiologist Louis Pierre Gratiolet (1815–1856) gave us this description of a kitten abandoning itself to the pleasures of drinking what must have been milk or cream.

"Observe a kitten advancing slowly and sniffing at some sweetened liquid. Its ears are erect, its widely-opened eyes express desire, its impatient tongue, licking its lips, tastes the desired object by anticipation. It walks cautiously, with outstretched neck. But now it has got hold of the longed-for object, its lips touch the balmy liquid, it laps it eagerly. The object is no longer desired, it is possessed, and the sensation which it awakens pervades the entire organism; the young cat then shuts its eyes, in contemplation of its own all-pervading pleasure. It falls back upon itself, hunches up its back, shivers voluptuously, and seems to cover up its body with its limbs, as if to possess the source of its enjoyment more entirely. Its head sinks in between its shoulders; one might fancy that it seeks oblivion of a world thenceforth indifferent to it. It resolves itself into the sense of taste, and the sense of smell, and withdraws into itself with a most significant completeness."

Books on cat care always warn us to give cats food and drink at room temperature to avoid causing digestive upsets. The effect on its hypothalamus in experiments where a cat is given cold liquids to drink would seem to bear out this warning. If it drinks cold (40° F milk, at the average temperature of refrigerators, there is an immediate drop in the temperature of the hypothalamus accompanied by peripheral vasodilation of the ear, and foot and toe pads of the forelimbs. This is followed by a drop in rectal temperature. Quite a lot of action merely from ingesting cold milk! The cat's body as a whole and not only its stomach apparently objects to cold food. Warm milk does not cause these changes.

There seems to be no basis, however, to the oft-repeated admonition

"Milk" by Theophile Steinlen.

that cats should always have fresh water, if one can judge from the cats themselves. Rather than drink from a clean water dish they much prefer to lap standing-water outdoors, flavored among other things with drowned worms and grasshoppers, decayed vegetation and algae. Even a fastidious indoor cat considers such water a treat, as it does the stale water in flower vases. Most cats, even Siamese, choose seasoned water at all times in preference to water fresh from the tap.

It has already been mentioned that the cat is a neat eater, and a gobbling cat is a rare cat. Chop licking is frequent in anticipation of a meal as well as after the partaking of one, and if the coming meal portends something better than usual there is excess salivation causing a good deal of swallowing. The average cat crouches on its haunches to eat, but an occasional one will leave its rear end elevated, making you wonder how it can swallow effectively. As Gratiolet observed, a cat also tends to shut its eyes as it eats or drinks. We assume it is done in pleasure but the Persians have another idea as to its meaning. They claim it is done out of ingratitude as if to say "I don't see what is being given me, so I won't have to show any appreciation." Another Moslem interpretation is more charitable. It states that it is because they like milk so much that cats always drink with closed eyes. Then when Allah asks them whether they have had their milk or not they stand a better chance of getting more because they can truthfully answer, "I did not see it."

A cat never "digs into" his meal immediately unless he knows what to expect. He will first sniff the food from all angles and if it isn't homogeneous he will extract the choice bits first regardless of how small they may be.

Feline stomachs have far stronger digestive juices than ours, and they easily soften swallowed bones so that they can be digested. Indigestible material such as fur and feathers is regurgitated in the same way that owls cough up their pellets. Food that disagrees is also regurgitated, and with some nervous individuals this is almost a daily occurrence. The cat that does this is not sick in the strict sense but is merely getting rid of the "butterflies in its stomach." Persons not acquainted with the mechanics of the procedure may think it is throwing a fit or choking to death because of the spasms it goes through. But though it may look and sound ghastly, as does coughing in the cat, regurgitation is a normal, common act. In fact it is so common that another word for vomiting is catting.

After the cat eats there is always the washing ritual with which everyone is familiar, but before this begins there will be a great deal of chop licking, as mentioned, the amount depending on how good the meal was. The folktale as to why the cat washes after eating was put into verse by Eva Beede.

You may have noticed, little friends,
That cats don't wash their faces
Before they eat, as children do,
In all good Christian places.

Well, years ago, a famous cat,
The pangs of hunger feeling,
Had chanced to catch a fine young mouse
Who said, as he ceased squealing,

"All genteel folks their faces wash
Before they think of eating!"
And, wishing to be thought well-bred,
Puss heeded his entreating.

But when she raised her paw to wash
Chance for escape affording,
The sly young mouse said his good-bye,
Without respect to wording.

A feline council met next day,
And passed, in solemn meeting,
A law forbidding any cat
To wash till *after* eating.

Like all carnivores cats have the capacity to gorge themselves at one meal after which they can go without food for days at a time; a week's fast means nothing to them. Provided with as many birds and mice as it wished to eat a laboratory cat was found to consume the equivalent of about 10% of its body weight each day, averaged over a period of time. However, it was capable of eating over 20% of its weight at one meal and in one period of 26.5 hours it consumed 17 mice.

Meat, being more easily broken down than vegetable matter, needs less time to be digested. Consequently feline intestines are short in comparison to those of herbivores. However, the inclusion in its diet of "people food" is said to be causing a gradual lengthening of the domestic cat's intestines to accommodate the less carnivorous fare. Already its intestines are supposed to be longer than those of the wild cat.

Cats urinate and defecate on the average of once a day, the frequency necessarily varying with the bulk and water content of the food eaten. Although they may have no well-defined territory they continue to have "calling places" where they leave their mark by urinating, and females as well as males spray at these spots despite what some books and veterinarians say to the contrary. Castration and spaying often do not change this habit, castration merely making the odor of the male cat's urine less obnoxious. The spindle tree, *Euonymus europeus*, shares this unpleasant odor with the tomcat and for this reason is frequently called the cat tree or cat-wood.

Other than spraying, cats bury both urine and faeces, first digging a hole and then covering it over. City cats who are unable to find a soft substrate in which to dig go through the burying motions regardless. All cats tend to visit a circumscribed area when they wish to defecate, often, unfortunately, the center of a flower garden. Such places have been designated as "scatoria."

> Belaud, that well-bred creature
> If constrained sometimes by nature
> To any less-than-proper act,
> Had such propriety, in fact,
> That 'neath the ashes he concealed
> What he was constrained to yield.
>
> JOACHIM DU BELLAY

Why cats treat their excrement as they do is told in a Canarese legend from the alpine forests of the Malabar Coast. Note the similarity to the cat-tiger tales in the chapter on cat enemies.

"A cat and a tiger once went out together for a walk. After they had strolled on through the wild jungle for some time the tiger began to feel hungry, and to think of the desirability of making a pounce on the cat. His sidelong looks soon aroused the suspicions of the cat, who, knowing not how else to elude the tiger's purpose, proposed that they should climb up and rest awhile in a tree, and then return home. To this the tiger readily agreed, only asking the cat to show the way, when, while the cat was well within reach, the tiger made a sudden grab for him. But the cat was too quick for the tiger, and instantly sprang forward on to a light branch of the tree where the tiger could not follow. Then the cruel beast crouched down at the root of the tree in watch until the cat would be obliged to descend. Long waiting, however, exhausted the tiger's patience, and at last he roused himself to depart, growling out as he slunk homeward: 'I cannot wait for you now, but as you cats always drop your dung in the same place, I shall be sure to catch you before long.' Then the cat cautiously descended from his perch of safety, and went round and told the whole of the cat world of what the tiger had said, and ever since then the cats have made it their custom to seek out every day a different place of egestion, and there dig a hole and drop their dung therein, and carefully cover it over with earth, so that the tigers may never know where they have been or where to find them again."

Social dominance is said to develop and be common among cats who compete for food, whether there are only two animals or many. Yet, through all the years that I have fed more than one cat I have never observed such a situation. One cat more hungry than usual will be able to shove aside another who isn't very hungry, but can seldom budge one who is, regardless of which one is higher in the pecking order in other matters. Never have I observed a perennial king, queen or bully of the food dishes.

Of course, laboratory experiments testing for food competition are more competitive than the routine feeding of a large group of cats; and the characters of the individual cats determine what the outcome will be. An experiment where only two cats at a time were used resulted in a more rapid manipulation of the problem box into which they were put than when one cat was tested alone. The outcome of the rivalry was of three types: (1) a struggle for the food by winner and loser; (2) a hoarding of the food by either cat; and (3) a sharing of the food with no aggression on the part of either.

When social dominance does appear during food competition it doesn't take the form of aggression. Only when the dominant cat is challenged and displaced downward in rank does aggression appear, and if dominance is reestablished aggression disappears or is greatly reduced. Where aggression does occur is among the cats lower in rank.

For example, in a competitive runway test with food as the goal, the two losing cats of three introduced in the runway may become aggressive toward each other but not toward the winning cat. This is a form of displaced aggression common among humans as well as cats. As Aldous Huxley advised, if you would know humans you would do well to observe cats.

XXIII
Wildness

"At whiles it seems as if one were somewhat as the cats, which ever have appeared to me to be animals of two parts, the one of the house and the cushion and the prepared food, the other that is free of the night and runs wild with the wind in its coat and the smell of the earth in its nostrils."

Una L. Silberrad c.1687. *The Book of Sanchia Stapleton*

NEVER having fully relinquished their wild traits to domestication, cats are able to choose between a life of freedom and independence and one of relative security and human intervention. Most choose the middle path when possible, retaining a cozy berth in a human household but roaming when they get the wanderlust. Others choose to remain close to the fireside their entire lives while still others consider a domestic existence stifling and leave it early never to return. Booth Tarkington's "Gipsy," reprinted here, is about such a cat, not too common yet common enough for everyone to know at least one like him.

Then there are cats who through accident or adversity are forced to become self-sustaining. Some, in particular those who have been mistreated by humans, often elect to live the rest of their lives on their own. Others like C. A. White's Jerry, whose story is also reprinted below, rejoice in regaining human companionship.

It is impossible to say whether cats feral from birth ever seek human habitations. Feral cats who seek help from people seem to be of two kinds: those who remain unapproachable and usually leave when they no longer need assistance, and those who appear to crave human companionship and ever so slowly come to accept it up to a point. The first could easily be those cats who are feral from birth, the second those who have already associated to some extent with humans.

I have had to trap some of the first type because of their continual ferocious attacks on other cats, but most remain aloof from cats and humans alike, coming and going as their needs dictate. A good percentage of the second type are pregnant or lactating females, and although they themselves may eventually become relatively tame, their kittens tend to remain half wild, no doubt because their introduction to humans came too late, that is, after the critical period for socialization.

One kitten of this type managed to survive and grow up on our farm. Spots never let us get close to her; she never entered the house even through the cat door, and she preferred to procure her own food rather than eat what we set out for her. We knew when she gave birth to kittens but were unable to find them. All our outhouses are equipped with cat doors. Too often animals had accidentally been locked up in them, so openings had been made which solved that problem and mouse problems at the same time. But the kittens were in none of these buildings.

One day I began the spring cleaning of a spare room in the house. In it was a heavy couch which I seldom moved to clean under. As I dragged it from the wall, there in the corner on the bare floor crouched Spots's three kittens, completely silent as their mother probably had enjoined them to be or their wild instinct dictated. They were not yet two weeks old. When I stooped to reassure them they reacted like young wildcats. I pushed the couch back in place and left them in peace. Spots had been entering and leaving the house without our being aware of it, most likely at night. Although she didn't trust us, something had told her that our home was the safest place in which to rear her children, and none of the house cats had given away her secret.

One of her kittens, now a mature cat of six years, is living with me now. Tri is more tame than wild but no one could describe her as a domestic pussy. She enjoys being petted up to a point, enjoys lying on a soft bed, and most of the time eats the food I give her. Yet she trusts no one but herself and bursts out of the house if the daily routine is upset in any way. She is completely on her own, avoiding contact with the other cats as she does with people.

For the past eight years all my cats have been strays or off-spring of strays. I no longer know what it's like to own a really tame cat except for the rare one who arrives before it has known adversity long enough to become altered by it. When one of these joins the household my first reaction to it is that it is mentally deficient. Fairchild, who came here a short time ago, is one of these—a thoroughly domestic cat, so trusting that I hesitate to discipline him in spite of the liberties he takes.

Finally there are those cats who, although they come from perfectly normal surroundings and perfectly normal domestic parents, are basically wild with the timidity, or rather extreme caution, and suspicion that exemplify wildness. The description of Gyp by W. H. Hudson, reprinted here, illustrates a cat of this type, and many are the cats like him, pedigreed as well as ordinary. They have little or none of the gloss of domestication to mask their primitive instincts, yet they retain a tie with humanity which keeps them living among us, unlike their similar brethren who seek a completely free existence like Tarkington's Gipsy.

Cat colonies with varying degrees of wildness are found in all parts of the world from the middle of large cities to the remotest islands. They are but another example of human unconcern and bungling. Introduced to various localities through design or negligence the cats become wild through necessity and often wreak havoc on native wildlife. Despite the hardships they endure, their tenacity for life keeps them alive and prospering sufficiently to reproduce and multiply. They are the ghetto-dwellers and crop sharers of the cat world except for those lucky enough to live in a land of plenty where wildlife has not been too badly decimated. There they regain all the beauty and grandeur of total wildness. If we can believe the reports, off-spring of cats gone wild gradually lose the varied coat colors and patterns of domestic cats and once again assume the grayish tabby pattern of their wild ancestors.

The question is often raised as to how long it takes a cat to become feral. Wildness is a trait that all cats possess; no matter how domestic they appear, wildness is an integral part of each. The cat that leaves its home for a few days or weeks (and this can be a male, female or neuter) is, to all purposes, feral during this time, and anyone meeting it would so consider it because of its actions. Consequently the question should be how long it takes a cat to become *irreversibly* feral and that is a futile and irrelevant question. It depends not only on circumstances but on the cat's heritage. What is important is that almost every domestic cat is capable of becoming wild and *succeeding* in its new role when circumstances demand it.

GIPSY

BOOTH TARKINGTON

On a fair Saturday afternoon in November Penrod's little old dog Duke returned to the ways of his youth and had trouble with a strange cat on the back porch . . .

This cat was, for a cat, needlessly tall, powerful, independent, and masculine. Once, long ago, he had been a roly-poly pepper-and-salt kitten; he had a home in those days, and a name, "Gipsy," which he abundantly justified. He was precocious in dissipation. Long before his adolescence, his lack of domesticity was ominous, and he had formed bad companionships. Meanwhile, he grew so rangy, and developed such length and power of leg and such traits of character, that the father of the little girl who owned him was almost convincing when he declared that the young cat was half broncho and half Malay pirate—though, in the light of Gipsy's later career, this seems bitterly unfair to even the lowest orders of bronchos and Malay pirates.

No; Gipsy was not the pet for a little girl. The rosy hearthstone and sheltered rug were too circumspect for him. Surrounded by the comforts of middle-class respectability, and profoundly oppressed, even in his youth, by the Puritan ideals of the household, he sometimes experienced a sense of suffocation. He wanted free air and he wanted free life; he wanted the lights, the lights, and the music. He abandoned the *bourgeoisie* irrevocably. He went forth in a May twilight, carrying the evening beefsteak with him, and joined the underworld.

His extraordinary size, his daring, and his utter lack of sympathy soon made him the leader—and, at the same time, the terror—of all the loose-lived cats in a wide neighbourhood. He contracted no friendships and had no confidants. He seldom slept in the same place twice in succession, and though he was wanted by the police, he was not found. In appearance he did not lack distinction of an ominous sort; the slow, rhythmic, perfectly controlled mechanism of his tail, as he impressively walked abroad, was incomparably sinister. This stately and dangerous walk of his, his long, vibrant whiskers, his scars, his yellow eyes, so ice-cold, so fire-hot, haughty as the eye of Satan, gave him the deadly air of a mousquetaire duellist. His soul was in that walk and in that eye; it could be read—the soul of a bravo of fortune, living on his wits and his valour, asking no favours and granting no quarter. Intolerant, proud, sullen, yet watchful and constantly planning—purely a militarist, believing in slaughter as in a religion, and confident that art, science, poetry, and the good of the world were happily advanced thereby—Gipsy had become, though technically not a wildcat, undoubtedly the most untamed cat at large in the civilized world. Such, in brief, was the terrifying creature which now elongated its neck, and, over the top step of the porch, bent a calculating scrutiny upon the wistful and slumberous Duke.

The scrutiny was searching but not prolonged. Gipsy muttered contemptuously to himself, "Oh, sheol; I'm not afraid o' *that*!" And he approached the fishbone, his padded feet making no noise upon the boards. It was a desirable fishbone, large, with a considerable portion of the fish's tail still attached to it.

It was about a foot from Duke's nose, and the little dog's dreams began to be troubled by his olfactory nerve. This faithful sentinel, on guard even while Duke slept, signalled that alarums and excursions by parties unknown were taking place, and suggested that attention might well be paid. Duke opened one drowsy eye. What that eye beheld was monstrous . . .

Gipsy had seized the fishbone by the middle. Out from one side of his head, and mingling with his whiskers, projected the long, spiked spine of the big fish; down from the other side of that ferocious head dangled the fish's tail, and from above the remarkable effect thus produced shot the intolerable glare of two yellow eyes. To the gaze of Duke, still blurred by slumber, this monstrosity was all of one piece—the bone seemed a living part of it . . .

Duke was so electrified by his horrid awakening that he completely lost his presence of mind. In the very instant of his first eye's opening, the other eye and his mouth behaved similarly, the latter loosing upon the quiet air one shriek of mental agony before the little dog scrambled to his feet and gave further employment to his voice in a frenzy of profanity. At the same time the subterranean diapason of a demoniac bass viol was heard; it rose to a wail, and rose and rose again till it screamed like a small siren. It was Gipsy's war-cry, and, at the sound of it, Duke became a frothing maniac. He made a convulsive frontal attack upon the hobgoblin—and the massacre began.

Never releasing the fishbone for an instant, Gipsy laid back his ears in a chilling way, beginning to shrink into himself like a concertina, but rising amidships so high that he appeared to be giving an imitation of that peaceful beast, the dromedary. Such was not his purpose, however, for, having attained his greatest possible altitude, he partially sat down and elevated his right arm after the manner of a semaphore. This semaphore arm remained rigid for a second, threatening; then it vibrated with inconceivable rapidity, feinting. But it was the treacherous left that did the work. Seemingly this left gave Duke three lightning little pats upon the right ear, but the change in his voice indicated that these were no love-taps. He yelled "help!" and "bloody murder!"

Never had such a shattering uproar, all vocal, broken out upon a peaceful afternoon. Gipsy possessed a vocabulary for cat-swearing certainly second to none out of Italy, and probably equal to the best there, while Duke remembered and uttered things he had not thought of for years . . .

(from *Penrod and Sam*)

THE PERMANENCE OF THE DOMESTIC INSTINCT IN THE CAT

C. A. White

That the common cat would return to its primitive feral state, if a company of them of both sexes were turned loose in a region where they could have no access to mankind, is probable, and perhaps certain. But that the domestic instinct has now become an integral characteristic of the species, is a matter that will hardly be questioned by anyone. Still, opportunities to test the real permanence of this instinct are not often presented. I had the good fortune, however, to meet with an interesting opportunity of this kind during the prosecution of my field work for the U. S. Geological Survey in the summer of 1883.

In the prosecution of that work I made the journey, together with my party of three other persons, in an open row-boat, from Fort Benton, Montana, to Bismarck, Dakota, a distance of more than 1,000 miles; nearly 600 miles of that journey being through a region which has so few inhabitants that no post-offices were established there. The only white people in the region were a few buffalo hunters, and the woodman who supplied the few passing steamers with fuel, and even these persons were rarely seen upon our journey.

Upon making our camp one night, about 100 miles above Fort Peck, a good-sized black-and-white male cat came to the boat, and, although shy at first, soon manifested gratification at meeting us. I at first supposed that he belonged to some settler, but on examining the neighborhood no trace of the recent presence there of white men could be detected. When we started upon our journey in the morning we left the cat on shore, but he followed along the bank, mewing piteously to be taken on board. The boat was headed for the shore, and as soon as it touched the bank the cat jumped on board, evincing delight at being in our company. For the next 100 miles he was our companion, and we became very much attached to him. He was extremely neat, and never soiled the boat in any respect while we had him. At times he would ask plainly, by such signs as he could command, to be set on shore; and then he would hurry back for fear of being left. He was gratified with our attention to him, and purred approvingly when we caressed him.

We would gladly have taken him to Washington with us, but as that was impracticable, we decided to leave him at the first place which should seem to offer him a good home. Upon reaching Fort Peck, which is now only an Indian trading-post, we found only one white man there, who was in charge of the store. To him we told the story of our cat, and begged him to give the wanderer a home. He consented, and upon going to the boat he at once declared our cat to be one which he, in company with a party of buffalo-hunters, had the year before taken to the place where we had found him. He said the cat was absent, probably on a hunt, when they broke their camp, and so Jerry, for that was the name we had given him, was left there, and had spent the year alone in the wilderness, hunting his own living.

Of course, I cannot say that Jerry had not associated with mankind in all that time, but the circumstances favour such a conclusion. If he had, after his abandonment, taken up with any settler, it seems hardly probable that he would have been so eager to join us. He seemed quite conscious that we would take him away from his haunt; and this shows that he formed no attachment to either persons or locality there. The love of locality is doubtless more observable in the cat than the love of persons; while the reverse is true of the dog. Cats are never so demonstrative in their expression of attachment as dogs, and I suspect that the associations of human domesticity has much to do with the attachment to locality which cats manifest. It is true that Jerry was an unusually intelligent cat, and his case may be a somewhat exceptional one. But I cannot help thinking that there is yet much for us to learn of the psychology of this alleged well-known animal.

[From a paper read before the Biological Society of Washington]

A CAT'S DISPOSITION

W. H. Hudson

Gip is a magnificent creature, a third bigger than an average-sized cat—as large and powerfully built as the British wild cat, a tabby with opaline eyes, which show a pale green colour in some lights. These singular eyes, when I first saw this animal, almost startled me with their wild, savage expression; nor was it a mere deceptive appearance, as I soon found. I never looked at this animal without finding these panther or lynx eyes fixed with a fierce intensity on me, and no sooner would I look towards him than he would crouch down, flatten his ears, and continue to watch my every movement as if apprehending a sudden attack on his life. It was many days before he allowed me to come near him without bounding away and vanishing, and not for two or three weeks would he suffer me to put a hand on him.

But the native wildness and suspicion in him could never be wholly overcome; it continued to show itself on occasions even after I had known him for months and had won his confidence, and when it seemed that, in his wild-cat, conditional way, he had accepted my friendship. He became lame, having injured one of his forelegs while hunting, and as the weather was cold he was pleased to spend his inactive and suffering time on the hearth-rug in my sitting-room. I found that rubbing warm, melted butter on his injured leg appeared to give him relief, and after the massaging and buttering he would lick the leg vigorously for ten or fifteen minutes, occasionally purring with satisfaction. Yet if I made any sudden movement, or rustled the paper in my hand, he would instantly spring up from the cushion at my feet and dart away to the door to make his escape; then, finding the door closed, he would sit down, recover his domesticity, and return to my feet.

Yet this cat had been taken in as a kitten and had already lived some two or three years in the house, seeing many people and fed regularly with the others [cats] every day. It is not, however, very rare to meet with a cat of this disposition—the cat pure and simple, as nature made it, without that little tameness on the surface, or veneer of domesticity which life with man has laid on it.

From *A Shepherd's Life*

ON THE CAT'S REVERTING TO THE WILD STATE

SIR WILLIAM JARDINE

There is perhaps no animal that so soon loses its cultivation, and returns apparently to a state completely wild. A trifling neglect of proper feeding or attention, will often cause them to depend upon their own resources; and the tasting of some wild and living food, will tempt them to seek it again, and to leave their civilized homes. They then prowl about in the same manner as their congeners, crouching among cover, and carefully concealing themselves from all publicity. They breed in the woods or thickets, and support themselves upon birds or young animals. Few extensive rabbit warrens want two or three depredators of this kind, where they commit great havoc, particularly among the young in summer. They sleep and repose in the holes, and are often taken in the snares set for their prey. I once came upon a cat, which had thus left her home: she had newly kittened in the ridge of an uncut cornfield. Upon approaching she shewed every disposition to defend her progeny, and beside her lay dead two half grown leverets. We have also known cats, which, though they sought their prey in the woods and fields, regularly carried it home before devouring it, and in this way various young game and hares were brought in.

(From *The Natural History of the Felinae*, 1837)

XXIV
Roaming, Homing and Territory

To keep a cat from roaming, butter its feet or cut off a piece of its tail and bury it under your doorstep." If only things were that simple! But cats are determined beasts and nothing will keep them where they don't want to be. As Andrew Lang observed:

"Every one is aware that a perfectly comfortable, well-fed cat will occasionally come to his house and settle there, deserting a family by whom it is lamented, and to whom it could, if it chose, find its way back with ease. This conduct is a mystery which may lead us to infer that cats form a great secret society, and that they come and go in pursuance of some policy connected with education, or perhaps with witchcraft. We have known a cat to abandon his home for years. Once in six months he would return, and look about him with an air of some contempt. 'Such,' he seemed to say, 'were my humble beginnings.' "

Peter and Boots provided me with personal experience in this cat trait. Day after day a grey Persian whom we got to know as Peter haunted us whenever we left the house. He chased and fought with our two Siamese and he tried to sneak indoors at every opportunity. He had appeared from nowhere and appeared to have nowhere to go, but we decided he had to leave if we were to have peace.

Neighbors living a mile away wanted a cat and were delighted with him. He was fed and housed royally and guarded from escaping until he could grow accustomed to his new home. It was useless. Peter had chosen to live with us and rushed back at every opportunity. We would have welcomed him gladly but he hated Tayi and Rimba and they despised him.

With the odds against us we decided to chance it and let him make his home with us. Both Tayi and Rimba had been neutered and we reasoned that if Peter was castrated they'd all live happily together. Naturally it didn't turn out like that: the feuding, if anything, stepped up in intensity. We were getting ready to move and to keep things from getting completely out of hand Peter was put into a huge indoor cage which he liked. Better yet, he didn't resent the other two cats when they visited him nor did they show their usual resentment toward him. By the time we moved we were certain we no longer had a problem, but of course we did. With Peter out of the cage the cats went back to their old routine of hate.

While we tried to bring amity between them Peter lived in the basement of our new home and was allowed to go outdoors during the afternoons. He never ran away and always came when called. He was one of the nicest and most intelligent cats that I've ever met except for his senseless intolerance of other cats; it was he who instigated all the fights.

We were wondering what to try next to solve the problem when a couple with young children visited us. All fell in love with Peter and he with them, and they begged for him. But his transfer to their home didn't work out any better than when our neighbors had taken him. He vanished from it during an unguarded moment and we never saw him again. I hope that he didn't leave with the idea of finding us once more, but no matter what, I hope he discovered the sort of home he desired and deserved. We learned much later that he had originally belonged to a family living only a couple of miles from our old home. Why he left them, only Peter would have been able to say.

When cats desert their homes they usually make a complete break with their past but sometimes they continue to revisit old haunts as Andrew Lang pointed out. This can lead to a cat's having more than one home, each family never suspecting that their pet is living a double or multiple life.

Boots demonstrated not only this double existence but how determined a cat can be about choosing its own home. She belonged to neighbors but spent more time with us than with them. We couldn't invite her indoors because Tayi and Rimba were adamant about having no more cats, and we didn't want the trouble we'd experienced with Peter repeated.

Winter came and Boots refused to go home, so we fed her and gave her a bed in the garage. Summer came and she was still with us. Another winter arrived and she spent it outdoors as she had the last. The next autumn her perseverance finally won her the home she wanted. Tayi and Rimba had developed kidney infections and a year's attempt to save them had proved useless. Boots moved in immediately with her two children and a foster child. She loved us deeply and during the remaining years of her life (she was elderly when she came to us) she amply rewarded us for giving her a home.

Cats know what they want and gamble everything in order to obtain it. This trait is well illustrated by those cats who, having been taken from a cherished family and home, endure severe hardships in an attempt to regain what they have lost. Many are the miles they travel and many are the miraculous tales that tell of these miles. None, however, sheds any light on what instinct or power makes possible these feats, nor do experiments on the problem. As in the study of bird migration scientists have been able to discover what doesn't make possible the homing ability but not what does. The senses of sight, hearing and smell do not contribute to it, nor does memory.

The little understood kinesthetic or muscular sense is thought to contribute to homing orientation. The sensory terminals or proprioceptors for this sense which governs body movement and position are located in the muscles, tendons and labyrinth of the ear (which see). However, when these are interfered with during experiments on the homing instinct some cats still manage to find their way home.

One folk formula for keeping a cat from returning to its old home was based on the kinesthetic principle. As Henri Fabre describes it in his essay on the homing power of cats which follows, the cat should be placed in a sack and spun round prior to being moved. This is supposed to confuse it sufficiently so that it will not attempt to find its way from the new home to the old.

Kinesthetic orientation in the cat is highly developed so it may take much more disruption than a spinning to eliminate it completely. It is conjectured that this orientation is the result of a sensitivity to the earth's geomagnetic field, and an experiment made on cats seems to prove it. After forcing them to take a turn of a predetermined number of degrees, it was found that when they reached an open field they turned the same number of degrees as the forced turn in the opposite direction. In other words they turned themselves back onto their original course.

These recent observations bear out those made by C. H. Hodge in 1893. One night he and his friends took a cat fishing with them in a boat. As it became bored the cat grew restless and, pointing its head toward home it meowed to indicate its desire to go back. The fishermen, deciding to test the cat's orientation, were unable to throw it off its bearings even when they first wrapped it completely in a heavy blanket before changing the boat's position. They were a mile from shore and it was a dark night but the cat always knew which way was home. The fishermen succeeded only in confusing themselves.

Tayi and Rimba, who usually accompanied us when we left home in the car, always knew when we once again approached it. They could be sound asleep but no sooner did the car make the turn onto the home stretch than they were alerted and wide awake. When we then reached a point about three miles from home they began to pace expectantly and as the car maneuvered the last few turns to get us to our doorstep they grew increasingly impatient, sitting at the car door and demanding to be let out.

In an attempt to determine how accurate the homing instinct is in cats, experimenters constructed a maze having 24 exits around the periphery. Cats were taken varying distances from their homes and placed in the center of it. It was found that the percentage of exit choices in the correct homeward direction varied inversely with the distance that the cats were from home. The choices dropped to chance after a distance of about eight miles.

Francis H. Herrick says of the cat's homing ability: "Probably all cats possess the homing power in varying degrees, and all with fixed abodes might possibly be induced to exercise it under certain conditions; yet in every case the possession of a power, and the tendency to use it should be clearly distinguished; though possession, in this case, be under the firm grasp of heredity, the *use* is determined by experience and the physiological state of the animal at the moment. Thus it is obvious that an animal with dependent young would have a double inducement to return to its home provided local attachments had already taken root; on the other hand, it is equally clear that, whenever an animal is forcibly removed from its abode, the diversions or accidents which are likely to attend it may be of such a character as to block or defeat any impulse to return. In every such case the only facts likely to be either known or knowable are that the animal on that occasion did or did not return; we are usually left in complete ignorance of the animal's inherent abilities, of its struggling impulses or even of its efforts, should any be made."

He concluded from some experiments that cats return to their homes by the most direct route rather than retracing the course over which they were taken away; that their abilities were not diminished by any previous treatment such as rotation, with the possible exception of anaesthetization; that they did most of their traveling at night. In these he corroborates Fabre's observations while his further conclusions verify facts on the subject already mentioned.

Like most people not intimately acquainted with them, Herrick believed that cats reserve all their affection for places, never wasting a thought on people. It does no good to dispute this fact even with documented anecdotes of cats seeking loved humans rather than homes, but there actually are just as many stories of these as there are of cats deserting humans to return to well-loved haunts.

The practice of dumping unwanted cats continues today as much as ever but automobiles now take them greater distances from home so that they are less apt to make their way back without mishap. The expression "the cat came back" is seldom heard today and is meaningless to many, but a few cats still do manage to come back, wanted or unwanted, and these are always newsworthy and fully reported by the press. And every time we hear of them we are filled with the unexplained wonder of such a gift. An even more remarkable ability discussed under psi is that of psi-trailing, the ability of cats to find loved ones who have moved to completely strange territory long distances away.

WILLIAM SWAINSON ON HOMING IN CATS

A most singular instance of the instinct of a cat for discovering its home is too remarkable to be omitted, particularly as it occurred under our own observation. This cat was an excellent mouser; and the house of a neighboring friend being greatly infested with rats, it was agreed that the animal should take up its residence for a time in his house, that it might be cleared, in some degree, of these troublesome pests. Pussy, however, had then a kitten about two or three months old; and as we thought she was more likely to remain in her new habitation if she had her little one as a companion, both animals were sent; and, that the mother should not discover her way back, both were tied up in a sack, and in that state conveyed to our friend's house, a distance of near a mile and a half from Tittenhanger Green. The mother, finding herself with her kitten, and in good hunting locality, made no effort to escape. To our utter astonishment, however, she made her appearance, next morning, at the breakfast-room door, at her usual hour! She had come —no one knew how—over fields and through coppices, as it was conjectured, early in the morning, by a route she never could have traversed before, and without any other guide but—instinct. Having partaken of her usual breakfast from the hands of her young mistress, she was seen no more that day; next morning, however, she was again at her post; and these daily journeys were continued for more than a week. On mentioning this to our friend, he stated that he always missed the cat at his breakfast hour; but that, soon after, she regularly returned to her kitten, which remained quietly in the house during the morning visits her mother paid to her real home. Our cat, like all good mousers, is such a thief, that, not wishing to kill it, we have frequently tied it in a sack, and turned it loose at a considerable distance from home; but, somehow or other, she invariably finds her way, "through brake and through briar," to Tittenhanger Green, where she now is.

(*On the Habits and Instincts of Animals.* 1840. London)

J. HENRI FABRE ON THE HOMING INSTINCT IN CATS

. . . to what extent does the Cat deserve his reputation of being able to return to the beloved homes, to the scenes of his amorous exploits, on the tiles and in the hay-lofts? The most curious facts are told of his instinct; children's books on natural history abound with feats that do the greatest credit to his prowess as a pilgrim. I do not attach much importance to these stories: they come from casual observers, uncritical folk given to exaggeration. It is not everybody who can talk about animals correctly. When some one not of the craft gets on the subject and says to me, "Such or such an animal is black," I begin by finding out if it does not happen to be white; and many a time the truth is discovered in the converse proposition. Men come to me and sing praises of the Cat as a travelling expert. Well and good: we will now look upon the Cat as a poor traveller. And that would be the extent of my knowledge if I had only the evidence of books and of people unaccustomed to the scruples of scientific examination. Fortunately, I am acquainted with a few incidents that will stand the test of any incredulity. The Cat really deserves his reputation as a discerning pilgrim. Let us relate these incidents.

One day—it was at Avignon—there appeared upon the garden-wall a wretched-looking Cat, with matted coat and protruding ribs; so thin that his back was a jagged ridge. He was mewing with hunger. My children, at that time very young, took pity on his misery. Bread soaked in milk was offered him at the end of a reed. He took it. And the mouthfuls succeeded one another to such good purpose that he was sated and went off, heedless of the "Puss! Puss!" of his compassionate friends. Hunger returned; and the starveling reappeared in his wall-top refectory. He received the same fare of bread soaked in milk, the same soft words. He allowed himself to be tempted. He came down from the wall. The children were able to stroke his back. Goodness, how thin he was!

It was the great topic of conversation. We discussed it at the table: we would tame the vagabond, we would keep him, we would make him a bed of hay. It was a most important matter: I can see to this day, I shall always see the council of rattleheads deliberating on the Cat's fate. They were not satisfied until the savage animal remained. Soon he grew into a magnificent Tom. His large round head, his muscular legs, his reddish fur, flecked with darker patches, reminded one of a little jaguar. He was christened Ginger because of his tawny hue. A mate joined him later, picked up in almost similar circumstances. Such was the origin of my series of Gingers, which I have retained for little short of twenty years through the vicissitudes of my various removals.

The first of these removals took place in 1870 . . .

We were somewhat anxious about the moving of the Cats. We were all of us attached to them and should have thought it nothing short of criminal to abandon the poor creatures, whom we had so often petted, to distress and probably to thoughtless persecution. The shes and the kittens would travel without any trouble: all you have to do is to put them in a basket; they will keep quiet on the journey. But the old Tomcats were a serious problem. I had two: the head of the family, the patriarch; and one of his descendants, quite as strong as himself. We decided to take the grandsire, if he consented to come, and to leave the grandson behind, after finding him a home.

My friend Dr. Loriol offered to take charge of the forsaken one. The animal was carried to him at nightfall in a closed hamper. Hardly were we seated at the evening-meal, talking of the good fortune of our Tomcat, when we saw a dripping mass jump through the window. The shapeless bundle came and rubbed itself against our legs, purring with happiness. It was the Cat.

I learnt his story next day. On arriving at Dr. Loriol's, he was locked up in a bedroom. The moment he saw himself a prisoner in the unfamiliar room, he began to jump about wildly on the furniture, against the window-panes, among the ornaments on the mantelpiece, threatening to make short work of everything. Mme. Loriol was frightened by the little lunatic; she hastened to open the window: and the Cat leapt out among the passers-by. A few minutes later, he was back at home. And it was no easy matter: he had to cross the town almost from end to end; he had to make his way through a long labyrinth of crowded streets, amid a thousand dangers, including first boys and next dogs; lastly—and this perhaps was an even more serious obstacle—he had to pass over the Sorgue, a river running through Avignon. There were bridges at hand, many, in fact; but the animal, taking the shortest cut, had used none of them, bravely jumping into the water, as its streaming fur showed. I had pity on the poor Cat, so faithful to his home. We agreed to do our utmost to take him with us. We were spared the worry: a few days later, he was found lying stiff and stark under a shrub in the garden. The plucky animal had fallen a victim to some stupid act of spite. Some one had poisoned him for me. Who? It is not likely that it was a friend!

There remained the old Cat. He was not indoors when we started; he was prowling round the hay-lofts of the neighborhood. The carrier was promised an extra ten francs if he brought the Cat to Orange with one of the loads which he had still to convey. On his last journey he brought him stowed away under the driver's seat. I scarcely knew my old Tom when we opened the moving prison in which he had been confined since the day before. He came out looking a most alarming beast, scratching and spitting, with bristling hair, bloodshot eyes, lips white with foam. I thought him mad and watched him closely for a time. I was wrong: it was merely the fright of a bewildered animal. Had there been trouble with the carrier when he was caught? Did he have a bad time on the journey? History is silent on both points. What I do know is that the very nature of the Cat seemed changed: there was no more friendly purring, no more rubbing against our legs; nothing but a wild expression and the deepest gloom. Kind treatment could not soothe him. For a few weeks longer, he dragged his wretched existence from corner to corner; then, one day, I found him lying dead in the ashes on the hearth. Grief, with the help of old age, had killed him. Would he have gone back to Avignon, had he had the strength? I would not venture to affirm it. But, at least, I think it very remarkable that an animal should let itself die of homesickness because the infirmities of age prevent it from returning to its old haunts.

What the patriarch could not attempt, we shall see another do, over a much shorter distance, I admit. A fresh move is resolved upon, to give me, at long length, the peace and quiet essential to my work. This time, I hope that it will be the last. I leave Orange for Sérignan.

The family of Gingers has been renewed: the old ones have passed away, new ones have come, including a full-grown Tom, worthy in all respects of his ancestors. He alone will give us some difficulty; the others, the babies and the mothers, can be removed without trouble. We put them into baskets. The Tom has one to himself, so that the peace may be kept. The journey is made by carriage, in company with my family. Nothing striking happens before our arrival. Released from their hampers, the females inspect the new home, explore the rooms one by one; with their pink noses they recognize the furniture: they find their own seats, their own tables, their own arm-chairs; but the surroundings are different. They give little surprised miaows and questioning glances. A few caresses and a saucer of milk allay all their apprehensions; and, by the next day, the mother Cats are acclimatized.

It is a different matter with the Tom. We house him in the attics, where he will find ample room for his capers; we keep him company, to relieve the weariness of captivity; we take him a double portion of plates to lick; from time to time, we place him in touch with some of his family, to show him that he is not alone in the house; we pay him a host of attentions, in the hope of making him forget Orange. He appears, in fact, to forget it: he is gentle under the hand that pets him, he comes when called, purrs, arches his back. It is well: a week of seclusion and kindly treatment have banished all notions of returning. Let us give him his liberty. He goes down to the kitchen, stands by the table like the others, goes out into the garden, under the watchful eye of Aglaé, who does not lose sight of him; he prowls all around with the most innocent air. He comes back. Victory! The Tom-cat will not run away.

Next morning:

"Puss! Puss!"

Not a sign of him! We hunt, we call. Nothing. Oh, the hypocrite, the hypocrite! How he has tricked us! He has gone, he is at Orange. None of those about me can believe in this venturesome pilgrimage. I declare that the deserter is at this moment at Orange mewing outside the empty house.

Aglaé and Claire went to Orange. They found the Cat, as I said they would, and brought him back in a hamper. His paws and belly were covered with red clay; and yet the weather was dry, there was no mud. The Cat, therefore, must have got wet crossing the Aygues torrent; and the moist fur had kept the red earth of the fields through which he had passed. The distance from Sérignan to Orange, in a straight line, is four and a half miles. There are two bridges over the Aygues, one above and one below that line, some distance away. The Cat took neither the one nor the other: his instinct told him the shortest road and he followed that road, as his belly, covered with red mud, proved. He crossed the torrent in May, at a time when the rivers run high; he overcame his repugnance to water in order to return to his beloved home. The Avignon Tom did the same when crossing the Sorgue.

The deserter was reinstated in his attic at Sérignan. He stayed there for a fortnight; and at last we let him out. Twenty-four hours had not elapsed before he was back at Orange. We had to abandon him to his unhappy fate. A neighbour living out in the country, near my former home, told me that he saw him one day hiding behind a hedge with a rabbit in his mouth. Once no longer provided with food, he, accustomed to all the sweets of a Cat's existence, turned poacher, taking toll of the farmyards round about my old home. I heard no more of him. He came to a bad end, no doubt: he had become a robber and must have met with a robber's fate.

The experiment has been made and here is the conclusion, twice proved. Full-grown Cats can find their way home, in spite of the intervening ground. They have, in their own fashion, the instinct of my Mason-bees. A second point remains to be cleared up, that of the swinging motion in the bag. Are they thrown out of their latitude by this strategem, or are they not? I was thinking of making some experiments, when more precise information arrived and taught me that it was not necessary. The first who acquainted me with the method of the revolving bag was telling the story told him by a second person, who repeated the story of a third, a story related on the authority of a fourth; and so on. None had tried it, none had seen it for himself. It is a tradition of the country-side. One and all extol it as an infallible method, without, for the most part, having attempted it. And the reason which they give for its success is, in their eyes, conclusive. If, say they, we ourselves are blindfolded and then spin round for a few seconds, we no longer know where we are. Even so with the Cat carried off in the darkness of the swinging bag. They argue from man to the animal, just as others argue from the animal to man: a faulty method in either case, if there really be two distinct psychic worlds.

The belief would not be so deep-rooted in the peasant's mind, if facts had not from time to time confirmed it. But we may assume that, in successful cases, the Cats made to lose their bearings were young and unemancipated animals. With those neophytes, a drop of milk is enough to dispel the grief of exile. They do not return home, whether they have been whirled in a bag or not. People have thought it as well to subject them to the whirling operation by way of an additional precaution; and the method has received the credit of a success that has nothing to do with it. In order to test the method properly, it should have been tried on a full-grown Cat, a genuine Tom.

I did in the end get the evidence which I wanted on this point. Intelligent and trustworthy people, not given to jumping to conclusions, have told me that they have tried the trick of the swinging bag to keep Cats from returning to their homes. None of them succeeded when the animal was full-grown. Though carried to a great distance, into another house, and subjected to a conscientious series of revolutions, the Cat always came back. I have in mind, more particularly a destroyer of the Gold-fish in a fountain, who, when transported from Sérignan to Piolenc, according to the time-honoured method, returned to his fish; who, when carried into the mountain and left in the woods, returned once more. The bag and the swinging round proved of no avail; and the miscreant had to be put to death. I have verified a fair number of similar instances, all under most favourable conditions. The evidence is unanimous: the revolving motion never keeps the adult Cat from returning home. The popular belief, which I found so seductive at first, is a country prejudice, based upon imperfect observation. We must, therefore, abandon Darwin's idea when trying to explain the homing of the Cat as well as of the Mason-bee.

(*The Mason-Bees* by J. Henri Fabre; translated by Alexander Teixeira de Mattos. c1914, Dodd, Mead)

NEIL B. TODD ON TERRITORY AND OVERPOPULATION

Precise measurements of the territorial requirements of domestic cats have not been made, but the best available estimates indicate an area of about 0.1 of a square mile. The Carpathian wild cat (*Felis sylvestris*), which is probably not specifically distinct from the domestic cat, is said to occupy approximately 0.2 of a square mile. This is an area circumscribed by sides 0.45 mile or 10 city blocks long, and in lieu of any other measurements will have to be accepted as of the correct order of magnitude. While Leyhausen states that tomcats may wander several miles during the mating season, it is doubtful that this is a common occurrence.

Considerably more is known concerning the behavior associated with territorialism. Apparently only male cats normally establish permanent, rigid territories, females being considerably less territorial. These territories are patrolled and marked by the free-ranging cat by the practice of spraying. Re-marking may occur at regular intervals, also when known marking spots have become diluted or masked by the spray of some rival male. Under normal conditions the territory of two males would not overlap, in fact would probably not be contiguous. Territory might be expanded by the marking and incorporation of neutral zones by a dominant male with a submissive male restricting his territory. In any event territorial expansion would probably not entail any serious aggression. Aggressiveness is ordinarily inversely proportional to the distance from the home site, as is also exploratory drive. Hence a mechanism is complete by which conflict is minimized. Two tomcats meeting on the borders of their territories will threaten each other through a series of fixed action patterns designed to intimidate a trespasser, and the net result is usually a mutual retreat. The male, however, will tolerate females in its territory but apparently not in the immediate proximity of its home site. In addition to the home site, marking points, and the borders of the territory, there may be a host of other points and areas distinguishable as secondary home sites or refuges; toilet areas, either distinct from or associated with marking spots; claw "sharpening" points; and possibly mating sites and advertising sites. The latter refers to another characteristic behavior of territorialism, advertising, which in the cat takes the form of caterwauling. It is not yet certain whether caterwauling is restricted to a few specific points or whether it occurs throughout an area in the range, but the former is possible.

In view of the description of territory for the wild or feral cat . . . it seems reasonable to ask what the situation is in an area such as Boston, where 150,000 cats are crowded together in an area of some 1,500 square miles. If 50 percent of the cats are males (perhaps a low estimate due to selection) and if 60 percent of these are castrated or immature, we are left with some 30,000 adult males occupying an area of approximately 1,500 square miles or 0.05 square mile each. The original estimate of 0.1 square mile per territory becomes an absurd ideal. This does not take into account the territorial requirements of females and neuters or the areas not suitable for territory, nor does it consider the number of cats that are partially or totally restricted by human limitations imposed on their freedom. These are factors very difficult to assess at present, but it will be seen that they tend to cancel each other to some extent, and it is safe to say that this estimate is a good approximation. This then means that the higher limits of population density have been reached or are being approached . . .

We note that crowding or restriction has reached the point where the establishment of the territorial requirements of all the males in the population becomes impossible. This is indicated by the vast number of territorial fights which occur between rival males. It is also indicated in the excessive spraying by some tomcats, which is best interpreted as overflow activity or displacement behavior . . . It might be mentioned here that neutering is not the answer to controlling spraying or even fighting, because these patterns having matured may persist. In some cases even sexual behavior continues as in the preoperated animal, but this is probably due to conditioning. More important, perhaps, neutering females seems to have the very undesirable effect of increasing enormously their territoriality while reducing their ability to adjust to a dominance hierarchy . . .

In summation it can be said that the establishment of territory and the evaluation of crowding through olfactory and other cues are characteristics which have been favored by selection during evolution to prevent overbreeding. Some species have moved away from the primitive condition, as new ecological niches became available, by shifting to dominance hierarchies. The domestic cat is one such species, but is really only in the first stages. The primitive and adaptive innate behavior of the cat is being modified by strong selective pressures, which are probably the underlying cause of much abnormal behavior. The natural selective process is being greatly hampered by indiscriminate random neutering, i.e., adaptive as well a nonadaptive individuals are being selected against, but, more importantly, vast numbers of neuter animals are being injected into the environment to add a new unstructured situation with which the cat must cope. Millions of years of feline evolution have gone into the development of behavior patterns adaptive to a bisexual system. The occurrence of neuters can therefore only add to the confusion. The following list may be tentatively offered as indications of territorial disruption:

1. Nonrandom breeding.
2. Aggressive behavior.
3. "Neurotic" behavior such as excessive spraying.
4. Urogenital disorders such as incontinence when these are of nervous origin.
5. Failure to bury feces and urine.
6. Eczemalike disorders resulting from excessive cleaning and washing, which appear as displacement activities.
7. Overeating.

From this it might be predicted that the tremendous selective pressures being applied to cats will lead to a less aggressive animal with increased tolerance for territorial restriction, a more sociable animal with formalized dominance hierarchies, and a general reduction in "neurotic" behavior and displacement activities.

("Behavior and Genetics of the Domestic Cat" 1963.
Cornell Vet. 53)

XXV
Psi and the Time Sense

CATS have always been considered "uncanny beasts" capable of seeing ghosts, having a foreknowledge of coming events, and any number of other unexplainable gifts. Their psychic powers have been wondered at and feared ever since they began to associate with man.

Do they actually possess the abilities with which they are credited? Parapsychologists have made limited investigations in an attempt to discover if cats possess psi to any extent, that is, whether they are psychic. Psi is an animal's extrasensorimotor communication with its environment and includes ESP or extrasensory perception and PK or psychokinesis. J. B. Rhine and S. R. Feather in a paper on "psi-trailing" in animals discussed the collecting and evaluating of material that could indicate whether cats and other animals possess psi.

"Five general types of behavior patterns which suggest psi as a factor have emerged in this collection: 1) behavior which suggests reaction to impending danger to the animal itself or to its master; 2) behavior which suggests reaction to the death of the master at a distance; 3) behavior which suggests anticipatory reaction to the master's return; 4) homing behavior; 5) 'psi-trailing' behavior . . .

"Psi-trailing is that in which an animal, separated from a person or mate to whom it has become attached, follows the departed companion into wholly unfamiliar territory and does so at a time and under conditions that would allow the use of no conceivable sensory trail. The distance being long enough, then the animal would have to be guided by a still unrecognized means of knowing."

The authors were extremely cautious in the acceptance of anecdotes which they believed could demonstrate psi-trailing. After investigating each they eliminated all in which the animals in question lacked sufficiently distinctive physical identification and those in which behavior was the only conclusive evidence for identification. They also disqualified accounts in which the distance covered was not great enough to negate the possibility of accidental meeting, and those in which details of the incident were unobtainable. Finally, if the incident had taken place too far in the past before being related they rejected it on the premise that the facts could be greatly distorted by the time lapse. It's surprising that *any* anecdotes survived such ruthless weeding. Here are two examples that did.

When Sugar's family moved from California to Oklahoma he was left behind with neighbors through necessity; he had evaded his owners when they tried to take him along in the car. Fourteen months later when Mrs. W. was in the barn at their new home, a cat leaped through its open window onto her shoulder when her back was turned. Taken unaware she pushed it off, but at the same time had the feeling that the cat was Sugar. After it had quieted down in their home she investigated and found that it had a left hip-joint deformity identical to the one that Sugar had. This along with its physical appearance and behavior proved to the family beyond a doubt that the cat was Sugar.

Months later the family with whom they had left Sugar visited them and they learned that Sugar had disappeared about two weeks after they themselves had left. Not wishing to disturb them the other family hadn't reported the fact. On looking at and examining the cat this family also was certain that he was Sugar.

Sugar was a strong, bold tom who put coyotes as well as dogs to flight, and besides this he was an extraordinary hunter who caught rabbits with ease. His bone deformity was such that it didn't handicap him in any way, so that, all things considered, he could have withstood the long trek to rejoin his family, with limited hardship. There is little doubt that the Oklahoma Sugar was the former California Sugar.

Chat Beau had to travel only 294 miles to rejoin his family. When Mrs. C. returned home to Louisiana from Texas where the family had gone to look for a new home, Chat Beau had disappeared. When the final move to Texas was made he had not yet made his appearance so they had to leave without him. Almost five months later he showed up in the yard of the Texas school where Mrs. C. taught and where her son was a pupil. Although the cat avoided all the other children, he allowed this boy to approach him and pick him up.

Chat Beau had been raised by the C's collie and when this dog and the schoolyard cat met they greeted each other and lay down to sleep together as they always had. The cat also exhibited behavior learned through association with the dog. It growled like one and bit when angry, and it came in answer to a whistle. Physically and behavioristically the cat was Chat Beau, even to the scar in one eye that prevented him from closing it completely and to tar on his tail that he had had before he vanished. He was, besides, a very tired, travel-worn cat who gave every indication that he had been on a long, hard journey.

To be successful in psi-trailing an animal must meet many difficulties besides orienting correctly, and, of course, its motivation must be very strong to begin with. As in the more usual homing episodes, it must be able to secure its own food, avoid or best its enemies, and traverse unknown and difficult terrain. In these and more minor difficulties a cat can easily bog down mentally or physically or both.

Observation of the trailing phenomenon either in the field or the laboratory is impossible due to the many complications involved so that this ability in cats and other animals will probably continue unsolved for years to come. In summing up such unbelievable feats as we now see them Rhine and Feather say: "If these animal cases occur as reported, psi would seem to be involved with much greater magnitude and consistency than it is even in the spontaneous experiences of humans. The reliability of psi capacity necessary to guide an animal such as Sugar in making the countless daily decisions necessary in a 1500-mile trip would be of an order so great as to suggest even that some qualitative difference in ability might be involved."

In regard to the other four behavior patterns that these workers list as suggesting psi, homing behavior is covered in another section where, however, the possibility of its being the result of clairvoyance is not discussed. In experiments testing for this, above-chance results were sometimes obtained when the investigator himself didn't know the direction to the cat's home. This excluded telepathy between himself and the cat and suggests clairvoyance on the cat's part. Only in a situation like this can one definitely be certain that the cat, and not the experimenter, is exhibiting psi.

The cat's ability to sense impending danger is best documented by the experiences of British cat owners during World War II. Long before air raid sirens sounded, British cats were somehow alerted to danger, and the families with whom they lived soon learned to heed their warnings. Usually the cats asked to be let into a well-protected part of the house and their unerring choice of a secure niche is as incomprehensible as their forewarning of a raid. No plausible explanation for this ability has as yet been given except ESP which itself is inexplicable.

Changes in atmospheric conditions could forewarn cats in the case of impending earthquakes, but here, too, ESP could be at work. Cats are said to become highly agitated well before the first tremor is felt, drawing back their ears, meowing, and trembling in their distress, their fur on end. They are said to leave the danger zone in ample time, sometimes succeeding in evacuating their owners as well. Cats who experienced air raids apparently didn't respond so emotionally as earthquake cats but that could easily be attributed to the repetitiousness of the event and its lesser magnitude.

Some cats' responses to changes in atmospheric conditions approximate those to earthquakes but in a far lesser degree. The many proverbs linking cats with weather are indicative of their strange behavior before a change in it. Sailors, for example, swore that when the ship's cat became overly frisky it was time to prepare for a gale.

If with her tail puss played in frolic mood,
Herself pursuing, by herself pursued;
"See!" cried my nurse, "she bids for rain prepare,
A storm, be sure, is gathering in the air;
If near the fire the kitten's back was found,
Frost was at hand, and snows hung hovering round;
Her paw prophetic rais'd above her ear
Foretold a visit, for some friend was near.

Rev. S. Bishop 1796

From observations and beliefs such as these it was but a short step for people to begin using cats to make rain, a practice found throughout the world. Napoleon, Mrs. Fanny de Shield's cat, was the only individual feline to actually gain fame as a weather prophet, and apparently he never erred. When he slept on his stomach, his head bowed down on the ground between his extended front legs, rain was in the offing. Dry weather was indicated when he slept on his side.

Alexandre Dumas's Mysouff is a good example of the cat's anticipatory behavior toward a master's homecoming. Every morning he escorted Dumas part of his way to work, and every evening he waited for him at the spot where he always left him. On those evenings, however, when Dumas decided not to go home at the usual time for some reason, only Mysouff's actions told his mother that he would be late. When she opened the door so that the cat could leave to meet and greet his master he remained curled up on his cushion. This was far different from the usual routine. Mysouff ordinarily expected to be let out punctually, and if he wasn't he would scratch at the door until he was noticed and served.

There are many instances of a cat alerting its people to the arrival of a loved member of the family who is away and actually not expected back until later. Call it psi or what you will, this and the other examples given above are not explainable completely, or at all, by anything now known.

Two laboratory attempts to test for psi in cats have been published: the first by Karlis Osis in 1952, "A Test of the Occurrence of a Psi Effect Between Man and the Cat;" the second by Osis and Esther Foster in 1953, "A Test of ESP in Cats." As pointed out in the introduction of the second paper it is "difficult to create the kind of psychological situation which would motivate an animal to use any possible clairvoyant capacity it might have . . . Food and danger, unfortunately, are the only stimuli easily available for laboratory tests. The laboratory situation seemed to make it necessary for us to use these stimuli in spite of the fact that according to the anecdotal material they are not the best ones for eliciting ESP responses."

Space does not permit a reprinting of the above papers, abstracts of which follow. For the average reader these will suffice. The first experiment indicated some psi functioning in which both man and cat participated; its significant findings probably resulted from telepathy but could also have come from psychokinesis exercised by the experimenter on the cat. The second experiment indicates that cats are probably clairvoyant.

"This paper is a report of a preliminary experiment in a program of research into the problem of whether animals possess ESP ability. The experimental animals used in the tests were six common domesticated cats. For each trail the animal was placed in an enclosed runway containing turns and obstacles, at the end of which were two food cups. It was the task of the agent in the experiment to try to influence the cat to choose that one of the two cups selected as the target.

"The experiment consisted of two sections: an exploratory section, in which one person worked alone handling the cats and serving as agent; and the main section, in which one person served as the agent while another handled the cats. The exploratory tests (1700 trials) gave statistically significant results. The total scores of the main series (2200 trials) were at the chance level, but other analyses yielded significant results. A comparison was made between some cats which, it was predicted, would score positively and others which, it was predicted, would score negatively. The difference between the two groups was statistically significant.

"Further analyses which showed evidence indicating psi effects were based on comparisons of scoring at different times of day and between the first and last half of the series for each cat, on the chronological distribution in each agent's scoring, and on the tendency of the cats to concentrate their success in the first group of trials of the experiment."

"In a previously published report (the abstract given above), Dr. Osis described an experiment with cats, the results of which suggested that both experimenter and cat contributed to the psi effect. The present experiment was an attempt to exclude the experimenter as far as possible as a source of whatever psi the results might show. In the main experiment, the animal was put into an enclosed runway at the end of which it had to choose between two food cups, one containing food and one not. The cups were placed according to a randomly selected order and the experimenter did not know which cup contained the food. The cat was given a mild electric shock for one or two of the failures in each run of ten trials. In part of the runs—those in which the testing conditions were assumed to be pleasant for the cat—it was predicted that the scoring would be above chance; and in those runs in which the testing conditions were assumed to be unpleasant for the cat, it was predicted that the scoring would be below chance. The overall results bore out this prediction: the total of 640 trials gave a statistically significant difference between high- and low-aim trials.

"An analysis was also done to determine the effect of side habit (that is, a rigid tendency to go to one side of the apparatus to get food). The cats were first divided according to whether they had been successful or unsuccessful subjects in the high-aim, low-aim section of the tests. It was found that the successful cats made higher deviations on those trials which showed less side habit than on those which showed more. The difference was statistically significant. An analysis of the data of the previously reported experiment showed similar effects."

THE TIME SENSE. All animals possess a built-in time sense, and that of the cat, who as yet is relatively unspoiled by domestication, still functions well. Time sense was discussed briefly under the cat's sleeping habits which tend to be as regular as its eating hours. A house cat not only expects but demands its meals at a regular time if there is any semblance of regularity in its home. However, if the household is one where the weekend routine differs from that of the rest of the week it will recognize and accept the change and never mistake one day for another.

Each Friday morning, sharp at eight,
He watches at the garden gate—
Our big black cat, so straight and grim
He minds us, when we look at him,
Of those tall andirons that grace
With beauty stern our chimneyplace.

As punctual as any clock
We see him marching down the walk;
Out to the gate, with footsteps spry
And long before we hear the cry
Of "Fish! Fresh Fish!" upon the air
We see Black Friday stationed there.

The reason why, you ask, perhaps,
He thus waits there? 'Tis for the scraps
Of nice sweet fish saved up for him
By our fishmonger, jolly Jim;

Oh, is not ours a favored cat
To have so kind a friend as that?

No other day does Friday wait
Out there beside the garden gate.
How keeps he tally of the day
That Jim the fishman comes our way?
Perhaps upon his ebon toes
He counts the passing days, who knows?

Some method of arithmetic
Is surely his—some mental trick
By which the time he calculates
And sits so patiently and waits
The day for which he's named, you know—
A name we think quite apropos.

LOUELLA C. POOLE

The time sense functions in matters other than creature comfort. Cats anticipate many periodical occurrences, some with pleasure, others with dread. They learn, like Dumas's Mysouff above, when to expect members of the family home and are waiting to greet them when they come through the door or at some predetermined spot. And they learn to avoid unpleasantries that also come with regularity. One cat who despised the weekly garbage collections for reasons only it knew, became extremely upset when these were imminent and hid before any noise or other sensory cue could have reached it to herald the event.

Few people like to credit examples of this sort for what they are—an unerring sense of time. By far the best cat anecdote about this unexplained phenomenon is given by Gustav Eckstein in "A Cat That Knows Monday."

"At the garage west of the college they said: 'There is a cat next door starts out every Monday night at 7:45.'

"So I went the following Monday, early, and waited. Surely enough, at 7:45 a yellow cat came down the walk to the curb, stood. A male. The traffic lights changed. He crossed. I do not say that he watched the lights, more probably watched the people who watched the lights. He crossed close to their feet. Not one of them noticed him, as they would have a dog. A dog joins a crowd. A cat employs it.

"At the other curb the people continued up the street. The cat cut between two bushes of a hedge and on over some rising ground. I followed him. We stayed together close along a brick wall. Then, pop, up onto a window sill he went—a window of a nurses' dining room where on Monday nights a large public plays at a bingo game.

"So Willy goes to bingo. I followed him three Mondays in succession. Apparently, that cat knows Monday. Apparently, that cat knows 7:45—though, of course, it could be merely some succession of events that leads up to Monday 7:45. I thought it might be food, but there was no food. Or a congregation of cats, but there were no cats. Willy was there at that exact time, apparently, to see and hear the human species gamble and scream.

"Queer, the sense of time . . ."

Willy's brain seems to have retained its time power.

I called on the two ladies who board and house Willy. They said confidently: "Oh yes, Willy knows Monday. And there is no reason that he should—except that he just knows Monday. Any other night Willy will go out much earlier, at 5 or 6 o'clock, and not return till 8 or 10 or midnight for his supper. But on Monday he stays in and promptly at 7:30 eats—wants that over. Gets back home at 15 minutes to 10—when the bingo game is finished.

"And Willy knows 8:10 in the morning—exactly!" The two ladies, it seems, take an 8:20 streetcar, and Willy, having spent the night out, aims to get in before the door is closed, prefers his breakfast and a quiet day of sleep. Said the older of the two ladies: "If he is somewhat early—say 5 minutes after 8—we can see him amble slowly up over the hill, perhaps stop to stretch a moment in a patch of sun. But if he is late—say 8 minutes after 8—he comes prancing."

XXVI
Friends and Foes

"The cat, like many other animals, will often form singular attachments. One would sit in my horse's manger and purr and rub against his nose, which undoubtedly the horse enjoyed, for he would frequently turn his head purposely to be so treated. One went as consort with a Dorking cock; another took a great liking to my collie, Rover; another loved Lina, the cow; while another would cosset up close to a sitting hen, and allowed the fresh-hatched chickens to seek warmth by creeping under her. Again, they will rear other animals such as rats, squirrels, rabbits, puppies, hedgehogs; and, when motherly inclined, will take to almost anything, even to a young pigeon."

HARRISON WEIR

THE ability of cats to make strange friendships is another of their characteristics that has fascinated man through his centuries of living with them. It is generally the cats themselves who make the first overtures toward these friendships. Many people think that they do it for strictly utilitarian purposes but evidence does not bear this out. True, a cat gets warmth from sleeping on the back of a horse but it can usually get warmth elsewhere under more comfortable circumstances. Affection is the deciding factor in favor of the horse. When deprived of her kittens a cat's maternal instinct does cause her to adopt foster children of another species but she will do the same when allowed to rear her own children. Something more than creature comfort must be sought to explain this drive—affection, love, call it what you will.

Love for each other is also common in cats, solitary animals though they are. You might say it develops into cat philanthropy considering the number of anecdotes telling about well fed cats who bring hungry ones home with them to eat. This is not a species trait; it is entirely individual. Most multi-cat owners find that the majority of their cats tolerate each other and nothing more. Jealousy is common.

When one cat does love another, it will make any sacrifice for that love. Rimba adored his mother Tayi and inconvenienced himself for her constantly. His love transcended sex itself. Some friends wanted to breed their female and brought her to visit him. He was intrigued by Whimwham and we put them in a room by themselves separated from the rest of the house by a screen door. Rimba didn't approve of his separation from Tayi. Fascinated by Whimwham he might be, but not to that extent. In short order he managed to open the door and without giving his crooning, rolling bride a second glance he ran and jumped on the bed where Tayi was sleeping, gave a weary contented sigh and a few placating licks to soothe her because of the nasty reception he received, curled up next to her and slept. Nothing would change his mind and Whimwham was sent home. No one was more surprised than we when Whimwham gave birth to three fine sons.

Adversity caused two adult males that I knew to be friendly. Hannibal and Muffin arrived at our farm in late autumn. They were very thin and wild and inseparable. They shared the food I put out for them without quarreling, groomed each other, slept together; one was never without the other. Muffin was the first to come through the cat door into the house and he soon ushered in Hannibal.

They had found a home and were content but not for long. By the end of a month both were sleek and plump and it was then that Muffin acted. He ambushed and attacked Hannibal constantly, and you could see how surprised Hannibal was over this change in attitude. He never fought back but took to sleeping in inaccessible places like the washbowl in the bathroom. He was clearly unhappy and bewildered and one day he left and never returned.

Almost every general cat book gives instances of cat friendships with each other and other animals, not only mammals and birds but reptiles, fish and others. Ida Mellen devotes an entire chapter of *The Science and Mystery of the Cat* to stories about them. Newspapers and magazines never tire of picturing and writing about these strange yet common occurrences. Because they are so well documented elsewhere

"Cat and Starling" by Harrison Weir.

only a few examples are given here, noteworthy because of authorship or date.

CAT'S ATTACHMENT TO A LEVERET

GILBERT WHITE

We have remarked in a former letter how much incongruous animals, in a lonely state, may be attached to each other from a spirit of sociality; in this it may not be amiss to recount a different motive which has been known to create as strange a fondness.

My friend had a little helpless leveret brought to him, which the servants fed with milk in a spoon, and about the same time his cat kittened and the young were dispatched and buried. The hare was soon lost, and supposed to be gone the way of most foundlings, to be killed by some dog or cat. However, in about a fortnight, as the master was sitting in his garden in the dusk of the evening, he observed his cat, with tail crect, trotting towards him, and calling with little short inward notes of complacency, such as they use towards their kittens, and something gamboling after, which proved to be the leveret that the cat had supported with her milk, and continued to support with great affection.

Thus was a graminivorous animal nurtured by a carnivorous and predaceous one!

Why so cruel and sanguinary a beast as a cat, of the ferocious genus of *Feles*, the *murium leo*, as Linnaeus calls it, should be affected with any tenderness towards an animal which is its natural prey, is not so easy to determine.

This strange affection probably was occasioned by that *desiderium*, those tender maternal feelings, which the loss of her kittens had awakened in her breast; and by the complacency and ease she derived to herself from the procuring her teats to be drawn, which were too much distended with milk, till, from habit, she became as much delighted with this foundling, as if it had been her real offspring.

May 9, 1776 in *The Natural History of Selborne*

(Richard Kearton comments on this last paragraph: "We have seen a cat trying to act the part of foster mother to a number of ducklings, for which she showed great affection, and this could not have been caused by gratitude for lacteal relief.)

HARES BROUGHT UP BY A CAT

Though similar instances to the following may not be very uncommon, yet there is something remarkable in it, as a curious fact in the deviations of nature, and a rare act of care in the animal creation, contrary to general instinct, and not unworthy the attention of the naturalist. Mr. Beames, who takes great pleasure and trouble in preserving the different species of game in his neighbourhood, had two young hares, very small in size, which had been found in the adjoining fields, and brought to his house. Whilst thinking what to do with them, and wishing they had not been brought from their seat, they were set down in the kitchen, when a cat, which was always remarked as a good one of her kind for killing vermin, &c. and had kittened a few days before, but whose young, except one, were destroyed, passed across the floor, and observing them, instead of making any inimical attempts upon them, as was expected, she approached with signs of affection. The young hares seemed much intimidated, discouraged her civilities, and seemed desirous of escaping; but each party being unmolested by the observers, the cat, by her persuasive attentions, reconciled their dislike, and brought them to return her civilities. They were therefore taken up and put in the place where the other young kitten was; and, on seeing it, shewed again signs of disgust, though their young companion, who could not yet see, appeared to entertain no jealousy at the approach of the strangers. The mother still continuing her soothings, encouraged her adopted family to partake, with her other child, of the sustenance she afforded, which they soon did. As they grew up, they followed their foster mother constantly about the house, with the other young cat, suckling with her, the old one never shewing more attachment to one than the other, they at all times playing together. After the hares were grown to near full size, one of them, of its own accord, quitted the kind abode of its tender nurse, and betook itself to seek, in its native fields, a more perilous support. The other the gentleman soon after also turned out, and had the opportunity of seeing this last frequently on its seat several months afterwards; so that we may suppose their natural temperament was not changed by sucking the milk of a carnivorous animal.

Scots Magazine, 1790. 52:340

The March 1797 issue of *Universal Magazine* tells of a friendship between a cat and a pigeon at the home of the late Robert James, Esq.

of Putney. The affection was reciprocal. "What rendered it more extraordinary was, that they were both found one day on the wall of the garden, and both became domesticated at Mr. James', where they continued to be inseparable companions."

A FRIENDLY RAT

W. H. Hudson

Most of our animals, also many creeping things, such as our "wilde wormes in woods," common toads, natterjacks, newts, and lizards, and stranger still, many insects, have been tamed and kept as pets . . .

The list of strange creatures might be extended indefinitely, even fishes included; but who has ever heard of a tame pet rat? Not the small white, pink-eyed variety, artificially bred, which one may buy at any dealer's, but a common brown rat, *Mus decumanus,* one of the commonest wild animals in England and certainly the most disliked. Yet this wonder has been witnessed recently in the village of Lelant, in West Cornwall. Here is the strange story, which is rather sad and at the same time a little funny.

This is not a case of "wild nature won by kindness;" the rat simply thrust itself and its friendship on the woman of the cottage: and she, being childless and much alone in her kitchen and living-room, was not displeased at its visits: on the contrary, she fed it; in return the rat grew more and more friendly and familiar towards her, and the more familiar it grew, the more she liked the rat. The trouble was, she possessed a cat, a nice gentle animal not often at home, but it was dreadful to think of what might happen at any moment should pussy walk in when her visitor was with her. Then, one day, pussy did walk in when the rat was present, purring loudly, her tail held stiffly up, showing that she was in her usual sweet temper. On catching sight of the rat, she appeared to know intuitively that it was there as a privileged guest, while the rat on its part seemed to know, also by intuition, that it had nothing to fear. At all events these two quickly became friends and were evidently pleased to be together, as they now spent most of the time in the room, and would drink milk from the same saucer, and sleep bunched up together, and were extremely intimate.

By and by the rat began to busy herself making a nest in a corner of the kitchen under a cupboard, and it became evident that there would soon be an increase in the rat population. She now spent her time running about and gathering little straws, feathers, string, and anything of the kind she could pick up, also stealing or begging for strips of cotton, or bits of wool and thread from the work-basket. Now it happened that her friend was one of those cats with huge tufts of soft hair on the two sides of her face; a cat of that type, which is not uncommon, has a quaint resemblance to a Mid-Victorian gentleman with a pair of magnificent side-whiskers of a silky softness covering both cheeks and flowing down like a double beard. The rat suddenly discovered that this hair was just what she wanted to add a cushion-like lining to her nest, so that her naked pink little ratlings should be born into the softest of all possible worlds. At once she started plucking out the hairs, and the cat, taking it for a new kind of game, but a little too rough to please her, tried for a while to keep her head out of reach and to throw the rat off. But she wouldn't be thrown off, and as she persisted in flying back and jumping at the cat's face and plucking the hairs, the cat quite lost her temper and administered a blow with her claws unsheathed.

The rat fled to her refuge to lick her wounds, and was no doubt as much astonished at the sudden change in her friend's disposition as the cat had been at the rat's new way of showing her playfulness. The result was that when, after attending her scratches, she started upon her task of gathering soft materials, she left the cat severely alone. They were no longer friends; they simply ignored one another's presence in the room. The little ones, numbering about a dozen, presently came to light and were quietly removed by the woman's husband, who didn't mind his missis keeping a rat, but drew the line at one.

The rat quickly recovered from her loss and was the same nice affectionate little thing she had always been to her mistress; then a fresh wonder came to light—cat and rat were fast friends once more! This happy state of things lasted a few weeks; but, as we know, the rat was married, though her lord and master never appeared on the scene, indeed, he was not wanted; and very soon it became plain to see that more little rats were coming. The rat is an exceedingly prolific creature; she can give a month's start to a rabbit and beat her at the end by about 40 points.

Then came the building of the nest in the same old corner, and when it got to the last stage and the rat was busily running about in search of soft materials for the lining, she once more made the discovery that those beautiful tufts of hair on her friend's face were just what she wanted, and once more she set vigorously to work pulling the hairs out. Again, as on the former occasion, the cat tried to keep her friend off, hitting her right and left with her soft pads, and spitting a little, just to show that she didn't like it. But the rat was determined to have the hairs, and the more she was thrown off the more bent was she on getting them, until the breaking-point was reached and puss, in a sudden rage, let fly, dealing blow after blow with lightning rapidity and with all the claws out. The rat, shrieking with pain and terror, rushed out of the room and was never seen again, to the lasting grief of her mistress. But its memory will long remain like a fragrance in the cottage—perhaps the only cottage in all this land where kindly feelings for the rat are cherished.

CATS AND HORSES

HARRISON WEIR

From time immemorial cats have been kept in stables, and when this is the case there is generally a friendly feeling between one or other of the horses and the cat or cats. Such I have known with the heavy, ponderous cart-horse and his feline companion; such was the case in my stable, and so in many others. Cats are as a rule fond of horses, and the feeling is generally reciprocated. Several of our "race winners" have had their favourites at home, among others the well-known "Foxhall." "Many famous horses have had their stable cats, and the great, amiable Foxhall has adopted a couple of kittens, if it would not be more correct to say that they have adopted him. A pretty little white and a tabby, own brothers, live in Foxhall's box, and when Hatcher, his attendant, has rubbed him over, and put on his clothing, he takes up the kittens from the corner of the box where they have been waiting, and gently throws them on Foxhall's back. They are quite accustomed to the process, and, catching hold, soon settle down and curl themselves up into little fluffy balls, much to their own satisfaction and to the good horse's likewise, to judge from the way in which he turns and watches the operation."

In Lawrence's "History of the Horse," it is stated that the celebrated Arabian stallion, Godolphin, and a black cat were for many years the warmest friends. When the horse died in 1753 the cat sat upon his carcass till it was put under ground, and then, crawling slowly and reluctantly away, was never seen again till her dead body was found in a hay-loft. Stubbs painted the portraits of the Arabian and the cat. There was a hunter in the King's stables at Windsor, to which a cat was so attached, that whenever he was in the stable the creature would never leave her usual seat on the horse's back, and the horse was so well pleased with the attention that, to accommodate his friend, he slept, as horses will sometime do, standing.

CAT AND ELEPHANT FRIENDSHIP

MARK TWAIN

The boon companion of the colossal elephant was a common cat! This cat had a fashion of climbing up the elephant's hind legs, and roosting on his back. She would sit up there, with her paws curved under her breast, and sleep in the sun half the afternoon. It used to annoy the elephant at first, and he would reach up and take her down, but she would go aft and climb up again. She persisted until she finally conquered the elephant's prejudices, and now they are inseparable friends. The cat plays about her comrade's forefeet or his trunk often, until dogs approach, and then she goes aloft out of danger. The elephant has annihilated several dogs lately, that pressed his companion too closely.

In a comment on the Zoological Gardens in Marseilles

All the larger carnivorous mammals and birds of prey are enemies of the cat—puma, tiger, lynx and other large cats; dog, wolf, coyote, fox; eagle and owl, to name a few. Smaller carnivores like the weasel and raccoon prey on kittens and young cats, but many an evening I've seen adult coons ambling leisurely around the house ignoring and being ignored by cats of different sizes. Cats have been known to kill weasels and to chase and route larger carnivores like coons and foxes much as they do dogs. Sometimes, too, they form friendships with them.

Ethologists have attempted to discover the cause of cat and dog enmity which they consider to be natural. In one study observations were made on wild, partly wild and tame dogs and cats in a location having few trees and buildings where cats could take refuge. The relationship between the proverbial enemies was found to range from continual aggression to mutual tolerance. It was decided that the behavior exhibited was due to rivalry in overlapping territories plus a natural antagonism between a predator and a prey that is capable of defending itself. Man's interference was thought to mask the natural relationship to some extent.

Another study considered the cat-dog situation in urban areas. The conclusions here were that cats in the city provide the stimulus that releases the chasing instinct in dogs while dogs provide the stimulus that releases the flight instinct in cats. In other words, each releases in the other drives that are ordinarily starved in the artificial urban environment. Cats restricted to indoor living were said to develop an abnormal timidity with the result that their escape drive was released by stimuli which would, under normal circumstances, be subliminal.

Folktales explaining the enmity of cat and dog are numerous and have been covered along with other cat vs. dog aspects in my previous book *Cats and Dogs*. The relationship of these two animals has been, is, and probably always will be one of interest to humans.

Not so well known to people in our part of the world is the hatred of the tiger for the cat. In the tiger's homeland this hatred is as proverbial as that of the dog for the cat. A. Locke in *The Tigers of Trenggam* says: "I have no doubt that if a buffalo, a cow, a goat, a dog and a cat were tied out spaced in a half-circle and a tiger approached so that he received the scent of all of them simultaneously, he would first kill the cat in preference to any other of the animals. An insane burst of rage seems to fill a tiger when the smell of a domestic cat reaches his nostrils."

A folktale explaining the intense hatred comes to us from northeast India and parallels the tale from the Khasis in the same region to be found in the section on the cat's domestication. Man and tiger were brothers who lived and worked in perfect accord. One day, however, they quarreled over a deer that each wanted for himself. They could come to no agreement and parted enemies, the tiger going into the jungle to live.

Unused to outdoor living he felt cold and damp in his new surroundings. He yearned for fire but pride kept him from going to man's home to ask for some. He sent the cat to steal it. But the cat found indoor life so much to her liking that she decided to remain. She didn't even bother to bring the tiger his fire. He was so enraged he swore to kill her if he ever came upon her. And that is why the cat is so careful to cover her droppings. She doesn't want the tiger to discover her whereabouts.

From Malay comes this tale about the tiger's hate. Cat had been on earth for some time before Tiger was created, and she was chosen to teach Tiger everything that she herself knew. She was very assiduous about her tutoring but Tiger's great size worried her, and so, being on the cautious side she refrained from showing him how to climb trees. Tiger was unaware of the omission and was delighted with Cat's instruction until he learned of it. He became so enraged that he swore he would kill Cat at the first opportunity. Because of this threat cats are careful to cover their droppings at all times while tigers carelessly leave their mark everywhere. The tiger has nothing to fear but the cat must keep its movements secret in order to avoid its cousin's revenge.

The Sinhalese tell a similar story about the cheetah and the cat. It is said that the cheetah kills its tutor whenever it can but is reverent enough not to make a meal of it. Instead, it places the dead body of each cat that it kills on an elevated spot and worships it.

XXVII
Miscellaneous Behavior and Intelligence

THE way an animal behaves at a given instant depends not only on how it is stimulated but on its background—genetics, anatomy, physiology and life history from birth onward. As Kuo pointed out in his study of the cat's response to the rat, it is as natural for cats to love rodents as it is to kill them. Similarly, cats can as easily love dogs as fear and hate them. The potentialities for either type of response are present in every cat.

It is a complex, highly intelligent creature so that its behavior can be predicted only in generalizations even when its environment is controlled. The generalizations, however, are fairly constant as can be seen by the ways in which it is described, the abundance of adjectives used to express its characteristics being an accurate guide to its varied behavior. Because of its complex nature which results in its acting differently to similar situations at different times there appear to be many contradictions to the terms applied to it, and human interpretation of the behavior naturally adds to these. But all the terms are applicable, and, sufficiently analyzed, provide a key to what a cat is.

The words most often used to describe it are: adaptable, affectionate, agile, aggressive, aloof, altruistic, amorous, aristocratic, asocial, bad-tempered, beautiful, brave, calm, capricious, cautious, clean, clever, cold, consistent, courageous, cruel, cunning, curious, dainty, deceitful, detached, devoted, dignified, domestic, egotistical, emotional, fastidious, "fraidy," freedom-loving, gentle, good-natured, gracious, grateful, greedy, haughty, high-strung, home-loving, hypocritical, imperious, impulsive, independent, indifferent, inscrutable, insolent, irascible, ironical, jealous, kind, liberty-loving, lovable, merry, monopolistic, moody, mystical, natural, neat, nervous, obstinate, orderly, patient, persevering, perverse, pesky, philosophical, playful, poised, polite, possessive, proprietary, proud, prudent, pugnacious, refined, resentful, reserved, resourceful, self-centered, selfish, self-sufficient, sensitive, serene, shy, sly, sneaky, snooty, spiteful, suspicious, sweet, temperamental, thieving, tidy, timid, treacherous, tyrannical, unaffected, uncooperative, ungrateful, unpredictable, unresponsive, untame, vain, well-mannered, wild, willful, witty.

To fully appreciate how and why the cat is all of these things, consider first of all its origin. Ancestors of the cat were solitary, hunting animals, and a large portion of the modern cat's traits necessarily stem from this fact. Predilection for a solitary existence makes it asocial, self-sufficient and self-centered and, in consequence, gives it an appearance of selfishness and jealousy. For the same reason it acts unresponsive, cold and detached to those around it, and perversely ungrateful and uncooperative.

Because a solitary animal must rely on itself alone, it is cautious and suspicious with a timidity arising from the need for these attributes rather than from fearfulness. Actually cats are among the bravest animals.

Because a social existence with its give-and-take is so alien to it, it appears greedy and possessive in the sense that it doesn't care to share anything with others, especially food, lodging and beloved humans. It cannot understand or tolerate interference, and people who are rebuffed for their meddling consider it to be spiteful and bad-tempered.

Finally, and what is perhaps most significant, the solitary way of life that was bequeathed to domestic cats makes them freedom-loving, independent animals asking only that they be allowed to live their lives as they wish. For this they are condemned the most, and labelled wild and willful and a host of other derogatory things, some already mentioned.

"Cats" by Hunt Diederich.

Humans can't forgive anyone for a take-it-or-leave-it attitude toward their advances.

Condemnation also stems from their hunting proclivities. Even those who defend cats consider their method of playing with their prey an act of cruelty. They deny that cats can be altruistic yet censure them for a concept that is equally abstract. As has been pointed out they are merely performing an instinctive act necessary for their survival when they play with their catch, an act originating from their hunting heritage like their cunning, agility, perseverance and courage.

The cat's heritage from its wild ancestors is, of course, over 3000 years in the past so that much of its behavior has been modified through domestication. Cats realize what is expected of them when they choose to live with man and govern themselves accordingly, never, however, giving up anything if they can avoid it. Their basic behavior has therefore undergone little change, but, freed from the need of providing for themselves they can indulge emotions that had to be kept in abeyance, such as charity towards other cats not so fortunate as they. Those interested in such modified behavior and individual cat personalities in general have only to read a few general and individual cat books for examples. Better yet, they have only to study their own cats and those of others.

AGONISTIC BEHAVIOR. Aggression and violence are such an integral part of our daily lives that we consider them inevitable. In an attempt to understand aggression ethologists have been studying it in various animals, and cats, with their well-defined responses and continual open antagonism toward each other, prove to be good subjects.

Threat and aggression, fear and escape, are inseparable companions and when behavioral scientists speak of agonistic behavior it is these to which they refer. In 1872, long before humans were as hostile as they are today, Darwin described feline agonistic behavior in *The Expression of the Emotions in Man and Animals*; in 1954 Konrad Lorenz in *Man Meets Dog* gave a more extensive description of the same thing, also in popular style. Both of these analyses are reprinted here. When possible, observation of animals in their natural environment is far better in obtaining correct interpretations than a laboratory experiment.

Charles Darwin 1872 In: *The Expression of the Emotions*

"Cats, when terrified, stand at full height, and arch their backs in a well-known and ridiculous fashion. They spit, hiss, or growl. The hair over the whole body, and especially on the tail, becomes erect. In the instances observed by me the basal part of the tail was held upright, the terminal part being thrown to one side; but sometimes the tail is only a little raised, and is bent almost from the base to one side. The ears are drawn back and the teeth exposed. When two kittens are playing together, the one often thus tries to frighten the other . . . All the above points of expression are intelligible, except the extreme arching of the back. I am inclined to believe that, in the same manner as many birds, whilst they ruffle their feathers, spread out their wings and tail, to make themselves look as big as possible, so cats stand up at their full height, arch their backs, often raise the basal part of the tail, and erect their hair for the same purpose . . .

"Rage or anger is not often seen, but may be observed when two cats are fighting together; and I have seen it well exhibited by a savage cat while plagued by a boy. The attitude is almost exactly the same as that of a tiger disturbed and growling over its food, which every one must have beheld in menageries. The animal assumes a crouching position, with the body extended; and the whole tail, or the tip alone, is lashed or curled from side to side. The hair is not in the least erect. Thus far, the attitude and movements are nearly the same as when the animal is prepared to spring on its prey, and when, no doubt, it feels savage. But, when preparing to fight, there is this difference, that the ears are closely pressed backward; the mouth is partially opened, showing the teeth; the fore-feet are occasionally struck out with protruded claws; and the animal occasionally utters a fierce growl . . .

"We can understand why the attitude assumed by a cat when preparing to fight with another cat, or in any way greatly irritated, is so widely different from that of a dog approaching another dog with hostile intentions; for the cat uses her fore-feet for striking, and this renders a crouching position convenient or necessary. She is also much more accustomed than a dog to lie concealed and suddenly spring on her prey. No cause can be assigned with certainty for the tail being lashed or curled from side to side . . ."

Konrad Lorenz 1954 In: *Man Meets Dog*

"In the cat, expressive movements are particularly highly developed. There are few animals in whose faces a knowledgeable observer can so clearly read a prevailing mood and predict what actions—friendly or hostile—are likely to follow. The face of the cat portrays so clearly and unmistakably the slightest degree of mental agitation that anybody who is familiar with this animal knows at once how he stands with it. How plain is the expression of trustful friendliness when, with erect ears and wide open eyes, a cat turns a smooth unwrinkled face towards its observer, and how clearly expressed by the facial musculature is every rising emotion, whether of fear or of hostility. The striped markings in the face of the "wild-colored" cat enhance the least movements of the facial skin and augment the vividness of the expression. This is one of the reasons why I prefer the wild-colored, "tiger," domestic cat to all others. The slightest vestige of mistrust—which does not yet border on fear—and the innocent round eyes become somewhat almond shaped and oblique, and the ears less erect; and it requires neither the subtle change of bodily attitude nor the gently waving tip of the tail to inform the observer that the mental state of the animal is undergoing a transition.

"The threatening attitudes of a cat are extraordinarily expressive, and are entirely different in their manifestation according to whom they are directed against, whether they apply to a human friend who has 'gone too far,' or to a feared enemy, perhaps a dog or another cat. They are different too, according to whether they are made purely in self-defense or whether they imply self-assurance in the animal and predict a forthcoming attack. Cats always announce their intention of attacking, and, except in the case of unreliable or mentally deficient psychopaths —which occur in cats just as in dogs—they never bite or scratch without giving previous unmistakable warning to the offender. Usually, indeed, the gradually increasing threatening gestures are suddenly exaggerated just before action is taken. This is evidently an ultimatum, 'If you don't leave me alone at once, I shall unfortunately be obliged to take reprisals.'

"The cat threatens dogs—or any other dangerous preying animals—by making its well-known hunched back. Standing on straight, stiff legs and making itself as tall as possible, it ruffles the hair of back and tail, holding the latter slightly to one side in order to make its whole dimensions appear larger to the enemy, almost as some fishes do in self-display or to intimidate a foe. The cat's ears are laid flat, the corners of its mouth are pulled backward and the nose is wrinkled. From its chest a low, strangely metallic growl issues, which culminates now and again in the familiar "spitting," that is, a forced expiration during which the throat is wide open and the incisors exposed. In itself, this threatening gesture is doubtless meant to be defensive; it is most frequently seen when a cat suddenly finds itself face to face with a big dog and has no time to withdraw. Should the dog come nearer in spite of this warning, the cat does not flee but attacks as soon as the dog has overstepped a certain, definite "critical distance." It hurls itself at the dog's face and with claws and teeth savages its most sensitive places, if possible the eyes and nose. Should the dog show the least sign of flinching, the cat regularly makes use of this slight breathing space to take flight. Thus the short feline attack is only to gain time while finding a way of escape. There is, however, one contingency in which a cat may make a prolonged and earnest attack in this hunchbacked attitude, and that is when she is defending her young. In this case she approaches her enemy when he is some distance away and she moves in a peculiar fashion, galloping with an up and down and sideway motion, for she must continually present her imposing broadside to the foe. Though this broadside gallop with laterally held tail is seldom to be seen in real earnest, it can very often be observed in the play of young cats. I have never seen it in mature tomcats except in play, for there is no situation in which they are obliged to attack an enemy like this. In the suckling female cat, this broadside attack brings with it an absolute and unconditional readiness for self-sacrifice, and, in this state, even the gentlest cat is almost invincible. I have seen large dogs, notorious cat killers, capitulate and flee before such an attack. Ernest Thompson Seton graphically describes a charming and doubtless true occurrence in which a mother cat in Yellowstone Park put a bear to flight and pursued him until he climbed a tree in terror.

"The threatening which precedes a battle between two cats, particularly males, is entirely different, but just as impressive and magnificent to watch. The animals stand opposed to one another stiff-legged as before, but in this case the hunched back and broadside attitude are almost entirely in abeyance. The threatening toms stand head to head, growling and screaming in their too familiar tones and swishing their tails. Apart from this movement, they stand like statues for an amazingly long time, up to many minutes. Each tries to break down the morale of the other, on the principle of "who can stick it out the longest." All other movements, particularly the advancing of the dominant cat, are carried out in slow motion. Slowly, very slowly, one animal moves forward by a fraction of an inch, screaming horrible threats into the face of the other, and it may be a long time before hostilities break out like an explosion, quick as lightning, which the human eye can scarcely follow . . .

"Another type of threatening, associated not with self-display but with gestures of humiliation, is seen when a cat is "teased" to the limits of endurance by a friendly human being. This type of inhibited threatening, which is accompanied by supplicating gestures of humiliation, is most commonly seen at cat shows or other such institutions, where the animals are in strange surroundings and must submit to being touched by judges and other people whom they do not know. A cat thus frightened shrinks down, making itself lower and lower, until its body is flat against the floor. Its ears are laid back threateningly and the tip of its tail moves angrily from side to side. If it is very wrought up, it may begin to growl in an undertone. In this mood, it seeks cover at any price and will dash behind a cupboard, the pipes of a central heating or up the chimney. If no such cover is at hand, it will press its back against the wall, lying half on one side. It will also take up this half-sideways position on the judging table at a cat show; it portends the readiness to hit out with a forepaw. The more frightened the animal becomes, the more sideways becomes its position, until finally one paw is raised from the ground and the claws are unsheathed for action. Should the fear of the cat mount still higher, this reaction leads to the last desperate means of defense which the animal has at its disposal: it rolls right over on to its back and turns all its weapons toward its aggressor.

"This last behavior is often seen during judging at cat shows, and even knowledgeable cat owners are constantly surprised how little notice an experienced judge takes of this dangerous-looking threatening of the small beast of prey and how complacently he touches the animal, which, with paw raised to hit, is singing from a widely opened throat the up-and-down melody of the tomcat song. Although the cat is saying unmistakably, "Don't touch me or I will bite and scratch in earnest!" at the critical moment it doesn't really do it, or, at the most, it only does it very half-heartedly. For the acquired inhibitions of the "good" tamed animal can stand up even to this sore trial. Thus the cat does not feign friendliness and then scratch and bite, but on the contrary it threatens to rid itself of the (from a feline point of view) insufferable attentions of the judge, and cannot bring itself to put its threat into action."

J. L. Brown and Hunsperger in their neuro-ethology experiments on cats discovered that the neural substrate for motivation of threat behavior overlaps that for escape, which helps to explain the similarities between threat and escape behavior. They also found that high intensity stimulations of certain parts of the cat's brain elicit attack while low stimulations in the same spots produced only threat, which explains the close resemblance of threat to attack behavior.

In the cat's brain threat behavior can be obtained from three separate areas with a gradation of response from the first to the third, anterior to posterior. Vocalization can be used as an example of this phenomenon. The spitting response graduates from pure spitting to a combination of spitting and growling and on into pure growling as one progresses from front to back. That is, there is a gradual change from the fear or defense response to that of attack. Growling is correlated more with aggression, spitting with defense and escape.

An enumeration of the indications of threat was compiled. There is no sequential order to these: they depend on the individual cat and are the result of the needs of the moment. Few, if any cats, will exhibit all the possibilities, and some may exhibit a response all their own. A threatening cat, then, announces its feelings by: opening its eyes wide, pupil dilation, fur erection, folding down of ears, folding back of ears, crouching, forward rotation of whiskers, lowering of head, protrusion of claws, arching of back, straightening and stiffening of legs, faster and deeper respiration, urination and defecation, growling and yowling, shrieking, spitting, standing up, lashing tail, quivering tail, erecting tail base.

In attack there is a forward rush with an explosive forward extension of the forepaws. The claws are protruded and first one paw and then the other strikes the enemy. The cat will then usually leap on its adversary, biting the nape of the neck and the ears and clawing at the eyes. It may use its powerful hind legs to knock over its opponent and attempt to disembowel it if conditions are favorable.

Holger Ursin studied escape and defense in normal, that is, not operated-on, cats, by means of stimulation experiments on three different groups: tame house cats, moderately wild cats, and extremely wild feral cats. The four stimuli used, grading from mild to extreme provocation, were (1) the sight of the experimenter, (2) opening the cage door and waving a stick, (3) poking with the stick, and (4) trapping in a net and then releasing.

Flight responses to these stimuli were broken down into (A) opening eyes, pupil dilation, raising ears, and rapid searching, (B) withdrawal, (C) flight, (D) wild flight. The defense responses were considered (E) flattening ears and crouching, (F) spitting, (G) growling, (H) striking with protruded claws (I) moving forward and attacking.

The results could have been anticipated by anyone with a knowledge of cats. No positive correlation was found between flight and defense for any group. In the feral group there was a negative correlation: depending on their individual characteristics the cats either fled or defended themselves, and there was little overlapping of the two reactions. (E) and (F) were exhibited by cats who withdrew, as well as those who defended themselves. The score for withdrawal definitely separated tame from feral. Tame cats always came towards the experimenter. My experience makes me wonder about this last observation. To me it is very uncatlike. None of my cats would ever approach anyone they didn't know well, let alone anyone who threatened them. Some, I know, would never tolerate being poked at, to say nothing of being trapped even if I were the one to do it. They'd bolt or attack like Ursin's feral group. I've had only one cat who was cringing and submissive, and she's that way to both people and cats. She could really be

"Cat Fight in a Larder" by Paulos de Vos. (The Prado, Madrid)

described as psychopathic, and because her fear of everything is so great she is unpredictable. Her usual reaction to any situation, however, is the same as that described by Lorenz for the tormented cat in the cat show. "Underdog" cats react like this frequently to dominant cats, and the display tends to send the bully off in disgust.

To get back to Ursin's experiment, each cat was consistent in its responses over the several months it was tested. He attributes the difference in actions between tame and feral cats to the critical period in their development, that period in the first weeks of their life which, if they are not in contact with and handled by humans, makes them untamable for ever after. This, of course, wouldn't explain the reaction of tame cats who later become feral and can be just as wild as those cats unfamiliar with humans. The violent action in these undoubtedly comes from traumatic experiences which the cats suffered at the hands of humans.

This last is not true in all cases. As noted earlier, some strays who have lived with me have never learned to trust anyone, spitting and striking out at both cat and human through pure nervousness, although unprovoked. Others who arrive at my door are in poor shape and have obviously been mistreated, yet are more trusting than cats I have owned since their birth, like the psychopath described above. She acts as if she were tortured every day of her life although she's never been hit. When petted, she cringes. It is definitely not true that you can tell how a cat has been treated by its expression and manner. Cats just aren't made that way.

WELL BEING: Happiness, Contentment, Affection and Related Feelings. Drawing again on Darwin we get this description of a happy, contented cat. "All the movements of a cat, when feeling affectionate, are in complete antithesis to those just described, [that is, in agonistic behavior]. She now stands upright, with slightly arched back, tail perpendicularly raised, and ears erected; and she rubs her cheeks and flanks against her master or mistress. The desire to rub something is so strong in cats under this state of mind, that they may often be seen rubbing themselves against the legs of chairs or tables, or against doorposts. The manner of expressing affection probably originated through association, as in the case of dogs, from the mother nursing and fondling her young; and perhaps from the young themselves loving each other and playing together. Another and very different gesture, expressive of

"The Arena" by Harold Weston. (The Phillips Collection, Washington, D. C.)

pleasure, has already been described, namely, the curious manner in which young and even old cats, when pleased, alternately protrude their fore-feet, with separated toes, as if pushing against and sucking their mother's teats. This habit is so far analagous to that of rubbing against something, that both apparently are derived from actions performed during the nursing period. Why cats should show affection by rubbing so much more than dogs, though the latter delight in contact with their masters, and why cats only occasionally lick the hands of their friends, whilst dogs always do so, I cannot say. Cats cleanse themselves by licking their own coats more regularly than do dogs. On the other hand, their tongues seem less well fitted for the work than the longer and more flexible tongues of dogs."

Enlarging on the cat's odd behavior of kneading when it feels particularly good, Darwin wrote further: "Kittens, puppies, young pigs and probably many other young animals, alternately push with their fore-feet against the mammary glands of their mothers, to excite a freer secretion of milk, or to make it flow. Now it is very common with young cats, and not at all rare with old cats of the common and Persian breeds (believed by some naturalists to be specifically extinct), when comfortably lying on a warm shawl or other soft substance, to pound it quietly and alternately with their fore-feet; their toes being spread out and claws slightly protruded, precisely as when sucking their mother. That it is the same movement is clearly shown by their often at the same time taking a bit of the shawl into their mouths and sucking it; generally closing their eyes and purring from delight. This curious movement is commonly excited only in association with the sensation of a warm soft surface; but I have seen an old cat, when pleased by having its back scratched, pounding the air with its feet in the same manner; so that this action has almost become the expression of a pleasurable sensation."

A contented cat also does a good deal of rolling. When alone it will roll from side to side as it sometimes does on rough surfaces in order to scratch itself; or it may roll over and over completely. If a loved and trusted person is present it will roll onto its back to present its under surface for an all-round and much appreciated tickle.

The caressing hand may meanwhile be licked, nibbled or bitten depending on the degree of the cat's exhilaration, and kicks of varying strength may also be delivered. Reserved cats accept their tickles with no outward display, while the more demonstrative cat all but swoons in its delight, looking at you with "melting eyes" and drooling as it hugs you with its front paws and sniffs noses.

An actively happy cat, young or old, will frequently chase its tail and play in wild abandon. Then, suddenly, with ears back and tail arched it will race away to nowhere, to lie down and begin calmly to wash.

Smiling and laughing are far less frequent in cats than in dogs even though they are capable of greater facial expression, unequalled, in fact, except by humans. Their more subtle and subdued humor seldom necessitates laughter. It is generally of a gentle teasing nature, not boisterous, and can be directed at people, other cats or other animals. Cats will always appreciate a joke with you or at you, but seldom one directed at themselves.

They usually show pleasure and amusement by a variety of facial expressions combined with body movements instead of by actual smiles and laughter. A cat's entire body from head through tail conveys its good feelings just as it expresses all its moods.

SELFISHNESS AND JEALOUSY. These are strong drives in the cat, because, as mentioned, it is an asocial animal. An extreme form of possessiveness is held sacred by all cats, and the most dominant tom, unless he is a rogue, would never think of snatching the catch from the lowest cat in the peck-order no matter how much he covets it. Farm cats often form a ring around a lucky hunter and his prey to watch enviously but never join in his game. The same rule applies to the hunter's right to eat his catch in peace. However, he may gladly share with others both the play and the booty of his own volition, especially if he isn't hungry. Kittens learn the basic do-not-touch rule of catdom early. A mother cat often angrily chastises her kittens who try to take from her a mouse that she wishes to keep for herself.

To a cat the possession of anything is indisputable—food, bed, territory, the humans it lives with. The difficulties people get into with cats are often the result of their not humoring this rule. Seldom is one good-natured enough to take an affront to its inborn rights without retaliating.

Roy Chapman Andrews described the extent to which a cat's jealousy can go in recounting his life with Lord Jitters, his famous white Persian.

"We discovered Queen, an English setter, in Carmel, New York.

She captured our hearts instantly but we were exceedingly uneasy as we brought her in the car to Pondwood Farm. How would Lord Jitters, the autocrat of our household, receive a dog? Although we had decided that we could not continue to be ruled by a cat and keep our self-respect, we fervently wished the ordeal of presentation were over.

"Lord Jitters left his post on the stone wall and, as usual, walked sedately out to the car to welcome us home. Suddenly he caught sight of Queen with Billie's arms round her neck. Frozen in astonishment, he turned a look on her that would have withered a cactus. Then he stalked, with indignant flirts of his tail, to the stone wall, where he proposed to watch proceedings . . .

"For forty-eight hours the Lord left the stone wall only at night. With cold eyes he gazed at us, jerking away if we tried to pet him, and refusing to eat in our presence. Even fillet of cod, his favorite dish, remained untouched during the daylight hours. With the delectable smell of fish in his nostrils, how he was able to resist I cannot imagine. But the hunger strike ended after dark concealed his movements; or at least I suppose it did, for in the morning the fish was gone, although he pretended it never had been there at all.

"Queen roamed the house and fields, always at our heels, but never approached Lord Jitters. Eventually time broke Jitter's resistance. In frigid silence he returned to the house, but not to his usual place on the bed in our room. Instead, he took up his residence in the guest room, there to sleep in lonely grandeur on a pillow. Billie and I hated to admit, even to ourselves, how much Jitter's conduct distressed us. His feelings were so deeply hurt that we wondered if he would ever forgive us. However, now that the break had been made, we decided we might as well 'die for a sheep as a lamb.' We had long wanted a black Persian kitten. Better get it now, for Lord Jitters could not be more disturbed than he was at present. The kitten arrived. It was only a month old—just a tiny ball of coal-black fluff punctuated by two yellow eyes. 'Smoke' was his name, but we eventually changed it to 'Poke-Poke,' because he always poked along behind everyone else. Jitters took one look, spat disgustedly in the little one's face, and walked away. I followed him into his room and endeavored to remonstrate. He stood stiffly just inside the door and heard me out. Translated, his reply was as follows:

" 'If you have quite finished, I will state my position once and for all. It is this. For three years I have given you my complete loyalty and affection. I assumed that I had yours. Evidently I was mistaken. Your introduction of these animals into my household has made it impossible for me ever to look upon either of you as I did in the happy past. I shall go my way and you will go yours. All I ask is to be let alone. Under no circumstances will I fraternize with these interlopers. So far as I am concerned they do not exist.'

"I bowed meekly and retired with a heavy heart. We hoped that time would bring a more tolerant attitude on Jitters's part and effect a cure to his injured feelings. In the weeks that followed Lord Jitters gave the most perfect exhibition of ignoring I have ever seen by man or beast. He would walk within a foot of Queen, never betraying by look or action that he knew the dog was even on the same planet. Pokie made a few kittenish attempts to play, without response from His Lordship. Only when he actually touched Jitters was there the slightest sign of recognition. It came in the form of a hiss and a smart slap from a white paw.

"Toward Billie and me his attitude eventually softened. He was polite but it ended there. The old companionship was gone. Never did he cross the threshold of our bedroom where he had always lived. No longer did he accompany us on walks through the woods. If we went on the pond we could never persuade him to enter the canoe. No more did he follow along the edge of the water while we were fishing, sitting patiently on a rock or picking his way daintily around the margin of an overflow. He had withdrawn completely within himself, devoted only to his own affairs . . .

"Lord Jitters retained his frigid attitude toward both Queen and Poke-Poke for many months. But as time wore on he became accustomed to their presence and accepted it as inevitable. Naturally he softened first toward the black cat. No one, animal or human, could resist the indolent sweetness of Poke-Poke's nature. Jitters seldom played with him—as a matter of fact, Pokie is too lazy to play much and Jitters too dignified—but he adopted a sort of protective big-brother attitude which is very amusing. Poke-Poke seldom washes himself because Queen and Jitters have taken the responsibility for keeping him clean. When Pokie's appearance becomes intolerable to Jitters, who is always immaculate, His Lordship sits down to it like a job which must be done and gives him a thorough cleaning from head to tail. Queen finishes the operation by nibbling up and down Pokie's back with her front teeth while he purrs ecstatically. With Queen, and other dogs which came later, Lord Jitters has never gone much beyond toleration. After all these years he has accepted the fact that they are permanent members of the family but he brooks no familiarity.

"Lord Jitters dearly loved to go for a walk with us up the wood road in the evening. After Queenie's arrival he no longer accompanied us. Eventually, however, he dropped back into his old habit. We are again a happy family. Queen dashes around in front; Lord Jitters precedes us sedately by a few yards, now and then jumping off the road to stalk a bug; behind, plodding along, with many a pause for rest, comes Poke-Poke. After a short distance he calls for us to wait. Then he asks to be picked up, for he is utterly exhausted from his unaccustomed exertions. During the remainder of the walk he rides comfortably, draped over my shoulder, interestedly watching the passing show. If he must take exercise that is the way it should be done.

"For a year after Queen and Poke-Poke arrived Lord Jitters never entered our bedroom. Then one morning, just as the breakfast tray was being brought up, he walked in as though he had never left it. Queen and Poke-Poke were already there, for they invariably arrive coincident with food. Jitters jumped on the bed.

" 'Good morning,' he said. 'I hope you slept well. Let's see what we have to eat this morning. Cream! Yes, I'll have a little, not too much—just a spoonful. And a piece of buttered toast with marmalade. No, not on the toast—there, on the side of the plate, where I can lick it as I wish.'

"Queen and Pokie backed off and made not the slightest effort to get their accustomed bits until His Lordship had finished. Then he jumped to the floor and, with a flirt of his plume, signified they had his permission to eat. After his initial appearance he returned to his accustomed place on our bed even though he had to share the room with Queen. One night he was restless and I put him out about eleven o'clock but let Queen remain. At first he could not believe that I really meant him to go. This was his room and who was I to dismiss him from it? When I gave a gentle push to his lordly rear, he favored me with what can only be described as a dirty look. About two o'clock in the morning a scratching and yowling at the door waked Billie and me. There was the Lord with a mouse. He jumped on the bed and deposited the limp rodent in Billie's lap.

" 'You evacuate me from my own room for no reason that I can fathom,' he said, 'but I return good for evil. I rid the house of mice while you sleep.'

"Having delivered himself of this reproof, he stalked out the door and down the stairs. For two nights he punished us by refusing to enter the bedroom . . ."

from *An Explorer Comes Home*

PLAY: "When I play with my cat who knows whether she diverts herself with me, or I with her! We entertain one another with mutual follies, struggling for a garter; and if I have my time to begin to refuse, she also has hers. It is because I cannot understand her language that we agree no better; and perhaps she laughs at my simplicity in making sport to amuse her."

Montaigne

Play is make-believe as well as activity and cats of any age can pretend and exercise better than most people. In the kitten, play is instructive besides being fun. In the grown cat it not only provides pleasure but keeps the animal physically fit and mentally alert. For this reason the indoor cat, in order to keep itself in readiness for any emergency, plays in excess compared to the cat with outdoor freedom, although boredom explains some of the excess.

No one, not even the worst aelurophobe, seems able to resist the appeal of a playing kitten, but the beauty and grace, and sometimes ludicrousness, of an adult cat in a similar display is often wasted on the observer. This in no way disturbes the cat; it couldn't care less how its actions impress anyone. It plays for its own satisfaction and remains indifferent as to whether humans wish to be bystanders or participants in its game, or neither.

A description of play in kittens (which is essentially the same as in adult cats) has been given by Konrad Lorenz along with its implications.

"A kitten is playing with its classical plaything, a ball of wool. Unfailingly, it begins to paw at the object, first gently and enquiringly with outstretched forearm and inwardly flexed paw. Now with extended claws, it draws the ball toward itself, pushes it away again or jumps a few steps backward, crouching. It lies low, raises its head with tense expression, glaring at the plaything. Then its head drops so suddenly that you expect its chin to bump the floor. The hind feet perform peculiar, alternately treading and clawing movements as though the kitten were seeking a firm hold from which to spring. Suddenly it bounds in a great semicircle and lands on its toy with stiff forepaws pressed closely together. It will even bite it, if the game has reached a pitch of some intensity. Again it pushes the ball and this time it rolls under a cupboard which stands too close to the floor for the kitten to get underneath. With an elegant 'practised' movement, it reaches with one arm into the space and fishes its plaything out again. It is at once clear to anyone who has ever watched a cat catching a mouse that our kitten, which we have reared apart from its mother, is performing all those highly specialized movements which aid the cat in the hunting of its most important prey—the mouse. In the wild state, this constitutes its 'daily bread.'

"If we now improve on our plaything by attaching a thread to it and letting it dangle from above, the kitten will exhibit entirely different prey-catching movements. Jumping high, it grabs the prey with both paws at once, bringing them together in a wide, sweeping movement from the sides. During this movement, the paws appear abnormally large, for all the digits with their extended claws are widely spread, and the dewclaws are bent at right angles to the paw. This grasping movement, which many kittens delightedly perform in play, is identical to the last detail with the movement used by cats to grab a bird just leaving the ground.

"Another movement, often observed in the play of young cats, is less easy to explain in its biological meaning, since its practical application is soon seen. In a lightning movement of upturned pads and claws the kitten reaches under the plaything and throws it in a high arc over its own shoulder, to follow it immediately with a jump. Or, particularly with larger playthings, the kitten sits before the object, rears itself stiffly erect, reaches underneath it with a paw from each side and throws it back over its head in a steeper and higher semicircle. Frequently the animal follows the flying object with its eyes and pursues it with a high leap, landing where it fell. The practical purpose of these two series of movements is the catching of fishes, the first series for smaller, the second for larger ones.

"Still more interesting and aesthetically beautiful are the movements of kittens playing either together or with their mother. Their biological meaning is less easily explained than that of the prey-catching movements, since, when cats play together, instinctive movements, whose practical application extends to many different things, are performed in colorful confusion on one and the same object.

"Behind the coalbox, a kitten sits watching her brother who is seated in the middle of the kitchen floor unaware of this scrutiny. Like a bloodthirsty tiger the watcher quivers with anticipation, whips its tail to and fro, and describes the movements of head and tail which are performed also by adult cats. Its sudden spring belongs to the realm of an entirely different set of movements, designed not for preying but for the fight. Instead of leaping on its brother as on a prey—an action which may alternately, of course, be performed—it assumes a threatening position while still galloping, arching its back and advancing broadside on. The assaulted kitten likewise humps its back and the two stand thus for some time, with ruffled hair and sideways bent tails. As far as I know, this never takes place between adult cats. Each of the two kittens behaves rather as though the other were a dog, but nevertheless their game goes on like a genuine tomcat fight. Clasping each other firmly with their forepaws, they turn wild somersaults over and over each other, at the same time moving their hind feet in a way that, in play with a human being, can prove extremely painful. Hugging its playmate in the iron grip of its forepaws, the kitten vigorously pushes both hind feet with unsheathed claws against it, repulsing it with a quick succession of kicks. In a genuine fight, these slitting, tearing blows are directed at the unprotected belly of an adversary where their action must be devastating. After their short boxing match the kittens release their hold of one another and now an exciting chase usually follows, in which another uncommonly graceful set of movements is seen. When the fleeing kitten sees the other getting very close, he suddenly turns a somersault that lands him, with a soft and absolutely silent movement, immediately underneath his pursuer. He digs his forepaws into its soft parts, scrabbling its face, at the same time, with his hind feet.

"How do these movements of play differ from those of real earnest? In their form, even the most practiced eye may fail to detect a difference, but nevertheless there is one. In these games, composed as they are of the movements of catching a prey, fighting a fellow cat and repelling a foe, serious injury is never done to the playmate acting one of these parts. The social inhibition against real biting or deep scratching is fully enforced during play, while, in a case of real earnestness, it is obliterated by the emotion evoking the particular series of movements . . ."

INTER-CAT BEHAVIOR: A knowledge of inter-cat relationships must be obtained principally from the communal living forced upon them by humans in crowded communities, homes and laboratories. Out of doors the adult cat usually follows a network of trails that he has laid out for himself in order to get from one place to another. Some of these trails will invariably be communal, used not only by more than one cat but other animals as well. To avoid contact with each other cats learn to use them at different times of the day. This is less difficult than it sounds. Spatial orientation in felines, that is, their ability to get around geographically, is well developed, the result of visual, olfactory, auditory and tactile senses working together. Even still-blind kittens less than a week old are capable of this orientation. Combined with an accurate time sense it is all that is needed for cats to avoid unpleasant encounters with each other. The periodic spraying of their territory, mentioned under elimination and territory, aids greatly in time, as well as territorial, demarcation.

When two strange cats do meet accidentally, what they will do about the encounter depends on what they discover about each other. The approach and greeting approximates that of most mammals—caution above all else, with an olfactory investigation of the anus, and nose to nose contact, also, perhaps, some whisker intermingling. A good deal of sniffing and circling takes place before the initial contact is made and may be repeated after it. The initiative is taken by the cat on whose territory—in time or place—the meeting occurs, and after the "come forward and be recognized" ritual is completed the intruder generally decides to leave and is allowed to do so. If he is reluctant to depart he may be given the "bum's rush" and if he doesn't care for such treatment there may be a fight irrespective of the sex of the participants. This is what takes place out of doors. What happens indoors is another matter.

A cat door allows my cats to come and go as they please. Naturally it also allows strange cats to do the same thing, and many take advantage of the opportunity. It isn't necessary for me to see the stranger to know that one has arrived. All the cats in residence will be perched on convenient observation posts peering in the interloper's direction. They are tense and jittery, as if they were the intruders, and act as if contact with the new arrival would be fatal. In spite of extreme caution the stranger also acts as if it is he that belongs and not the residents. Not even the more aggressive cats dispute his rights to partake of bed and board, but once again outside the house, let him beware. If he is accepted as a permanent resident his immunity indoors vanishes and seldom does a newcomer dispute the dominant cats' positions.

This is as good a place as any to voice my dissent about the belief that cats crawl away somewhere to die. Granted they do want to be left alone when sick—some *will* leave if not allowed the peace and quiet they desire; but I have found that if they can possibly make it, they will use all the strength left them to crawl home to die. This even applies to strays who don't wish to become permanent residents anywhere. In fact one new stray who still hadn't the temerity to come indoors finally found the courage and was allowed to enter the house one night to die.

Although mutual indifference to each other is the commonest behavior, as soon as there is more than one cat dominance may develop. Unlike with humans, however, the hierarchy may differ for different things. For example, one cat may have priority for a resting place but a low rating when all the cats are milling around and bickering while waiting for food.

Boots, the old female who waited so determinedly to be taken in by us, was one of the rare cases—top cat in everything—and she played the role of benevolent tyrant. Tolerating no dissension, she was on the spot chastising both participants indiscriminately as soon as a quarrel developed. No one ever questioned her authority on any matter, not even an evil tomcat that we had at that time. When she died, Red One, a huge castrated stray, took over, and things were much the same as in her reign. It was only after he died that the pattern changed. No one wanted the difficult job and no one does yet, four years later. In consequence there is seldom much peace among the cats. Squabbles are omnipresent and a new bad-tempered tom, a partial boarder, plays havoc with those afraid to stand up for their rights. Only Specs, a castrated tom, puts him in his place if he's not feeling too lazy. None of the cats shows any politeness toward any other cat anymore. No longer does one approach another and with gentle licks insinuate himself so that he can share a coveted sleeping spot. Bullying and fear prevail and apparently will continue to do so until a successor to Boots and Red One comes along.

A strange relationship—something between that of worker and parasite and slave and master—can develop between two cats under experimental conditions. It was described by J. F. Masserman in his paper on "Experimental Neuroses" and seems to have no counterpart in cats living a more or less normal existence.

"Two cats, each of which had been trained to manipulate a switch to obtain food, were placed in a single cage. The cage was equipped with a barrier between the switch and the foodbox, so that the animal which essayed to work the switch could not reach the food-box until after its less enterprising partner had eaten the pellet. Under these circumstances some pairs of cats evolved a form of cooperative effort; they alternately worked the switch to feed each other. This cooperation, however, lasted no longer among cats than it does among men. One animal sooner or later showed tendencies toward 'parasitism'; it ate the pellets produced by its partner's efforts but refused to leave the food to manipulate the switch. The worker animal, finding its own 'cooperative' behavior completely unrewarding, in turn ceased to produce food. Both animals, the parasite usually near the food-box and the worker near the switch, lolled about the cage for hours in a travesty of a sit-down strike. But as hunger increased, the relatively undernourished cat that had worked the switch usually would discover that if the switch were depressed six or eight times in rapid succession to release as many food pellets, he could scramble back to the box in time to get the last pellet or two before the parasite partner gulped them all. In these experiments the end result was that the worker animal labored hard for a meager living while supporting its parasitic partner in leisure—a form of relationship apparently accepted by both animals. A few workers learned to jam the switch so that food was provided without further effort. They thus found a 'technological' solution to a 'socio-economic' problem."

But cats can be as completely unselfish as they can be selfish. Dilly, a stray tom, was living with us when Calicat arrived with her kittens, seeking help. He was all solicitude when he realized how sick she was, and, gentle soul that he was, he took over the care of her kittens. He groomed them (and her, too), played with them, taught them, stayed with them when she went hunting and sat with them when she was home so that she could rest and recuperate. He did everything but nurse them and he did it lovingly although you could see he was bored with his self-infected responsibilities and anxious to leave and carry on the pursuits of his sex. When Calicat was run over and killed he continued his task without her as best he could and it certainly wasn't his fault that only one of those completely wild kittens survived to maturity.

Rimba, as pointed out in the Friends and Foes chapter, was continually inconveniencing himself for his mother. A complete pacifist at heart, he could fight fiercely if necessary. One day a strange cat chased Tayi, and Rimba felt he must do something about it, but what and how? It didn't take him long to figure out. Maneuvering in the best military fashion, he ran between pursuer and pursued, intercepting the stranger head on, then attacked so ferociously that the other cat didn't try to do anything but escape which was all that Rimba desired. All cats are imbued with good common sense and take the path of least resistance if at all possible, unless extremely aroused. It is then that they become dangerous.

Behaviorial Development in kittens is complicated by association with humans. Increased stimulation through human handling not only speeds up their physical development—such as opening of eyes, emergence from nest area, coordination, even color change in the Siamese—but produces changes in their psychological development. In the stress of adapting to many humans a kitten may learn to be less fearful of strangers but its play and social behavior suffer. It doesn't play as much as kittens having only a one-person-contact and it makes much fewer natural social contacts.

Handling makes young kittens better able to meet all the stressful conditions encountered in a human household, but it makes them less tractable to confinement. Experimenters also claim that discipline must begin before they are six weeks old, training after six weeks having no permanent effect on them. However, if they are removed from their mother and litter mates too soon they are permanently damaged emotionally. As they mature they become aggressive and unpredictable both toward people and other cats, are easily frightened and tend to be overly active. They lack the power of concentration that most cats have and are psychotic in many different ways. The wool eaters of catdom are said to belong to this class of cats.

Reared normally, without too much human interference, developmental behavior in the kitten is complicated enough. As in other animals there are critical periods during which whatever happens will determine its future behavior. One of the most obvious of these is the already discussed socialization period which determines its reaction toward people. If first introduced to them *after* this period, the chances are that the cat won't accept them and will always be relatively wild in their presence.

As it matures the kitten learns to practice restraint when necessary, to pretend and dissimulate. The last the adult cat can do to perfection as when caught consuming the chops laid out for the evening meal. From past experience it knows it is doing the wrong thing. It's not a matter of forgetting because its memory is phenomenal, apparently capable of spanning its lifetime. It's merely that things of this sort seldom trouble it. The human idea of right and wrong is not the cat's, and, refusing to accept the alien creed, it will take what it wants when it wants and display complete innocence when caught. It isn't a thief as much as an opportunist, and although it does have a sense of guilt and shame it doesn't always display it when humans think it should. It likewise is credited with a sense of duty and trust and a moral sense, all difficult things to evaluate even in humans.

Insult, neglect, injustice, punishment, reproof—the cat is extremely sensitive to all of these and most cats must suffer from all of them through callousness or misunderstanding on the part of humans. The family pet can be as misunderstood as other members in the household where it lives.

Its insatiable curiosity, actually a sign of intelligence, often earns it much more than mere reproof. Literally poking its nose into everything new and different, it can't fail to bring about disaster some of the time. Although satisfaction is said to bring back the cat killed by curiosity I have never seen or heard of one satisfied enough to resist investigation of almost anything, and it is that fatal urge combined with impulsiveness that leads to tragedy, such as when a cat sees an interesting sight outside an open upper window. Seeming never to have heard of its proverbial cautiousness it will leap out of the window for a closer examination of what intrigues it. Overwhelming concentration rather than impulsiveness may explain such acts, but regardless of what it is, it can end in the cat's death. Under ordinary circumstances cats never act so stupidly since they are fully capable of reasoning from cause to effect as researchers are now finding out.

INTELLIGENCE. Just how intelligent the cat is and how much it can learn is still being argued. Up to the 1930s it was considered, if not abysmally stupid, close to it, by most scientists because of their inadequate methods for measuring feline intelligence. Today's experiments on cats tend to take into consideration their physical and psychological make-up, and evaluations and opinions as to their capabilities have consequently changed drastically. Experimenters now find that if cats want something badly enough, they are able to accomplish far more and show greater powers of thought than was ever thought possible.

In the past, experimental attempts also met with failure and reduced the cat to neurotic ineptitude or pure resistance and recalcitrance because the attempted training frightened the animal or was too rapid and intensive for its age and capacity. Recently, many experiments on cats are actually designed to produce psychotic results so that these can be studied and equated to human neuroses. The following, however, has been discovered about normal cats, if any laboratory cat can be considered normal.

Cats readily learn to respond to auditory stimuli (buzzers, bells, tones), to visual stimuli (light intensities, flickers, etc.), and to tactile stimuli, such as electric shock avoidance. Once a response of any sort has been learned, they can apply it to a similar problem. In other words, they can generalize and by so doing speed up their responses. Their learning ability is highly flexible. As situations change and new ones develop they can adjust to them by unlearning, or inhibiting and modifying, previously learned responses much as humans do. They are aware of the succession of events and have a limited counting ability.

Because of their natural curiosity, their agility, and the flexibility of their forepaws they are adept at mechanical problems and selective learning—trial and error. However, if not upset or frightened (for example by being placed in strange surroundings) they will attempt to grasp the problem set before them and solve it by reasoning rather than by hit or miss trial and error. Their brain is capable of analyzing what their senses register, and they can even form an association when cause and effect are separated temporally, spatially, or both. In their ability to solve complex problems (such as oddity problems and those presenting ambivalent cues) they are sometimes superior to or as good as monkeys and usually exceed other animals below the primates.

A cat's intelligence is such that it realizes the limits of its abilities. Almost never does one attempt the impossible; rather it will employ strategy to overcome its incapacities, and it is an excellent strategist, often outwitting humans.

Of great advantage to the cat is its ability to learn through observation. The elaborate laboratory experiments used to determine its imitative capacities really aren't necessary. Anyone who owns a cat can observe them. Through a close scrutiny of humans the household cat soon learns to manipulate mechanical devices such as latches, where the learning is to its advantage. It would eventually learn such things without *any* help but it learns much more rapidly from observation, especially from other cats rather than humans. Its being shown how to do something doesn't produce as good results as when it observes that same thing being done by another. Its abhorrence of being forced to do anything probably accounts for this more than any other factors.

Illuminating in its simplicity, *Nature* in 1889 had this to say of observational learning in cats, not that it was considered such in those days. "Two cats were on a roof, from which it was necessary to jump. Tom made the spring, but Tabby's courage failed and she drew back with a cry of distress, whereupon Tom leaped back, and, giving a cheerful mew, as much as to say, 'See how easy it is,' jumped across again, followed this time by Tabby."

Books could be filled with anecdotes and experiments which prove the superior mental powers of cats. Here are only two, both published 40 years ago but as good as, or better than, anything done since. The first is Frances Pitt's observation of a cat in its natural environment. The second is one of many experiments carried out on cats by D. K. Adams, one of the first researchers to point out the errors in experimental methods used on this difficult animal. As in the classical primate experiment some of his cats learned to reach food suspended above them by maneuvering and mounting a box. Both Pitt's and Adams's descriptions of feline behavior reflect their knowledge of cat character.

1. "The adult cat who spends much time watching mouseholes, who catches rats, and even rabbits, is a highly *skilled* hunter. Long experience has developed her inherent talent into art, and her performance is tempered with judgment and discretion. Watch an 'old hand' pounce on a rat, such as the tabby-cat I saw at work one day. She was a keen huntress, some three years of age, *not* of the overfed, pampered, fireside-pet description, but of the most sporting type. Something moved in a straw-rick. The cat, which was passing by, paused, listened, while her tail tip twitched and the pupils of her eyes dilated. The scuffling noise was repeated, coming from a spot in the side of the rick about two feet from the ground. Puss crouched slightly and then waited in a rigid attitude. I saw something grey move in the straw. It was a nearly full-grown

rat with its head toward the cat. She remained immovable, the only thing betraying her tense excitement being that uncontrollable tail-tip, nor did she stir until the rat turned, when she sprang like a flash, to seize the rodent by the back of the neck and drop down with it kicking in her grasp. She bit firmly into its neck, nor did she relax her grip until sure her dangerous prey was killed.

"The way the cat waited until it was safe to spring, until she could do so with the certainty of getting the rat so it could not bite her, was eloquent testimony to her judgment. If her actions did not display forethought and intention it can only be said that they had all the appearance of it.

"Now I contend that such an episode gives us a far truer insight into the mind of the cat that scores of experiments of the 'find the outlet from the basket' type."

2. "The liver was suspended (in the cage) at a height of 85 cm., and the box was 50 cm. east of the point directly under the liver, with its long dimension at right angles to the direct line to that point. As soon as she was put in (the cage), Tabs climbed on the box and stretched repeatedly toward the liver. She shortly gave over this reaching, and walked around the room. After more than a minute of this, she stood up under the liver and reached toward it. Then she sat under it, and looked from it to the box and back again several times. Then she suddenly got up, ran to the box and started to pull it straight toward the liver. It was about 12 cm. away when she dropped the string, wandered off into a corner and sat down to wash without another glance at the liver. After more than a minute of this she suddenly paused and became rigid for a period of four or five seconds, in the posture of washing, with one hind leg sticking up at an angle of about 80 degrees from the horizontal, and with the liver throughout this period in her line of regard. Her ears were pricked forward and there was no relaxation from the awkward posture. At the end of this period of immobility, she abruptly got up and ran to the box, climbed on it and reached toward the liver. After several such futile efforts, she sat down and looked from the liver to the box, on which she was sitting, several times; then, again abruptly, she got down off the box, took hold of the nearer string, and pulled the box squarely under the liver, a distance of more than 30 cm., inasmuch as she had previously left the box with its nearest part about 12 cm. away from the point directly under the liver. She climbed on the box at once and got the liver." The time involved was under five minutes.

Further Reading

Cat-care books cover the essentials of cat biology, and so do most general cat books; but for the non-specialist reader there are no books that deal with the subject in much detail except Mivart's *The Cat* and Mellen's *The Science and the Mystery of the Cat.* Consequently, for those who wish to go farther than this book has taken them I have only one suggestion: locate a library that has the periodical *Biological Abstracts.* In it you will find references to all aspects of cat biology.

There are, however, two drawbacks to this. First, the references will usually be difficult to locate, and second, they may prove to be too technical. It is for these same reasons that I decided not to include here a bibliography of the hundreds of articles and books from which this book grew. The references listed below were selected for their general interest and will be understandable by the non-specialist for the most part. They can also be located relatively easily and are of sufficient length to warrant a search for them.

Cat anatomy and physiology texts are common enough and popular enough to have at least one example in most public libraries and the same is true for cat-care books. None of these is listed here except for

Whitney's book on cat-care which deals in greater detail with cat biology than other similar books.

Here then is a beginning for further reading on the natural history of the cat. Happy and successful hunting!

ADAMS, DONALD KEITH. 1929. Experimental studies of adaptive behavior in cats. Comp. Psych. Monog. 6:1–168.

BLOOM, FRANK. 1960. *The Urine of the Dog and Cat; Analysis and Interpretation.* N.Y.: Gamma Publ.

BLOM, FRANK. 1960. *The Urine of the Dog and Cat; Analysis and Interpretation.* N.Y.: Gamma Publ.

CORONOIS, J. D. 1932. Development of behavior in the fetal cat. Genetic Psych. Monog. 14(4):283–386.

FIREMAN, JUDY, ed. 1976. *The Cat Catalog.* New York: Workman.

FOX, MICHAEL W. 1974. *Understanding Your Cat.* New York: Coward McCann.

GALLICO, PAUL. 1972. *Honorable Cat.* New York: Crown.

GAY, MARGARET C. 1969. *How to Live with a Cat.* New York: Simon and Schuster.

HERRICK, FRANCIS H. June 1922. Homing powers of the cat. Sci. Mo. 14(6):525–539.

MELLEN, IDA M. 1940. *The Science and the Mystery of the Cat.* N. Y. Charles Scribner's.

MILLARD, ADELE. 1976. *Cats—In Fact and Legend.* New York: Sterling.

MIVART, ST. GEORGE. 1881. *The Cat; an Introduction to the Study of Backboned Animals Especially Mammals.* Lond. John Murray.

MOELK, MILDRED. 1944. Vocalizing in the house-cat; a phonetic and functional study. Am. J. Psych. 57:184–205.

OSIS, KARLIS. 1952. A test of the occurrence of a psi effect between man and the cat. J. Parapsychology 16:233–256.

OSIS, KARLIS and FOSTER, ESTHER BOND. 1953. A test of ESP in cats. J. Parapsychology 17:168–186.

POCOCK, R. I. 1907. On English domestic cats. P. Z. S. London 107:143–168.

POCOCK, R. I. 1951. Catalogue of the genus *Felis.* Lond. British Museum.

RHINE, J. B. & FEATHER, S. R. 1962. The study of cases of "psi-trailing" in animals. J. Parapsychology 26:1–22.

ROBINSON, ROY. 1959. Genetics of the domestic cat. Bibliographia Genetica 18:273–362.

ROSENBLATT, J. S. & SCHNEIRLA, T. C. The behavior of cats *in* Hafez, E. S. E. 1962. *The Behavior of Domestic Animals.* Baltimore: Williams & Wilkins.

ROSENBLATT, J. S., TURKEWITZ, G. & SCHNEIRLA, T. C. Early socialization in the domestic cat as based on feeding and other relationships between female and young *in* Foss, B. H. ed. 1961. *Determinants of Infant Behavior.* Lond. Methuen.

SCHNEIRLA, T. C., ROSENBLATT, J. S. & TOBACH, E. Maternal behavior in the cat *in* Rheingold, Harriet L. ed. 1963. *Maternal Behavior in Mammals.* N. Y. John Wiley.

SEARLE, RONALD. 1976. *More Cats.* Brattleboro, Vt.: Stephen Greene Press.

STRICKLAND, JAMES H. 1963. The integumentary system of the cat. Am. J. Vet. Res. 24:1018–1029.

WHITNEY, LEON F. 1953. *The Complete Book of Cat Care.* N. Y. Doubleday.

WILKINSON, G. T. 1966. *Diseases of the Cat.* N. Y. Pergamon (a section of this is devoted to cat nutrition).

WILSON, CHARIS & WESTON, EDWARD. 1947. *The Cats of Wildcat Hill.* N. Y. Duell, Sloan & Pearce.

ZEUNER, F. E. 1963. *A History of Domesticated Animals.* Lond. Hutchinson.

Index

A

B

C

D

E

F

G

H

I

J

K

L

M

R

U

V

W